"Pascal Baudar is a culinary visionary who is also excellent at clearly explaining his ideas and methods to make them accessible. I am in awe of this book as well as his two earlier ones. Get ready to be inspired."

—Sandor Ellix Katz, author of *Wild Fermentation* and *The Art of Fermentation*

"*Wildcrafted Fermentation* is an amazing, passion-based work! Looking outside at the snow-covered ground, I'm more eager than ever for the return of musk mustards, lamb's quarters, and other wild plants to add to ferments. And I especially appreciate the use of the Latin names for plants and the cheerful and repeated reassurances that nothing can go wrong—just what a nervous fermenter wants to hear. This is a stunning book."

—Deborah Madison, author of *Vegetable Literacy* and *The New Vegetarian Cooking for Everyone*

"Pascal Baudar is back. His distinctive approach to wildcrafting is enhanced this time by connecting wild plants to the transformative power of lactic acid fermentation. In doing so, Pascal elevates commonly found roots, shoots, seeds, weeds, and leaves to foods with astounding flavors. He encourages the reader to explore the 'flavorshed' of their own region while understanding how to responsibly be part of their local ecology. The book is exciting, creative, and beautiful. Perhaps more importantly, it offers inspiring, adaptable recipes that employ solid and safe techniques. It is a must-have for both foragers and fermentation enthusiasts."

—Kirsten Shockey, coauthor of *Fermented Vegetables*, *Fiery Ferments*, and *Miso, Tempeh, Natto and Other Tasty Ferments*

"With a rare combination of humility and wisdom, Baudar shares his deep immersion into the seam between wild foods and fermentation so that we all may embark on or enhance our own exploration of these lost arts. Risks of error deter many people from attempting either wild food harvesting or home ferments, but Baudar puts all of our instinctive concerns in perspective, cautioning us to follow some basic rules and encouraging us not be afraid to experiment.

"My favorite recipe titles include Fermented Forest Floor Paste and Roasted Oak Bark Hot Sauce. Those who doubt the utility of his innovative creations need look only at the earth around them. The possibilities, as he suggests, are limited only by the *eye* (and palate) of the beholder."

—Evan Mallett, chef/owner, Black Trumpet bistro; author of *Black Trumpet*

T0354254

Also by Pascal Baudar

The New Wildcrafted Cuisine:
Exploring the Exotic Gastronomy of Local Terroir

The Wildcrafting Brewer:
Creating Unique Drinks and Boozy Concoctions
from Nature's Ingredients

Wildcrafted Fermentation

Exploring, Transforming, and Preserving
the Wild Flavors of Your Local Terroir

PASCAL BAUDAR

Chelsea Green Publishing
White River Junction, Vermont
London, UK

Project Manager: Alexander Bullett
Project Editor: Benjamin Watson
Copy Editor: Laura Jorstad
Proofreader: Eliani Torres
Indexer: Linda Hallinger
Designer: Melissa Jacobson

Printed in the United States of America.
First printing February 2020.
10 9 8 7 6 5 4   24 25 26 27 28

Our Commitment to Green Publishing
Chelsea Green sees publishing as a tool for cultural change and ecological stewardship. We strive to align our book manufacturing practices with our editorial mission and to reduce the impact of our business enterprise in the environment. We print our books using vegetable-based inks whenever possible. This book may cost slightly more because it was printed on paper from responsibly managed forests, and we hope you'll agree that it's worth it. *Wildcrafted Fermentation* was printed on paper supplied by Versa Press that is certified by the Forest Stewardship Council.®

Library of Congress Cataloging-in-Publication Data
Names: Baudar, Pascal, 1961- author.
Title: Wildcrafted fermentation : exploring, transforming, and preserving the wild flavors of your local terroir / Pascal Baudar.
Description: White River Junction : Chelsea Green Publishing, 2020. | Fermentation basics — Getting started: Exploring your local terroir — Exploring local and ethnic flavors — Delving deeper into local ingredients — Fermenting with the environment — Foraged and fermented soups, pastes, spreads, and sauces — Wilder cheeses — Creative dishes and plating.
Identifiers: LCCN 2019044579 (print) | LCCN 2019044580 (ebook) | ISBN 9781603588515 (paperback) | ISBN 9781603588522 (ebook)
Subjects: LCSH: Cooking (Wild foods) | Fermentation. | Food—Preservation. | LCGFT: Cookbooks.
Classification: LCC TX652 .B3334 2020 (print) | LCC TX652 (ebook) | DDC 664/.024—dc23
LC record available at https://lccn.loc.gov/2019044579
LC ebook record available at https://lccn.loc.gov/2019044580

Chelsea Green Publishing
White River Junction, Vermont, USA
London, UK

www.chelseagreen.com

To my wonderful children, Felicia and Luc;
my daughter-in-law, Denise; and you, too, Garrett!

And, of course, to my granddaughter, Olivia.

Olivia,
the future belongs to you—
make this world a better place.
Shape it the way you dream it should be!

CONTENTS

Discovering Fermentation

I grew up in Belgium, and the sour flavors of lacto-fermentation were not a big part of my culinary education. Maybe a couple of times a year we would eat choucroute garnie (garnished sauerkraut) purchased in jars or cans at the store. It was cheap and easy to prepare, just an already cooked sauerkraut with sausage and salted pork. The idea of raw fermentation, as well as the concept of probiotics and the health benefits associated with the process, never entered the picture. I even think my mom served it when the food budget was particularly low that week; it was cheap canned food.

My favorite part was the meat—the cooked sauerkraut wasn't exactly my cup of tea. Even cooked, it still had that strange sourness I wasn't accustomed to. I'm pretty sure that if I had asked my parents or even my grandparents how sauerkraut was made, they would have had no clue—it was already a lost practice. But if you study the various components of this garnished sauerkraut, you'll realize that it was solid *paysan* (peasant) food based on extremely traditional food preservation techniques: salting and fermentation. Salted meat and sausage were important staples in the old days, and fermented cabbage was one way to get you through the winter and add a decent amount of vitamin C that could prevent scurvy as well. That purchased jar was pure food preservation history and probably a very luxurious meal for my ancestors.

Once I left home, I never thought of purchasing lacto-fermented products. Of course, I still ate and drank a lot of fermented products like cheese, wines, beers, salamis, and so on . . . but not fermented vegetables.

I rediscovered fermentation 30 years later when I moved to America and specifically to Los Angeles. At the time I was living near Pasadena, which has a large Asian population and quite a lot of Asian grocery stores and restaurants.

One day, as a dedicated foodie, I decided to be adventurous and took the kids to a Korean barbecue restaurant. A couple of minutes after we sat down, the waitress placed on the table a dozen beautiful little pickled condiments in small bowls; the colors ranged from bright yellow to deep red. I wasn't sure what they were and was definitely intrigued. (I've always loved tasty surprises.) I could see sliced orange roots sprinkled with chives submerged in a reddish liquid; unusual yellow squares, which I assumed were also from a root vegetable; pungent cucumbers with a generous amount of red chili flakes; some sort of boiled greens with seeds on top; and many other foods. All of them were super pretty.

One caught my attention, as the bowl was noticeably bigger. It was some sort of leafy vegetable immersed in red sauce, but I could also see little bits of garlic and chili flakes. I didn't know what to make of the odor, though—it was a bit repulsive and intriguing at the same time.

I took a bite, and utter confusion established itself on my taste buds. It was sour, sweet, sugary, spicy, salty, fishy, and yet, in an odd way, it kind of made sense. Part of me rejected it and another part of me loved it. The flavors were extremely remote from anything I'd experienced to that point. Originally, I had expected vinegar-based pickles, but this was another universe of flavors altogether. I tried the other colorful condiments; some did use vinegar and were more familiar to my European palate, while others were quite unusual.

I liked a few of them, but some were definitely more challenging. One thing for sure: I could not shake the strange sensation the first one gave me—it was as if my body craved it. I asked what it was, and I was told it was fermented cabbage in a spicy sauce called kimchi.

Overall it was a great evening and we left the restaurant quite fulfilled, but it didn't take long, maybe a few days, before my culinary curiosity took me to the local Korean supermarket. There I examined various shelves of completely unknown food: bags of dried seaweeds of all sorts; dehydrated herbs and mushrooms; a whole aisle of seeds and grains; numerous containers of brown and red pastes; and, of course, a whole section of fresh and frozen fish. My head was spinning—for a Belgian country boy, this was a brand-new unexplored food universe.

I focused on my quest to find kimchi, not sure if I could even recognize the concoction amid the tremendous variety of colorful jars and boxes covered with unknown writing. But in the end, I didn't have to search long. As I walked into a new aisle, I was welcomed by rows of glass and plastic containers of all shapes and sizes, each labeled KIMCHI in English. And there it was: I could see the cabbage leaves submerged in the reddish liquid. My quest was over! I purchased the smallest jar and took it home.

I'll be honest, it was not love at first bite. It actually took me weeks to get used to the strong fermented taste of raw kimchi and the countless variations on that condiment. It was a completely alien flavor profile, but the more I ate it, the more I craved it until it eventually became a love affair.

Fermentation had entered my life! In retrospect, I probably should have started with milder raw ferments (kimchi can be quite "out there" in terms of smell and taste), but once you love kimchi, you've pretty much arrived; most other plant-based ferments are much milder.

Fermenting and Wild Food

Yet lacto-fermenting still seemed a very dangerous, esoteric, and complex process to me. Very little information existed at the time detailing how ferments are made. This soon changed, however, with the invention of the internet, and the timing suited me perfectly.

As I explained in my book *The New Wildcrafted Cuisine*, in the mid-1990s I became interested in wilderness survival skills and took many classes with anyone who could teach the subject locally. Of course, wild food was often part of the curriculum, largely from a survival perspective. With a very few exceptions, most of the dishes created were pretty basic and somewhat bland. We're talking stews, boiled greens, wild flour pancakes, and so on.

Tasting plants directly exposed me to the incredible flavors that wild edibles can provide, but in the classes and workshops I attended, they were not truly explored to their full potential.

Still, for me, it was very much like a spiritual awakening. I became fascinated with researching wild edibles and exploring their true flavors through culinary applications. One of the things that frustrated me very early on was the fact that, unlike commercial products, wild edibles are available for only a short period of time. You'll find some vegetables and fruits available all year long at the grocery store, but lamb's-quarter (*Chenopodium album*) or local chickweed (*Stellaria media*) will be available for only a month or two.

Strangely enough, aside from freezing, dehydrating, and smoking, the whole subject of wild food preservation techniques wasn't explored very much in the survival field. Yet if you think about it, these are essential skills. Through traditional and modern food preservation techniques, you can preserve your wild harvest—but you'll realize very fast that you can also create an infinite number of flavorful preserves ranging from delicious pickles, jams, canned condiments, syrups, and spice blends to liqueurs, country wines, and even traditional beers. And this is pretty much where fermentation came into the picture for me: as one of many possible preservation techniques for the wild edibles I collected during the year.

I'm one of those lucky people who love to research and figure out how to do things from books or online research. With the appearance of the internet in the mid-1990s, fermentation enthusiasts began posting tutorials about fermentation. Following online instructions, I made my first sauerkraut, which was a success. I was thrilled, to say the least, and to this day lacto-fermentation is one of my favorite food preservation techniques.

Why? Because it's one of the easiest and safest ways to preserve food: Nature provides everything for you. All you need are plants, salt, and sometimes water. Depending on where you live, you can make your own salt by dehydrating seawater or even using seawater for fermentation. Just don't do it with seawater from Los Angeles! Way too much pollution. I usually go all the way to Oregon to collect pristine seawater.

After I made my first sauerkraut, my next project was a wild food kimchi, which ended up absolutely delicious. I was totally hooked.

Exploring Wild Flavors Through Fermentation

Since that first sauerkraut, as you'll see in this book, I've made countless types of ferments using local wild edibles ranging from sauerkraut blends to kimchis, hot sauces, savory pastes, plant-based cheeses, dehydrated spices, and much more. Twenty years later I'm still amazed to find new uses for wild plants through fermentation.

Fermentation has also been a great teacher. I've learned about patience and the ability of time to transform the original flavors into new ones. It is truly fascinating. For example, some of the spicy pastes in this book are much better after many months of fermentation. My "wild" habanero hot sauce is way too spicy to consume in the beginning, but after two or three months of fermentation at room temperature, it is heavenly.

Not all the experiments I've done ended up delicious. While working on this book, I did make quite a few mistakes, but this was all part of my education. For example, I found out that fermenting stinging nettle (*Urtica dioica*) is an exercise in moderation. My first sauerkraut mixed with stinging nettle smelled like . . . cow pie. If you're a country boy, you'll know exactly what I'm talking about. I could not get past the smell even to try it. But used in smaller quantities, stinging nettle is quite awesome.

If you embark on a journey to explore local plants, be safe—but you can be bold, too! Make sure you correctly identify the plants and that they're not toxic, but otherwise the sky is really the limit. I'm sure you'll experience a few failures in terms of flavors as you go along, but it's all part of the learning process. Every time I make a mistake, I learn something. What I like about fermentation is the fact that the mistakes are related to taste, not food safety. Fermentation is an extremely safe process.

The delicious, unique flavors and recipes you can create will make any past failures completely worth it. If you are a chef, a home cook, or a foodie, exploring local plants through wild fermentation will allow you to create tasty condiments that are truly yours and cannot be found anywhere else. Fermentation is an incredible tool if your quest is to create a cuisine unique to you and your environment.

How to Use This Book

Fermentation has always been a big part of my research into the culinary uses of wild edibles, both yeast (fungal) and lacto (bacterial) fermentation. You can research wild flavors through cooking and creating beverages of all sorts, but lacto-fermentation is especially fascinating because, like wild yeast, the bacteria are readily available, and it not only is a remarkable preservation technique but also produces foodstuffs very good for your health.

Still, for me the real bonus is the way fermentation can transform flavors. Wild natural flavors can be quite phenomenal on their own, but through the process of lacto-fermentation they can be transformed and raised to new levels.

Although I live in Southern California, most of the plants featured and fermented in this book can be found pretty much anywhere in North America and in some parts of Europe. I'm sure the information here will be applicable in many other countries and regions as well. Aside from a couple of selections, I have deliberately omitted recipes that are so hyperlocal that they can't be reproduced anywhere else.

If you live in North America, most of the plants used are even considered invasive weeds—dandelion, curly dock, mustards, wild radish, and so on.

They are also extremely common. If you are interested in exploring your local terroir more deeply, you can easily find edible plants identification books featuring your region online. A simple online search for "New York wild edibles book," for instance, turned up three volumes.

Think of the recipes and methods as collections of ideas, concepts, and possibilities. I think most of them can be easily reproduced and adapted to your own environment.

If you live in Colorado and decide to ferment beets in "forest floor" materials, it will never taste the same as my own forest floor ferment, because I live in California. You'll be dealing with a different environment and different herbs. That's the beauty of it. In Arkansas you may try making a nut-and-plant-based fermented cheese using pecans and other local nuts and seeds to explore your own local flavors.

Fermentation is a natural process, and from an artistic perspective you can go even deeper. As you'll see in this book, once you know the basics of technique and food safety, you can bring nature itself into the process and start fermenting with wild plants, leaves, bark, wood—and even tree trunks. It may seem extreme, but it really isn't; the ingredients and vessels that you use will contribute flavor accents to the fermenting process.

The real idea—and fun—behind this book, though, is to use fermentation as a medium to explore the true flavors of your environment. Not just what you can find in the store, but what nature can provide you as well.

For a cook or chef, the creative possibilities offered by the simple process of lacto-fermentation are infinite. While I stick mostly to common wild edibles, realize that if you use something truly local and native that hasn't been used in fermentation before (like yucca flowers in my region), you're inventing a new flavor, which in itself is an integral part of a very exciting culinary journey.

I hope you like the book and can't wait to see your fermented creations!

A Quick Note to Fermenters

Most of my ferments are made using regular jars. When I started my fermentation journey many years ago, I used commercial fermentation systems and traditional fermenting crocks, but over the years I slowly switched to using regular Mason-type jars and lids.

If you're a purist, many of the ferments in this book can be done with commercial systems or kits, and I've even listed some that I recommend on page 21.

Some of the ferments can be considered a bit unusual and are breaking the conventional rules. If you are new to fermentation, I advise you to start with very simple recipes, such as sauerkraut-type ferments, so you can build your confidence in the process and understand the basic principles. Once you're armed with knowledge about the process and food safety procedures, a lot of creativity becomes possible both in the ferments themselves and also in the methods you use.

In this book you will find regular procedures but also some unconventional ones such as fermenting in a tree trunk, in leaves, with a smaller amount of salt than usual, or without keeping the ingredients under the brine. I think the main difference between regular fermentation and what I do is the fact that, in many instances, I work very closely with many of my ferments, shaking or stirring the contents to distribute acidity during the process, checking the pH, and so on. Personally, using regular Mason jars or other methods, I have *never* experienced any spoilage or mold issues and I've done a huge amount of ferments.

But it's really up to you. If you prefer to use commercial kits with air-lock systems on top, most of the recipes would still work, though some may be challenging.

Most of the mistakes I've seen from people in the fermentation field are gross errors such as ingredients floating over the brine, or leaving the ferment *unattended* for many days or weeks. If you establish a close relationship with your creations and take care of them, it's really hard to experience failures.

Done properly, fermentation is probably the safest way to preserve food.

Learn and understand the basic principles, have fun, and create!

Use of Latin Names

In this book, the first time I name a plant or wild ingredient used, I will add the Latin botanical name, then I'll simply use the common name.

This is not a plant identification book, but most of the plants used in the recipes, with a few exceptions, were chosen because they're common in North America and Europe.

On Picking Wild Plants, or Foraging

Like many of our human activities, foraging can be done for good or evil; it can help the environment or intensify sustainability issues. Over the years I've learned to streamline my activities so as to minimize my impact on nature. It's been a learning curve with trials and errors, but these days I actually think foraging can be done in such a way that you help your local environment by removing non-native plants (pretty much 90 percent of what I pick) and harvesting sustainably or growing the native plants you need. As far as I can remember, at this point I've pretty much replanted all the plants I used in this book in much larger quantities than I'll ever use, mostly on private lands owned by friends.

You don't need to be a fanatic tree-hugger to see that our planet faces real problems such as pollution, climate change (natural or not), human expansion, loss of natural habitat, species extinction, and much more. At this time in our evolution, we absolutely need to be part of the solution, and this responsibility even applies to the simple act of picking wild plants. We must make sure that our picking wild plants for food, drinks, or medicine is done carefully, with environmental health and integrity in mind.

Picking plants and berries for food or making drinks can connect us back to nature: It is a sacred link that, as a species, we all share. We are here because our ancestors had a very intimate relationship with nature, knew which plants to use for food or medicine, and in many instances knew how to sustainably interact with their wild environment. No matter where we live, it's part of our cultural DNA.

I personally don't think the impulse to protect nature at all costs with a look-don't-touch mentality will work. Growing up in Belgium, I came by my love for nature through a deep interaction with my wild surroundings. If you truly love something, you will take care of it and make sure it is still there for generations to come.

When I was a kid, raising animals, growing food in our garden, and picking up wild berries, nuts, and plants weren't considered weird or special; they were a normal part of life. The knowledge was used by elders, who would pass it on to the next generation. In many modernized countries, this cycle of transferring knowledge has been lost. Very valuable and nutritious foods such as dandelion, mallow, and other plants are looked upon as "weeds," and TV commercials gladly promote the use of toxic chemicals to destroy them. The people I've seen trashing the wilderness are the product of our current society. If you don't know or understand the value of something, you simply won't care for it.

So do it the right way! Respect the environment, learn which plants are rare or illegal to pick, don't forage plants in protected areas (natural preserves and the like), work with native plant nurseries, and educate yourself on how to grow native plants and remove non-natives.

If you take from nature, work with her and make sure you always plant more than you'll ever take. That way future generations will have the same creative opportunities you presently have—or more.

CHAPTER 1

Fermentation Basics

For readers who are new to fermentation, I thought it would be a good idea to explain in very simple ways how the process works. You can find much more information online or in such books as *Wild Fermentation* or *The Art of Fermentation* by Sandor Katz.

Here's the simplicity of it: Go to the store and buy a peach, tomato, cucumber, cabbage, or cauliflower, then leave it on the table at room temperature for a few days or weeks. It will rot. This is due to the presence of countless microorganisms on the surface of fruits and vegetables that are competing with one another for survival.

While a lot of microorganisms can lead the food to rotting, some of them—the *Lactobacillus* bacteria—are beneficial and can help you preserve food. The challenge of lacto-fermentation is to find ways to promote the growth of beneficial bacteria and inhibit the ones that promote rotting.

The solution for that challenge is quite simple: Add salt.

For some magical reason salt inhibits the growth of the "bad" microbes prone to spoiling the food, while the "good" ones can tolerate it. By mixing salt with your vegetables/fruits or placing them in a brine, you're promoting the growth of microbes that will help preserve your food while wiping out most of the bad ones. It's already a tremendous advantage to start with.

A lot of the traditionally fermentable foods such as tomatoes, cabbages, peppers, and radishes contain a decent amount of sugar. That's important, too, because lacto bacteria love sugar and the addition of salt also induces osmotic pressure, which helps facilitate the extraction of "sugary" juice from your foods. That's the second advantage. You've already eliminated a lot of the bad guys by using salt, and because you use ingredients that contain sugar, you are now feeding the good ones.

The lacto bacteria eat the sugar present in the vegetables or fruits and convert it to lactic acid, which then acts as a preservative, further inhibiting the bad guys. That's the third advantage. It's also why vinegar works well as a preservation method, because microbes that can spoil food don't like an acidic environment. In the process this acidic environment will give ferments their typical sour and tangy flavors.

The last and final advantage of this food preservation technique is the fact that bacteria prone to spoiling food don't like an anaerobic environment, which is why fermentation is usually done within closed containers such as jars or crocks.

So lacto-fermentation really provides you with a lot of advantages in your quest to preserve food:

1. Use of salt to inhibit the growth of bad guys.
2. Use of sugary ingredients to feed the good bacteria (*Lactobacillus*).
3. Production of an acidic environment by the conversion of sugar to lactic acid by lacto bacteria.
4. Fermentation in closed containers, which also inhibits the bad bacteria from spoiling the food.

Of course, there are some exceptions or clever methods to work around the advantages used. For example, you don't always need to add pure salt, and some people will ferment vegetables using celery juice (which contains sodium) or seaweed. But the basic principles behind fermentation will stay true.

At normal room temperature (70–75°F / 21–24°C), the fermenting ingredients will go through various stages. The first 10 days are usually the most active. From day 1 to day 3, you may notice some very light bubbling occurring; then there's another 2-to-3-day period of very active fermentation. The process will then slow down and by around day 10, the bubbling will be practically nonexistent.

Fermentation is a process that was mostly used by people to preserve food during the cooler temperatures of winter, but you can do it at any time of the year. Leaving your ferment at room temperature for too long can alter the texture and taste—particularly for someone like me who lives in Southern California. The next step, after the initial fermentation, is to place your ferment in the fridge. Due to the low temperature, the fermentation process will continue, but extremely slowly.

How long can you keep your ferment in the fridge? For a very long time! It's often based on your own preferences. The ferment continues to evolve over time. Fermented salsas are usually eaten within a week; after that they can become too mushy. I've eaten sauerkraut that had been stored in the fridge for a year and was still crunchy. Some people enjoy kimchi after several years.

My own personal preference is to try to eat ferments such as sauerkraut or kimchi within 2 to 5 months, but I don't have any rules as to when you can start eating them. For example, I like to eat some of my fermented raw soups or salsas after 3 or 4 days of fermentation, and many of my lacto-fermented cheeses are at their best flavors within 10 days. Taste your ferments as you go along and you'll learn how you like them, young or old.

Some people advocate that, for optimal health benefits, it's best to eat ferments after a couple of months. They're probably correct, but you can also ferment for flavors—and this book is mostly about flavors. The health benefits are a bonus.

About Salt

Due to the importance of salt in the fermentation process, one of the first question people ask me in my workshops is "How much salt should I use?"

It's a very valid question. People new to fermentation are often afraid that if they don't use the appropriate amount in their ferments, it could lead to undesirable conditions such as molds or a "bad" fermentation (rotting).

The first person who showed me how to make sauerkraut used tablespoons as a unit measure, and to this day a lot of the recipes I find online use tablespoons as well. Still, it's really not the proper unit of measurement to use, because of the wide variation in types of salt. You'll find a lot of recipes telling you that the rule for sauerkraut-type ferments (mixing vegetables with salt) is to use 2½ to 3 tablespoons for every 5 pounds of vegetable.

That's all good until you start weighing how many grams or ounces a tablespoon of your salt is. For example, my favorite salt is pure sea salt from Korea made from dehydrated seawater. It's very fluffy and light. One tablespoon is the equivalent of 12 grams. But if I go to the store and buy regular salt, which is much denser, 1 tablespoon can weigh up to 20 grams. My Korean sea salt is close to half the weight of the regular sea salt I buy at the supermarket.

Thus if I used tablespoons as a measure with my favorite sea salt when making sauerkraut, I would end up with much less than the amount asked for in the recipe.

If you do some research online about measurement units and how much a tablespoon of salt converted to grams is, you end up with 17 grams. So even if I used regular sea salt from my local supermarket, I would still end up using more than the recipe asked for.

That's why, in this book, I will continue to use tablespoons as a measurement unit, but provide the weight in grams as well. For your part, what you should probably do is measure how much 1 tablespoon of your favorite fermentation salt weighs; that way, when a recipe asks for 40 grams of salt and 1 tablespoon of your salt weighs 20 grams, you'll know to use 2 tablespoons.

By the way, fermentation is very forgiving. Despite using various types of salts and tablespoons as a measurement unit, I have never had a fermentation go bad. And I'm pretty sure I had some wide variation when I started fermenting years ago.

Speaking of salts, another question people often ask is, "What type of salts should you use for fermentation?"

Go for pure sea salt with no additives in it if you can. Regular table salt is often heavily processed to eliminate minerals and can even be bleached.

Pure sea salt can be hard to find in some locations. Yesterday I wanted to buy some salt for a fermentation workshop, and I could not find sea salt containing just "salt." All the sea salts offered for sale included additives such as an anticaking agent, iodine, dextrose, and so on. Iodine can inhibit the growth of lactic acid bacteria in a ferment—not a good thing.

I try to use natural ingredients as much as possible. Check the label and look at the ingredients list: It should simply say "sea salt." Other mineral-rich natural salts such as pink Himalayan salt, Celtic salt, or naturally harvested gray sea salt like Guérande salt can be used, too.

Types of Ferments, Mold, and Food Safety

Now that we've looked at salt and measurement units, let's talk about the various types of ferments you'll encounter in this book and how to avoid issues such as mold.

Most people think of ferments as either sauerkraut/kimchi types or brine-based products such as lacto-fermented dill pickles or carrots, but in this book, because we are dealing with ingredients that are usually not found in regular stores, you are going to encounter all kinds of ferments, from soups, hot sauces, and spicy pastes to fermented stems, flowers, and seedpods, smoked wild oats, and even loose roots. Each type of ferment will require a specific amount of salt and spices, and different techniques to avoid mold or spoiling.

My viewpoint on mold is simple: It's never acceptable! It's usually the result of a gross error—say, you didn't keep your ingredients under the brine for a sauerkraut-type ferment, or in the cases of sauces, liquids, and loose ingredients in a jar, you forgot to shake or stir the contents.

If you don't keep your vegetables under the brine and leave the ferment alone, you allow (bad) bacteria or fungus (mold) to come in contact with air and create a situation in which they can potentially thrive and take over. That's how you end up with mold on top or other unfavorable issues.

I've *never* had any mold in over 10 years of fermentation in jars or crocks, and that's including a lot of experimental fermentation. There is no reason for it if you work closely with your ferment.

As a forager I work with a wide variety of unusual ingredients, shapes, and textures such as fibrous roots, stems, tough leaves, aromatic sticks, and so on. My challenge is to find fermentation techniques that I can work with to create safely delicious ingredients and condiments.

For example, our local wild mustard roots may be too tough to eat as is, but if you ferment them in a spicy brine, the resulting fermenting liquid can be used to make gourmet soups, salad dressings, and sauces.

Here are the various lacto-fermentation techniques I use.

Sauerkraut-Type Ferments

This category includes chopped or shredded ingredients such as cabbage mixed with salt and massaged to extract the juice, which will serve as the fermenting brine. The ingredients are then transferred and packed into a jar and usually kept under the brine using a weight.

These types of ferments are an easy way to explore wild flavors by simply mixing the cabbage base with wild greens such as spicy mustard leaves, radish leaves, dandelion, perennial pepperweed (*Lepidium latifolium*), garlic mustard (*Alliaria petiolata*), and so on. The flavors of these ferments can be further enhanced by the addition of spices (wild or not), aromatic seeds, or herbs. If you have a lot of such ferments in your pantry or fridge, you can also blend them together.

Brine-Based Ferments

You've seen these types of ferments with carrots, cauliflower, dill pickles, whole peppers, and so on. The technique is useful when you can't extract the juice and create a brine by massaging the ingredients with salt.

If you're a wildcrafter, this approach is perfect for edible roots such as burdock (*Arctium* spp.), specific fruits, or bulbs. It's very easy—you just need to create a salt brine, often with the addition of spices and aromatic seeds. Place the ingredients into the fermenting vessel, then add the brine and spices. Make sure the contents stay under the brine, and let it all ferment.

Liquid Ferments

Liquid ferments such as soups, hot sauces, or salsas cannot really be placed under a brine. The solution is to stir or shake the contents daily. I do it at least twice a day but often much more, though I have the advantage of working from home.

For example, let's say you decide to make a habanero/garlic hot sauce. You place your ingredients in a blender with the amount of water and salt called for in the recipe, push the button, and turn everything into a liquid.

Pour the contents into a jar and close the lid, but not too tight, so the fermentation gases can escape. Two or more times a day, screw the lid down tightly and shake the contents for a few seconds, then unscrew the lid a bit. The fermentation process will make the contents acidic. After around 10 days the fermentation gases will slow down considerably, and the contents will be acidic enough that mold won't be an issue. Close the lid tightly and place the jar in the fridge if you want, though I've fermented hot sauces for weeks and even months at room temperature. I still shake the jar from time to time if I ferment at room temperature, but after 3 to 4 weeks, it's not even a must. If you still see any pressure, just unscrew the lid a bit to burp the jar and close it again.

Fermenting Pastes

Some ferments are neither solid nor liquid. Good examples are fermented garlic, spicy chili pastes, or various relishes. Sometimes the paste is so thick that you can't shake it inside a jar as you would a liquid sauce.

The solution is to work with the ferment. Simply remove the lid and, using a clean fork or spoon, stir the contents two or three times daily; then screw back the lid, but not too tight, so the fermentation gases can escape. From my experience, some pastes won't have a lot of fermentation gases, while others, such as my dandelion harissa, can have a very active fermentation.

When the initial fermentation is complete, place your jar in the fridge. Some people set a layer of plastic or parchment paper on top of the paste to minimize contact with oxygen.

"Loose Ingredients" Fermentation

This is a technique I use with ingredients such as mustard, radish, or similar roots. The roots may be too tough to eat, but they're still loaded with flavors that can be extracted.

All you have to do is crush the roots in a *molcajete* (stone grinder) or cut them in small pieces, mix them with a salty brine and spices, then ferment the contents. It really works!

For optimal flavors I'm not always interested in a huge amount of liquid; my jar may be half full, but the crushed roots fill it. The solution is to shake, shake, shake. At least three times a day I close the lid tight and shake the jars for a few seconds, then unscrew the lid a bit. Sometimes I even place the jar upside down with the lid closed for a few hours.

The method works extremely well. The contents become acidic during the initial fermentation of around 10 days, and you won't experience issues such as mold. After that period I still shake it from time to time.

The jar is then placed in the fridge, but I've fermented such concoctions for 2 to 3 weeks at room temperature.

As a note, I'm probably stirring or shaking some of my ferments too much, but better safe than sorry.

Doing It

Fermentation is extremely easy to do and safe. Let's examine each technique with step-by-step photos.

METHOD 1:
BASIC FERMENTATION—SAUERKRAUT

This is how you make a regular sauerkraut. All you need for the fermentation process to occur is cabbage, salt, and a quart jar. That's the beautiful simplicity of it.

Ingredients for a 1-quart jar (946 ml)

1 large green cabbage
   (a bit less than 2 pounds / 900 g)
Salt

Equipment

Knife and cutting board
Large mixing bowl
1-quart jar with lid (washed and clean)
Pasteurized stone or weight to keep
   ingredients under the brine
   (pasteurize by boiling for 12 minutes)
Canning funnel (optional)
Wooden cabbage pounder (optional)

Procedure

From a hygiene perspective, because people often touch ingredients at the store, remove the outer leaves of the cabbage. Set aside a clean leaf to be used later for keeping the shredded cabbage submerged in the brine.

Quarter the cabbage and slice into thin strips. Some people remove the tough core inside each quarter before slicing (I do). Place an empty bowl on a scale and tare the scale (press the button that resets to zero). Add the sliced cabbage to the bowl, and calculate the weight. The amount of salt used for sauerkraut is usually around 2 teaspoons (11 g) salt for a pound (454 g) of vegetables. If you end up with around 1¾ pounds (800 g) of sliced sauerkraut, for instance, you would use around 1 tablespoon (17 g) of salt.

Add the salt and massage/squeeze the cabbage forcefully with both hands until the cabbage becomes very watery. I like to do it in a couple of steps. Massage for 3 minutes, let the cabbage rest for 5 minutes, then do it one more time until it's quite juicy. The idea is to extract enough juice so that you can keep the ingredients submerged in the created brine. It usually requires around 5 minutes of massaging—sometimes a bit more if the cabbage was dry from long storage.

Place a canning funnel on top of the jar (optional) and pack the cabbage inside it. You can use your hand or a wooden cabbage pounder. The goal is to eliminate air pockets but also to have liquid (brine) covering the contents. Try to leave around 1½ to 2 inches (2.5–3.1 cm) headspace (space between the brine and the rim of the jar). When you're done, cover the top with the folded leaf you set aside at the beginning. I also like to position a pasteurized stone on top, or some similar weight.

Instead of a rock, you can also purchase online all kinds of weights made of ceramic or glass to keep ingredients under the brine.

Remove any floating particles. Place the lid on top and close it, but not so tight that fermentation gases can't escape. Place the jar in a somewhat shaded area of the kitchen. It's a good idea to set a plate under it in case the fermentation process pushes some of the liquid over the top.

These days I just close the jars and burp the contents as necessary, but if you're just starting out with fermentation, try the method of not closing the lid too tight at first until you get comfortable with the process. If you forget to burp a closed jar for too long, you can end up with quite a mess because of the pressure building up inside. Also check the section on commercial fermentation kits (page 20), which can make it easier.

For the first 3 or 4 days (if I don't use a weight), I like to open the jar once a day and, using a clean fork or spoon, push down the contents to release all the air bubbles and keep the ingredients under the brine. After the initial fermentation (around 10 days in Southern California), I screw the lid tight as the fermentation gases should be practically nonexistent. Place the jar in the fridge.

As you eat the contents, it's a good idea to transfer and pack the contents into a smaller jar. The less airspace above your sauerkraut, the longer it will keep. I've eaten a sauerkraut that was a year old and still crunchy.

Remove the outer cabbage leaves and set aside a fresh one. You will use it later to keep the ingredients under the brine.

Quarter the cabbage. Some people remove the tough core inside each quarter before slicing (I do).

Slice each quarter into thin strips. Some people like their sauerkraut chunkier, while others prefer very thin strips.

Place an empty bowl on a scale and tare the scale (press the button that resets to zero). Then add the sliced cabbage to the bowl and calculate the weight.

Add the appropriate amount of salt based on the weight—2½ to 3 tablespoons of salt for every 5 pounds of vegetables.

Massage/squeeze the cabbage forcefully with both hands until it becomes very watery.

Place a canning funnel on top of the jar (optional) and pack the cabbage inside it.

Use your hand or a wooden cabbage pounder to pack the contents into the jar. The goal is to eliminate air pockets but also to have liquid (brine) covering the cabbage.

When you're done, cover the top with the folded leaf you set aside at the beginning.

I also like to position a pasteurized stone (boiled for 12 minutes) or similar weight on top. Remove any floating particles.

Place the lid on top and close it, but not so tight that fermentation gases can't escape.

After around 10 days of fermentation, close the lid tight, then place the jar in the fridge, where it will keep for months.

Alternative Ways to Keep Ingredients Under the Brine

Another method to weigh down the cabbage under the brine is to use a widemouthed Mason jar as the main fermentation vessel, then place inside it a smaller (½ pint) jar to keep everything weighted down. You can even add rocks or water inside the smaller jar if you want. Cover everything with a cloth and secure it with a twine or a rubber band. Ferment at room temperature, in a location out of direct sunlight.

Another technique used to keep ingredients submerged in the brine is to use a ziplock bag filled with water. It works, but I just don't like the idea of having plastic in my ferment.

As a note, I've rarely used these methods; they do work, but I like my simple method of using a regular lid. However, quite a few people will ferment this way.

Commercial Fermentation Systems and Kits

Most of my fermentation projects are done using regular canning jars with standard lids and bands or European jars with rubber seals, clamp-top lids, and clear glass. But as I explain throughout the book, I like to work closely with my ferments, supervise the contents daily, stirring or shaking the contents and burping the jar to release gases when necessary.

I don't recall experiencing any issues or even getting mold, and I've used this method for close to 10 years. That said, some people may opt to purchase a fermentation kit, which can offer specific advantages.

All commercial kits operate more or less the same way and are quite efficient. You place or screw the apparatus on top of a Mason jar and have some sort of system allowing the fermentation gases to escape. Some kits also include a mechanism or weight to push or keep the ingredients under the brine, thus reducing the possibility of mold. They work very well for ferments such as sauerkraut or kimchi. In the case of fermented sauces or pastes, having a means to keep the ingredients under the brine is not a necessity, but an airlock or mechanism allowing the gases to escape is quite helpful.

Purchasing a commercial kit is a good option for someone who does not have the time or desire to be as closely involved with the ferments as I do. I admit that I can be a bit obsessive in my relationship to my ferments, and my way may not be for everyone. Some people may just want to let the ferments do their thing without having to check on them daily. With a fermentation kit the contents will stay under the brine and you won't have to stir or shake them. Even if you mostly use jars, it's also useful to have such a system at home (I do) if you travel from time to time.

There are many commercial kits available and sold online, but here are four that I've personally used and recommend.

Kraut Source Fermentation Kit. I love this kit for the aesthetic, and it's quite effective, too. The system comprises a stainless steel unit placed on top and secured with a regular jar band. It allows fermentation gases to escape and also includes a mechanism to keep the ingredients under the brine. The stainless steel unit is dishwasher-safe and easy to use. My package came with salt and a recipe book (www.krautsource.com).

The Easy Fermenter Kit. The company sells various kits, and I received what they call The Easy Fermenter Kit. This basic kit includes everything you need to start fermenting: Three Easy Fermenter Lids, which are placed on top of the jar and set up to allow fermentation gases to escape; three beautiful glass weights to keep the ingredients under the brine; one oxygen extractor; and a guide/recipe booklet (www.nourishedessentials.com).

Masontops Complete Fermentation Kit. This very attractive kit is composed of a set of four pickle pipes, which allows fermentation gases to escape. You also receive a fermentation guide booklet, a set of four glass weights to keep the ingredients under the brine, and a very pretty wood vegetable tamper (www.masontops.com).

Pickle*Pusher Complete Mason Jar Fermentation Kit. The kit comprises a three-piece airlock system that allows fermentation gases to escape and an ingenious pickle pusher kit to keep the ingredients under the brine. I like the basic airlock setup if I do sauces or pastes (www.ultimatepicklejar.com).

Kraut Source Fermentation Kit.

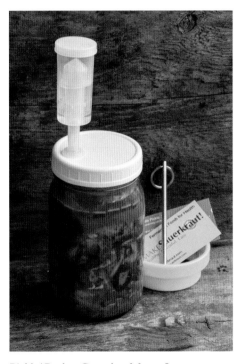

Pickle*Pusher Complete Mason Jar Fermentation Kit.

Most Common Questions Regarding Sauerkraut

I COULD NOT GET ENOUGH JUICE OUT OF MY CABBAGE TO MAKE A BRINE. WHAT DO I DO?

You can make a brine composed of 1 to 2 tablespoons (17–34 g) salt in 1 quart (1 L) water to cover the vegetables. I usually use around 1½ tablespoons (25 g) of salt per quart of water, which would be close to a 3 percent brine (see table 1.1).

MY BRINE WAS ABSORBED BY THE CABBAGE. DO I NEED TO ADD MORE?

This usually happens after the initial 10 days of fermentation; the contents are acidic enough that it's not a problem. As you eat your fermented ingredients, just transfer them to smaller jars whenever you can to limit the amount of oxygen, which will help keep them longer.

WHEN IS MY KRAUT READY TO EAT?

There are no rules; it's whenever you like to eat it. Some people say that ferments such as sauerkraut should be aged for a minimum of 20 days for best flavors and also to get the maximum probiotic benefits. That said, I like young crunchy and salty sauerkraut, so I don't mind eating it after a couple of weeks of fermentation.

My spicy, kimchi-like concoctions are usually fermented for anywhere between 4 days in summer and up to a week in the colder winter temperatures, then placed in the fridge and eaten pretty fast—usually within 2 weeks, but I've also aged these types of ferments for months.

HOW LONG WILL IT KEEP?

A sauerkraut will keep for many months properly stored in the fridge. I've had sauerkraut that was still crunchy and delicious after a year.

WHAT ABOUT TOPS WITH AN AIRLOCK?

An airlock is a device placed through a hole in a jar lid that allows fermentation gases to escape, protects the contents from outside bacteria or critters that could be interested in your ferment (flies), and creates an anaerobic (no oxygen) environment.

The main advantage to using an airlock is the fact that you don't need to burp the contents of your jar (unscrew the lid to let pressure off) and you don't risk having excess pressure if you forgot to "burp" the jar that day.

It's really not a bad idea to use them. Personally, I don't use airlocks for lacto-fermentation in jars, because I like to work closely and supervise my ferments daily, but if you're gone most of the day at work or travel from time to time, you probably should purchase some.

You have a lot of different options available online; do a search for "fermenting supplies." Amazon is also a good place.

METHOD 2:
BRINE-BASED FERMENTATION

If you can't extract and create your brine by massaging the ingredients with salt, you can solve the problem by creating a brine from scratch. For example, you can't just put salt on root vegetables such as carrots, radishes, or turnips, or vegetables like cucumbers, cauliflower, or bell peppers and expect to extract enough liquid through massaging and squeezing. It doesn't work; these vegetables cannot produce enough of their own brine.

The solution is simple. Instead of trying to create a brine through massaging/squeezing your ingredients as you would with sauerkraut, you create a brine by just mixing salt and water (unchlorinated).

Place your ingredients, such as carrots, cucumbers, or mixed vegetables, into a jar, then add the brine and various spices for flavoring. It's that easy. The lactic acid bacteria present on the ingredients will start digesting the sugar and turn the brine acidic, which in turn will guarantee food preservation because the bad bacteria that can spoil the contents can't survive in that acidic environment.

Traditionally, to keep veggies crunchy and crisp, tannic leaves from grapes, black tea, or horseradish are usually placed on top with the added purpose of keeping the ingredients under the brine. I don't find tea leaves or horseradish in the wilderness, but we have a lot of possible alternatives such as oak, currant, wild grape, or willow leaves, oak bark, and probably many more interesting possibilities to play with. Be aware that a little bit can go a long way. For example, our local coastal oak leaves are extremely bitter, and my first attempt to use them didn't work very well; however, my sauerkraut with roasted oak bark was quite delicious. Adding a tannic element in the jar is not a must, but it helps with texture. Some tannic leaves or spices such as bay, mugwort, or cloves can be used to add flavors as well. Locally, I often use our California bay leaves.

Like sauerkraut, ferment at room temperature until the initial fermentation is complete and no more fermentation gases are present.

Table 1.1 Brine Calculator

Brine (%)	Pint (0.47 L)	Quart (0.95 L)	Gallon (3.78 L)
2	9 g	19 g	76 g
3	13 g	29 g	114 g
3.5	17 g	33 g	132 g
5	24 g	47 g	189 g
10	48 g	95 g	379 g

Note: 2% brine: kimchi, sauerkraut, cauliflower, carrots, salsa, and green beans. 3.5 to 5% brine: bell peppers, onions, and cucumbers. 5 to 10% brine: pepper sauces/mash.

The recipes will vary a bit, and there is conflicting information in books and online. Most recipes ask for a 2 to 3.5 percent brine—the exceptions are a few ingredients such as pickling cucumbers, radishes, bell peppers, or onions, which are more prone to spoiling and require a stronger brine: at least 3.5 percent and up to 5 percent. A lot of pickle medley recipes call for a 3.5 percent brine.

The brine pickling method is quite useful when dealing with wild edibles and can be used with unusual ingredients such as roots, stems, seedpods (for instance, wild radish), and others. In this book most of the recipes will ask for a 3 to 3.5 percent brine (1½–2 tablespoons salt per quart / 29–33 g per liter).

I've observed that it takes a bit longer than a regular sauerkraut, from 10 days to 2 weeks. Once it's complete I place my jar in the fridge, where it will keep for many months.

The rule of keeping ingredients under the brine will apply to these types of ferments, but if you pack the jar nicely it's not always necessary to add a weight on top. If you ferment a mix of vegetables or wild food ingredients, try to combine components that have similar texture and density—for example, cauliflower with carrots or broccoli with garlic.

Spices are usually added to brine pickles. The most common ones include cloves, bay leaves, juniper berries, mustard seeds, coriander, peppercorn, allspice, dill, chili flakes, garlic, thyme, and tarragon. You can even buy classic pickling spice mix at your regular supermarket.

As a wildcrafter, this is where you can have fun and add some truly local flavors. Wildcrafted spices I commonly use include: California juniper berries (*Juniperus californica*); wild fennel (*Foeniculum vulgare*) leaves and seeds; bur chervil (*Anthriscus caucalis*); black mustard (*Brassica nigra*) seeds; California bay laurel leaves (*Umbellularia californica*); various local sages; yarrow (*Achillea millefolium*); local mugwort (*Artemisia douglasiana*); roasted mesquite wood or oak bark, pinyon pine branches, or pine or fir needles; California sagebrush (*Artemisia californica*); wild celery (*Apium* spp.) seeds; and many others. Even after 20 years of wildcrafting, I continue to discover new possibilities.

Some of your local wild spices may have distinct peculiarities that you'll need to research and experiment with. For example, our local juniper berries are really flavorful unripe (and dried), but if fully ripe, they just taste sugary with little flavor. California bay leaves need to be slowly dehydrated at room temperature for a month; some people react badly (myself included) to fresh bay leaves, probably due to specific terpenes (aromatic chemical compounds) or other agents that evaporate during the slow dehydration process.

BASIC PICKLE BRINE

Here is the procedure for making a basic brine pickle. We'll use simple ingredients like carrots and common spices.

Ingredients for a 1-quart jar (946 ml)

4–5 medium-sized carrots

1–2 garlic cloves

1 regular bay leaf or ½ California bay leaf

1–2 dried chili peppers (optional; I use Japanese or arbol chili peppers)

1 fresh dill sprig

Around 2 cups (475 ml) water (not tap water, which often contains chlorine)

Brine

Brine note: I use 1½ tablespoons of salt to 1 quart of water (26 g salt per liter). It's a bit less than a 3 percent brine. For this recipe you'll use around 2 cups (475 ml) of water, more or less, depending on how much your jar is packed. So you're looking at ¾ tablespoon (15 g) of salt for 2 cups of water. If you need a bit more water, just use 1 tablespoon (17 g)—you can't go wrong.

Equipment

Knife and cutting board

1-quart jar with lid (washed and clean)

Canning funnel (optional, but it helps)

Procedure

1. Clean your jar, lid, and screw band thoroughly and set aside. I use regular hot water and dish soap.
2. Clean your carrots gently with cold water. I don't peel them, as a lot of the lacto bacteria will be present on the surface. You want those bacteria! Cut the carrots into sticks, measuring the length necessary by comparing them with the jar size. The sticks should be around 5¼ inches (13 cm) in length. I usually cut each carrot in four or six strips.
3. Crush your garlic cloves (or cut them in half lengthwise) and place them at the bottom of the jar, then add the rest of the ingredients. I add the bay leaf, optional chili peppers, and dill as I fill the jar and not all in the same location, so the flavors distribute evenly in the jar. You should end up with around 1 inch (2.5 cm) headspace.
4. Prepare your brine by dissolving ¾ tablespoon (15 g) of salt into 2 cups (475 ml) of water.
5. Pour the brine into the jar. If you did a good job packing your ingredients into the jar, they should stay submerged under the brine and there would be no need for a weight on top. If that's not the case, you can add a pasteurized stone or similar weight on top to keep them under the brine. Screw the lid on top, but not so tight that fermentation gases can't escape.
6. Place the jar in a somewhat shaded area of the kitchen. As a note, these days I simply close the jars and burp the contents as necessary, but if you're just starting with fermentation, try the method of not closing the lid too tight at first so gases can escape until you get comfortable with the process. If you forget to burp a closed jar for too long, you can end up with quite a mess because of the pressure building up inside. Also check the section on commercial fermentation kits; one of these can make things easier.

7. When the initial fermentation is completed and you don't get much gas emanating from the ferment, usually 10 to 15 days, screw the lid tight and place the jar in the fridge. The pickled ingredients will last for several months and the flavors will continue to develop. But you can eat them young, too; I usually eat the contents after 2 to 3 weeks of fermentation.

It's completely normal for the brine to become cloudy during the fermentation process, and the contents will take on sour/tangy flavors.

I often serve my fermented carrots with a tad of seasoned rice vinegar or homemade apple cider vinegar. To make a seasoned vinegar, just combine ¼ cup of vinegar with 4 teaspoons maple syrup, honey, or sugar and ½ teaspoon kosher salt. A little goes a long way, but it's quite delicious.

I add the bay leaf, chili peppers, and dill as I fill the jar and
not all in the same location, so the flavors get distributed evenly in the jar.

METHOD 3:
CHUNKY OR LIQUID FERMENTS—
SOUPS, HOT SAUCES, AND SALSAS

As explained earlier, the problem with liquid ferments such as hot sauces or salsas is the fact that you can't really keep the ingredients under the brine. You have a higher risk of spoiling, because some of the contents will be in contact with air/oxygen, which can promote the growth of bad bacteria or mold.

But it's really not an issue if you work with your ferment. The solution is to stir or shake the contents daily. I do it at least twice a day until the initial fermentation is done and the contents are acidic enough. You'll know it is done when you don't get any substantial fermentation gases being released inside the jar and very little or no pressure on a closed lid. I've never had any mold or spoilage issues using this method.

Note that not all ingredients need to go through a full initial fermentation. For example, salsas don't age very well, and the contents can quickly become mushy. Two to 4 days of fermentation is often enough. If I just want to get the benefits of probiotics and a tad of sour flavors, some of my soups are just fermented for a couple of days.

Hot sauces require more salt because peppers are more prone to molding. I usually double the amount of salt that I should be using in my fermented hot sauce recipes, which works perfectly, as many hot sauces such as sriracha or Tabasco are quite salty in the first place. I usually end up with a sauce that is close to a 5 percent brine, or around 3 tablespoons of salt per quart (47 g salt per liter). I never add vinegar to my hot sauces, and some are fermented for up to 3 months at room temperature before being placed in the fridge.

BASIC FERMENTED SALSA

You'd better wear gloves for this one. I once made a large quantity of salsa without using gloves. My jalapeños were superhot (I didn't taste them, silly me), and it ended up being quite a painful experience; the burning sensation in my hands lasted hours.

A fermented salsa is a rather short ferment, usually 2 to 4 days. The longer you age it, the softer and mushier your ingredients will become. I would advise you to make it quite chunky, but that's really just my preference. Some people age their salsa, but I'm not a fan of it; I like it when it's still young, slightly sour, and crunchy.

Ingredients for a 1-pint jar (475 ml)

5 ounces (142 g) diced tomatoes
    (around 2 medium-sized tomatoes)
1½ ounces (42 g) diced white or red onion
    (around ¼ medium-sized onion)
2 ounces (57 g) diced bell pepper
    (around ½ small bell pepper)
2 ounces (57 g) or 2 small (or 1 large)
    diced jalapeño peppers (remove seeds
    if you want)
½ ounce (14 g) chopped cilantro
    (usually 1 bunch)
Salt (see directions)

Equipment

Knife and cutting board
Disposable gloves
1-pint jar with lid (washed and clean)
Canning funnel (optional, but it helps)

Procedure

1. Place the diced tomatoes, onion, bell pepper, and jalapeños in a bowl, add the chopped cilantro, and mix well. You should end up with around 11 ounces (312 g).

2. Usually for fermentation purposes, you follow the rule of 2 teaspoons (11 g) of salt for every pound (2.3 kg) of vegetables. Because this one is going to be a short ferment, however, we're changing the rule and you're going by flavors—you need to make it a tad too salty. Mix ½ teaspoon (2.5 g) of salt with your ingredients first and taste. A bit too salty is all right; the saltiness will go down a bit with the fermentation process.

3. Once you've mixed in your salt, transfer the contents into a food processor for a less chunky salsa or directly into a pint jar. Close the lid, but not too tight, so the fermentation gases can escape. A couple of times a day, screw the lid tight and shake the contents for a few seconds, then unscrew the lid a bit. As an alternative, you can also open the jar, stir briefly with a clean fork or spoon, then screw the lid back on (not too tight).

    For chunky-type ferments such as salsa or hot sauces, don't fill more than around 75 percent of the jar—sometimes bubbles created during the fermentation process will push the ingredients upward. Not a problem if you monitor your

After the initial fermentation, place in the fridge or, if you're making hot sauce, continue fermenting at room temperature. A salsa is a shorter ferment—usually 2 to 4 days.

ferment during the day, but I've had a couple of overfilled jars create a mess in the morning due to a very active fermentation during the night.

4. The fermentation process will make the contents acidic. For a salsa, we're going to stop the fermentation after 2 to 4 days and place the jar in the fridge. For better texture, I like to eat my salsa within 5 days. Other ferments such as hot sauces will be fermented for around 10 to 15 days, at which point the fermentation gases will slow down considerably, and the contents will be acidic enough that mold won't be an issue. After that period, close the lid and place the jar in the fridge if you want—though I've also fermented hot sauces for weeks at room temperature. I still shake the jar from time to time if I ferment at room temperature, but after a couple of weeks it's not a must. (I'll still do it maybe once or twice a week.) If you feel any pressure on the jar's lid, just unscrew it a bit to burp the jar and close it again.

METHOD 4:
FERMENTING PASTES

Some pastes are so thick that you can't really shake the contents into a jar. This was the case for my Ethiopian-inspired spice paste and my harissa sauce.

Pastes can also be a bit tricky and, from experience, need to be monitored well. Some may ferment very slowly, and some may react like a sourdough with extensive swelling and bubbling. That was the case with my fermented harissa chili paste. The harissa was barely fermenting for 7 days, but on day 8 I woke up with the jar's lid about to explode. For the next 3 days, I had to stir the inside two or three times a day to remove the air pockets forming and keep the paste down in the jar. Luckily, my jar was only 60 percent full originally, so I didn't have any spillage.

The basic method is similar to that for chunky or liquid ferments, but instead of shaking the contents, you need to stir them several times a day with a clean spoon or fork to remove any air bubbles forming in the paste due to fermentation activity. This also serves to mix the top part, which is more exposed to air, with the fermenting acidic paste below.

After 10 to 15 days, when the initial fermentation is complete, you can place the paste in the fridge. Try to use an appropriate jar size to minimize the amount of oxygen present. It's not a must, but I like to place a perfectly cut piece of plastic wrap on top; some people use parchment paper or a piece of plastic cut from a ziplock bag. Less contact with oxygen will help your ferment keep longer.

Open the jar and stir the contents with a clean fork or spoon.

METHOD 5: FERMENTING
LOOSE INGREDIENTS IN A JAR

This method was directly inspired by unusual wild ingredients such as roots. Good examples are the mustard and wild radish roots (*Raphanus sativus*) I forage locally. They're too tough and fibrous to eat, but they are packed with flavors.

To really extract and explore the taste of the various tough roots I use, my solution is to crush them using a stone grinder and mix them in a ferment comprising maybe 60 percent roots and 40 percent brine. I also use this method with mixed ferments that represent whole environments, which can be composed of roots, dry stems, leaves, aromatic sticks, and barks.

In many such ferments I'm mainly interested in creating a flavorful brine with spices, which I then use to make soups, sauces, salad dressings, and so on. For maximum flavors, I don't fill the jar with brine, and I use as much root material as possible. But there are really no rules as to how much brine to use; it's up to you. Most of my brine in these types of ferments consists of 1 teaspoon salt (5.5 g) per cup (236 ml) of water, which is a 2 percent brine (23 g salt per liter), but you can go higher.

Needless to say, there are a lot of loose ingredients that are not placed under the brine and are in contact with air within the jar. The solution for such "extreme" ferments is to really work with them and shake, shake, shake, then shake some more. I probably will shake the contents two to three times daily and from time to time will even place the jar upside down for a couple of hours (or longer). The idea is to make sure that, as the fermentation progresses, all ingredients inside are well marinated into the forming acidic brine and don't spoil.

These days I usually keep the lid closed so I can monitor the pressure, then shake and burp the jar as necessary (see the following section, "Using Lids as a Pressure Gauge").

Prepare your brine, add your spices, crush your roots (if you used roots), then place all your ingredients in a jar and close the lid.

About Lids

Fermenting in Mason jars with a closed lid could be somewhat controversial in fermentation circles, but it really isn't if you have experience and carefully monitor your ferments. I don't advise you to do it if you're new to fermenting (it's probably better if you unscrew the lid a bit so fermentation gases can escape), but otherwise closed lids can be an interesting way to know if a ferment is active or not.

Using Lids as a Pressure Gauge

When the lid of a ferment is screwed tight, the fermentation gases can't escape and create internal pressure, which will push the lid upward. With experience, though, you can gauge how active a fermentation is by pressing on the lid with your index finger. If the pressure is excessive, you can "burp" the jar by unscrewing the lid; from there you can decide to leave the lid unscrewed a bit so fermentation gases can escape or close it again if you want to monitor the pressure further.

Please note that it takes discipline and constant monitoring (sometimes several times a day) to use this method. If you're a forgetful person, it's definitely not for you. Neglecting a very active ferment for a day or two can create a mess or be downright dangerous. Either your lid will bend and pop off the jar with force, lots of liquid or fermenting ingredients bursting out (which is usually what happens), or the jar will explode. Jar explosion is pretty rare but can occur. You really need to supervise and burp every day to release the pressure.

The method is quite useful for the following reasons:

It can let you know that a fermentation has started. Very often, I'll close the lid in the beginning and, upon verifying that the ferment is now active, I'll burp the jar and leave the lid unscrewed a bit until the next time I stir or shake the contents. Because I didn't have existing recipes for my wild fermented ingredients and I experimented quite a lot, finding out if a fermentation had started correctly was quite important in some instances. If after 3 to 4 days nothing is happening, it's a cause for concern. I might try the recipe again, but next time I would use a starter by incorporating liquid from an active ferment, such as sauerkraut juice.

Sometimes a ferment will start very slowly. My dandelion/harissa sauce was barely fermenting for the first 5 or 6 days, with just a bit of pressure on the lid. I would stir the contents daily and even checked the acidity (the pH was 3.7), but there was very little indication of fermentation. So on day 4 I added a bit of sauerkraut juice to the paste and closed the lid again. The mild pressure continued for another 3 or 4 days; then, on day 8, I woke up to a lid that was about to blow. It can happen that fast. I burped it with no problem (in the sink . . . just in case) and had another 3 days of crazy active fermentation when I had to burp the jar three times daily.

You may also notice, as can be the case with paste, that a fermentation is active and constant but doesn't produce a lot of pressure. You barely need to burp it every couple of days. It's totally okay; some ferments can be like that.

Using the lid as a gauge is also useful to determine if an initial fermentation, usually around 10 days, is done. I often close the lid when I think it's finished and check the pressure at the end of the day or the next day. If there is barely any pressure or none at all, I know it's time to place my jar in the fridge for aging.

Personally, I find this method quite helpful and I use it a lot, but as I said earlier, it's much better if you're an experienced fermenter and you know you have the discipline necessary to monitor your ferments daily. Used responsibly, there is also something very personal about this approach: It really helps reestablish a close relationship with your ferments. You can "feel" how ferments react to temperature, how adding some acidic elements such as lime or lemon juice can influence the process, the peculiarity of some recipes, and so much more!

How to Unscrew a Stuck Lid

If you do a lot of fermentation in jars, you will encounter from time to time a lid that is stuck or really hard to open. The bands and lids you buy at the store are usually made of tin-plated steel that, over time, can rust due to contact with salted brine and the acidity of the ferment itself. This can make it difficult to open a jar.

Screwing the lid excessively tight when placing a ferment in the fridge can also make it hard to open later on, as cold temperatures have a tendency to contract the metal band.

My solution is to place the top of the jar and lid band under very hot water for 10 seconds or more. The heat will cause the band to expand a bit and allow you to unscrew it. In the worst-case scenario, if you can't do it with your hands, use a jar opener after the hot-water treatment.

Purchasing a jar opener is a really good idea; one day you will need one for that especially stubborn jar. I've used my Pampered Chef Jar Opener for the last two years and I've never experienced a jar I could not open . . . eventually.

My lids and bands get reused often as I do more ferments. Over time you may experience bands with excessive rust. Simply replace the bands with new ones, which can be purchased separately.

Rusting lids is not just a fermentation issue. Anyone who does canning and pickling eventually needs to replace the bands. If the issue is really bugging you, do some searching online for alternative tops when fermenting in jars, such as stainless steel lids and bands or plastic tops with airlocks. You also have the option of purchasing a commercial system such as those described on page 20.

Avoiding Rust on the Lid Band

There are solutions if you want to avoid rust on your lid bands. During the initial fermentation of 10 days or so, I'm not too worried, but it can become an issue when you store your ferments in the fridge or, in the case of hot sauces, you ferment at room temperature for a long time.

The answer is quite simple. After the initial fermentation you need to clean the band and sides of the jar. Once the band is dried, place some parchment paper on top of the jar, screw on the lid and band, then store in the fridge. If you keep opening the jar to retrieve some of the ingredients inside, inspect the parchment paper and replace if necessary.

I've also seen people using plastic wrap instead of parchment paper, but I haven't tried it myself.

Checking the pH

If you start experimenting with new wild edibles, low-salt fermentation, or unusual ingredients such as fermenting leaves or working with roots, it's a *very* good idea to invest a bit of money in pH test paper strips. (I use Hydrion strips. that measure acidity ranging from 3 to 5.5 pH.) Even better, purchase a pH meter.

A few years back, pH meters used to be expensive, but these days you can buy one for less than $20 and they are useful if you deal with pastes or hot sauces. The pH strips use a color system, and in the case of colorful sauces, you won't be able to get an accurate reading.

A pH meter or paper strip will give you a reading on the pH scale (*pH* stands for "potential hydrogen"), which measures how acidic or basic a substance is. The pH scale ranges from 0 to 14. The lower the number, the more acidic the ingredients. For example, vinegar has an acidity level of around 3. A sauerkraut or kimchi usually comes in at around 3.3.

It's important to know the acidity because of one specific bacterium, *Clostridium botulinum*. This bacterium is found in the form of spores in soil and also on the surface of some ingredients such as roots, fruits, and vegetables. It can lie dormant for years, but under the right conditions, such as the absence of oxygen in a jar, the spores may grow out into active bacteria again, in the process producing neurotoxins. The poisoning that results from ingesting contaminated ingredients is called botulism, and it can be fatal. Even when treated, it is fatal for 5 to 10 percent of people in developed countries. Untreated, you have a 50 percent chance of death. Not something to sneer at.

But on the good side, *C. botulinum* cannot grow below a pH of 4.6, which is one of the reasons why fermentation works so well. Ferments such as sauerkraut or kimchi quickly reach an acid level well below 4.6, thus making botulism a non-issue.

In this book I may repeat myself here and there on the issue of botulism and pH, but I think it's an important subject. As you'll see, I've had some real surprises when substituting wild edibles for common ones in no-salt fermentation recipes from reputable books. Sometimes, despite an active fermentation, I could not get the pH below 4.6, which is a big no-no.

Spending around $20 for a lifesaving device is a worthy investment, so if you decide to experiment, make sure to test pH levels. When I want to investigate a new ferment, I usually test my unusual recipe or ingredients when the fermentation process starts and again when the initial fermentation (around 10 days) is complete. If the pH isn't below 4.2, I won't use it. In some cases it's even a good idea to check the pH again after a couple of months and before you eat it. I once had an unusual ferment that had a pH of 4.3 and ended up close to 4.6 after 3 months in the fridge.

As a final note, you can influence the pH in a recipe by incorporating from the start acidic ingredients such as lemon or lime juice or adding sugary elements that you know will ferment well and create an acidic environment. That's why I make a dandelion sauerkraut but not a ferment from pure dandelion leaves. The lacto bacteria will eat the sugar present in the cabbage and convert it to lactic acid. In my experience, just fermenting dandelion leaves didn't create a low enough pH.

Breaking the Rules

I've been fermenting for so long and experimenting with ferment types ranging from regular sauerkraut to sauces, pastes, and soups that, over time, I've developed my own techniques to ensure that none of my ferments will get moldy or go bad. I don't recall any failure in the last 10 years.

If you are new to fermenting, I highly suggest that you start with the traditional methods and advice such as keeping everything under the brine, removing any organic elements floating on top, using the prescribed amount of salt, and so on. Heck, purchasing a small fermenting crock may not be a bad idea, either. I just like jars because they're so much fun for creating experiments in various sizes, and the resulting amount is perfect for my use. If you have a large family or own a restaurant, larger containers such as crocks can make sense.

But here is the scoop:

From my perspective, the key to successful ferments is to work with them. The vast majority of mold issues I see discussed on fermentation forums happen because people follow a recipe, which may include keeping things under the brine. Then they leave the ferment alone for a considerable amount of time, only to discover some mold floating on top of the brine. All kinds of things can happen if you don't supervise or work with your ferment. For example, the ingredients may absorb the brine and then be exposed to air, or your airlock can run dry. If you're using a water-sealed crock and forget to add water on the side, you may have issues. In my early days of fermentation, I experienced that problem when fermenting in crocks for 2 to 3 months. It was quite heartbreaking to open the lid and see some mold floating on top of the brine.

Since I started working closely with my ferments, however, I have never experienced any failure.

So yes, in the beginning, if you do a sauerkraut-type ferment, keep things under the brine, but recognize that it's not the only safe technique. If you don't supervise your ferments, you may not notice that some small pieces have started floating on top after a while. These days I don't even add a stone or glass weight on top of my sauerkraut; instead I push the ingredients under the brine using a clean fork or spoon at least once daily. As the fermentation process makes the contents acidic in just a few days, experiencing mold or anything "going bad" becomes less of an issue. If you make fermented salsas, hot sauces, liquid soups, and so on, stirring or shaking the jar will do the job. Based on my own personal experience, the first 10 days are usually the most crucial; after that, the contents are generally acidic enough.

Five Knife Cutting Techniques Every Wild Fermenter Should Know

Let's face it, a lot of the common fermented foods are quite easy to prepare. Shredding cabbage to make sauerkraut is a cinch, and roots such as carrots, radishes, or beets are quite tender and easy to slice. There is a good reason why these foods are fermented: They actually taste good and have the right texture at the end of the fermentation process.

But when you start entering the universe of wild edibles, you are going to deal with different parameters—toughness, stringiness, chewiness, and so on. It's probably why not many people have experimented with fermenting wild food. Many years ago I fermented mustard leaves mixed with shredded cabbage, and the end result was quite inedible: It was extremely tough to chew. And yet I presently use the same ingredient to make a delicious ferment. The only difference is that I apply the right cutting techniques. Often the flavors are there to start with; the challenge is to prepare the ingredients properly prior to the fermentation so the texture and mouthfeel will work at the end.

Ever heard of *chiffonade*? Probably not, unless you're a chef or experienced cook, but I learned the term while researching how to deal with some chewy wild edibles. Ten years ago I would have thought that the leaves of perennial pepperweed, black mustard (*Brassica negra*), or curly dock

(*Rumex crispus*) were inedible due to the fact that the leaves, once fermented, were so tough that eating them was a real jaw workout. Then I experimented with the chiffonade cut and it opened up a brand-new universe of edible leaves, fermented or not. It's so simple: Twist the leaves and slice them in very thin strips. The tougher the leaves, the thinner you want those strips to be, and with experience you can become a true slicing artist. That simple technique turned my tough leaves into fermented delicacies.

The same can be said of some roots. Wild turnip (*Brassica rapa*) or burdock roots are tough, but using proper knife cutting techniques and slicing them thinly or applying a julienne cut makes them quite edible. Understanding and applying proper knife cutting techniques were a true epiphany in regard to fermenting wild edibles, and opened up many new creative possibilities for me. If an ingredient is too tough or chewy, experiment with different cuts; chances are, you'll end up with a tasty solution.

The Five Basic Cuts and Their Uses

1. **Chiffonading.** Perfect for tough leaves such as mustard, radish, perennial pepperweed, and many others.
2. **Slicing.** Great technique for roots that are tough but not too stringy. Also works well with stems. My favorite technique for fermenting cattail (*Typha*) or black mustard stems.
3. **Julienne cutting.** Another good technique for dense and fibrous roots. Sometimes slicing and cutting will work on the same ingredients, but you can choose a specific technique for aesthetic purposes.
4. **Chopping and mincing.** Works well for onions and peppers, also some bulbs or stems. Keep chopping these ingredients and you end up mincing them. Mincing works beautifully with delicious herbs such as parsley, basil, wild chervil, chickweed, and so on.
5. **Dicing.** I mostly use this technique for somewhat softer roots such as daikon or radish. You'll see recipes using dehydrated diced daikon roots with wild spices later on in this book.

There is one more technique I use on roots that are very savory but too hard and stringy to eat as is. By pounding, chopping, or crushing them, you can extract their flavors through fermentation in savory brines. The resulting brines can be used for soups, sauces, salad dressings, and so on.

To chiffonade, twist leaves and slice thinly. This is a great technique for tough or chewy leaves like mustard, wild radish, dandelion, and many others. One of my most used knife techniques for wild food.

Slicing is perfect for roots and fibrous or stringy stems. Lay your root or stem on the board and slowly cut down to create uniform pieces. Experiment: The tougher the ingredient is, the thinner you may need to slice it.

The julienne cut works great with large roots. Slice the roots horizontally, then one more time vertically to create long, thin strips. Depending on how tough your root is, you can create very small strips. Think of them as tiny French fries.

Chopping and mincing are good techniques for ingredients such as garlic, peppers, and onions or aromatic and savory herbs like wild chervil, chickweed, and parsley. Simply cut your ingredient into pieces. Keep chopping and you're basically mincing—creating tiny little tasty bits.

Dicing: Create a julienne cut and then cut it once more. You can make large, small, and tiny cubes. For fermentation purposes, large cubes work great with soft roots such as daikon while small cubes are great for tougher roots.

Making a Culture Starter

For most ferments, such as sauerkraut or kimchi, all you need are vegetables or fruits, salt, and sometimes water. The lacto bacteria are already present on the ingredients, and a successful fermentation is assured. But for some recipes you will need a starter culture. Good examples in this book are fermented cooked greens or mushrooms. The ingredients are cooked or steamed, and any bacteria present in the first place are killed during the cooking process— thus you'll need to add a source of live bacteria (starter) to obtain an active fermentation. I also use a culture starter when I make my fermented nuts and seed cheeses.

There are various ways to introduce a live culture. Some people use whey or use the contents of probiotic supplement capsules purchased at the store. For my part, and in this book, I use the active brine from basic ferments such as sauerkraut; sometimes, if I have at hand some fermenting vegetables such as carrots, I may use that brine as well. But most of the time I create my own culture starter by using cabbage. It's cheap and convenient, and if your diet is plant-based, it's a good alternative to whey.

CULTURE STARTER

Making a culture starter is as simple as making a basic sauerkraut (fermentation method 1, page 16). The only difference is that I may use more liquid than necessary because I'm more interested in the fermenting brine than the ingredients.

For my purposes, I want to use the young and very active fermenting brine created during the initial fermentation. That's when you get a lot of bacterial activity. I can start using the brine when I see that it's active and fermentation gases are present; the timing is normally from day 3 to around day 10, depending on the temperature. In all honesty, I have used the brine of an aged ferment (a couple of weeks old) as a starter and it did work, but I would need to experiment more before concluding it works every time.

Ingredients for a 1-quart jar (946 ml) (around 75 percent full)

1 small green cabbage
   (around 1½ pounds / 680 g)
1 tablespoon (17 g) salt
Around ½ cup (118 ml) water

Equipment

Knife and cutting board
Large mixing bowl
1-quart jar with lid (washed and clean)
Canning funnel (optional, but it helps)

Procedure

1. Remove the outer leaves of the cabbage. Quarter the cabbage and slice it into thin strips. Add it to the bowl and sprinkle on the salt.
2. Massage the cabbage, squeezing forcefully with both hands until it becomes very watery. I like to do this in a few steps: Massage for 3 minutes, let the cabbage rest for 5 minutes, then do it one more time until it's quite juicy.
3. Place a canning funnel (optional) on top of the jar and pack the cabbage inside it. You can also just use your hand or a wooden cabbage pounder. The goal is to eliminate air pockets, but also to have liquid (brine) covering the contents. The jar should be around 75 percent full.
4. Next, add the water. Try to leave 1 to 1½ inches (2.5–3.8 cm) headspace (the space between the brine and the rim of the jar).
5. Place the lid on top and close it. When making a starter, my technique is either to shake the contents at least once daily and burp the jar as necessary or open the jar, stir the contents at least once daily, then close the lid again (burping as necessary). If you want, you can also unscrew the lid a tiny bit to let fermentation gases escape, which is probably a more workable arrangement if you don't work at home as I do.

Once the fermentation is active, you can start using the brine. Sometimes, if the ferment was only 2 or 3 days old and I used most of the brine for starter, I make another generation of culture starter by adding a new brine composed of a bit less than 1 teaspoon (4 g) of salt per cup; I let this ferment with the cabbage for another couple of days before I use the new fermenting brine.

After that, the cabbage is either composted or used for other culinary applications such as soup. Don't just throw it away!

Once the fermentation is active, you can use the liquid as a culture starter.

CHAPTER 2

Getting Started: Exploring Your Local Terroir

*T*erroir is an interesting French word. As I was writing this book, I looked for a possible synonym in the English dictionary, but there is none because no English word has the same meaning. It originates from the word *terre*, which means "land."

It is mostly associated with winemaking, but if you start exploring local flavors, you'll realize that we all have a specific terroir. The Lexico definition is as follows:

Terroir:

1. The complete natural environment in which a particular wine is produced, including factors such as the soil, topography, and climate.
2. The characteristic taste and flavor imparted to a wine by the environment in which it is produced.

However, if you start exploring local edible plants—fruits, mushrooms, berries, and their wild flavors—you'll realize that the definition is truly applicable to everything that grows. Each environment is unique. If I pick up a dandelion in my local forest and one in my backyard, chances are the flavors will be slightly different. In fact, yesterday I found a bunch near a pristine natural source of water and, probably due to soil composition, it had a bit of a salty taste.

Everything plays a role in terroir: location of plants, altitude, climate, soil, temperature, time of year, and so on. A wild mustard growing in March will be tender with some sweetness. The same plant growing in June or July, even in the same location, will have a tendency to taste more bitter due to the lack of rain, higher temperatures, and exposure to the sun.

So, for our purpose, *terroir* can be defined as:

> The complete natural environment in which your local edibles grow, including factors such as soil, topography, and climate. The term also encompasses the types of plants and the characteristic taste and flavor imparted by this environment.

The current environment can be vastly different from what it was hundreds of years ago. After all, in our modern age, you can have breakfast in Paris and eat dinner in New York the same day. With our help, plants have traveled all over the world as well and have seen new lands as opportunities. This all happened very quickly. The first farmers in colonial America surely imported some of their seeds from England and other European countries. A bag of wheat or barley grains could also contain a lot of unwanted seeds, sometimes as much as 1 percent.

As a modern wildcrafter I look at the present environment as what it actually is, a mix of native and non-native plants. Some of the non-native plants can also be considered *invasive*, which is defined by Merriam-Webster as:

> Tending to spread, especially in a quick or aggressive manner: such as a non-native organism; growing and dispersing easily, usually to the detriment of native species and ecosystems.

Here in Los Angeles it's plain to see; I just need to go outside my apartment and look at the local hills surrounding the city. They are covered by various types of mustard flowers, wild oats, foxtail grass (*Hordeum murinum, H. jubatum*), and many other non-native plants. Probably 90 percent of the flora covering the hills is non-native and often invasive.

But guess what? Most of those invasive plants are edible and nutritious. In many instances we've just forgotten how to use them properly.

The Mediterranean hoary mustard (*Hirschfeldia incana*) and the black mustard covering my local hills were even used as crops in the old days. Black mustard is still a crop in some part of India and Africa, where the seeds are used in traditional curry. But locally these plants are considered a noxious weed destined to be uprooted or sprayed with chemicals.

To be honest, there was some trial and error involved in my own quest for local flavors. In the beginning I saw all plants as equal, but over the years of interacting intimately with my environment and educating myself on local ecology, I've come to take a different approach.

I still love all plants, but I can use wildcrafting as an opportunity to help the environment. In fact, I would say that close to 90 percent of what I collect

Close-up of a 5-acre (2 ha) field full of wild radish, curly dock, perennial pepperweed, and mustard. These are pretty much exclusively non-native plants, but they can be turned into delicious and healthy food.

is non-native and often invasive. The plants are easy picking because they are extremely plentiful, but many of them are also very flavorful and nutritious. Good examples are wild fennel, nasturtium (*Tropaeolum* spp.), water mint (*Mentha aquatica*), black mustard, chickweed, feral figs and olives, lamb's-quarter, mallow (*Malva* spp.), curly dock, and countless others.

It's an interesting perspective when you realize that some people in Los Angeles can't afford decent food, yet we are surrounded by many invasive "weeds" that are highly nutritious.

Using wildcrafting and exploring local flavors as a tool to help protect the environment also make you part of the solution. In fact, you could even invent a modern and truly local cuisine with the same goals. Foraging can sometimes be controversial if not done properly—and truthfully, commercial foraging can indeed create environmental concerns. I saw it as an issue with plants like ramps and fiddleheads while teaching in Vermont. The capitalization of natural resources such as American ginseng (*Panax quinquefolius*) or local white sage (*Salvia apiana*, sold for smudging) provides other real examples. When money is involved, foraging can get a bad name, but it doesn't have to be that way. Even when I was working with local chefs and restaurants, I would say that 95 percent of the edible plants I provided were in fact non-native. The rest were sustainably harvested and even planted on private property.

So what are the solutions and the right approaches to wildcrafting?

I like to concentrate on the culinary uses of local non-native and invasive plants, then use native plants in small quantities, such as for flavor accents. Over the years, through friends and students attending my workshops, I've also gained access to thousands of acres of land in which I plant native plants and even create native gardens. If you pick up acorns, walnuts, or berries, why not try planting some as well? One mature oak or walnut tree will probably provide more nuts for the next generation(s) than you'll pick up in your lifetime. Plant a few and you're actually planting much more than you'll ever take from nature. Put together a small nursery at home, too; it's a fun hobby and you'll learn tons in the process. I grow white sage, black sage, mugwort, yarrow, yucca, and tons of other native plants at home, which I transfer to my native gardens later on. Local native plant nurseries are also there to help you and can be great resources for native plants and education.

You don't have to be an extremist; some actions really have no impact on the land. Still, always be aware of the law. For example, on BLM (Bureau of Land Management) acreage, visitors can harvest special forest products in reasonable amounts for personal use without a permit, but harvesting more than small amounts does require a permit or a contract. Some national

Black walnuts sprouting in my native plant nursery, about to be placed into a pot.

forests also allow visitors to pick edible plants and berries for personal use, while others will require a permit. And natural preserves should not be touched. You need to check.

Within all the parameters of dos and don'ts, there are a lot of ethical and sustainable solutions. Some actions are also plain common sense. Removing an invasive plant such as black mustard, wood sorrel (*Oxalis* spp.), or perennial pepperweed is a good thing.

Education

The main problem you'll encounter if you want to explore local flavors is education. Plant identification is really a lost skill in our modern day: being able to label a plant and make sure it's fully edible (and also not rare or endangered) is key.

On the good side, you can probably start eating your finds on day 1. Simply go for a hike; if you know even a tiny bit about edible plants, I'm sure you'll come back with something to play with. Many common "weeds" that you have around, such as dandelion, are very nutritious food.

Mix a bit of that dandelion with cabbage, make a sauerkraut, and voilà! You've just opened the door to a new world of possibilities: fermenting with what nature can provide!

You have tons of options to get educated. Nowadays tons of books about foraging are available for purchase online, and you're pretty much guaranteed to find one related to your local area. You can also find many groups about wild plant identification on social media such as Facebook. Some are more related to the protection of native plants, such as those from the native plant societies of New York, Oregon, Colorado, and many other states; others are more related to the medicinal and culinary uses of plants. Good examples are the groups Edible Wild Plants and Foragers Unite on Facebook. You can post pictures of your plant and get proper identification.

Nothing beats one-on-one education, though, and with a small amount of research, you should be able to find a local expert throughout the US or even Europe who can teach you about medicinal or edible wild plants. Learn a couple of plants a week, play with them, and guess what? By the end of the year, compared with most people, you'll already be an expert.

Through the application of fermentation to wild edibles, you are exploring a new territory. You won't find a wild mustard sauerkraut or a dandelion hot sauce at your local supermarket, but you can also go much further and discover brand-new flavors as well.

For example, in Mexico the original food preservation techniques were mostly dehydration, smoking, and some alcoholic fermentation. I could be wrong, but my research indicates that lacto-fermentation was only introduced with the arrival of Europeans. So take a native plant like yucca (*Hesperoyucca whipplei*) and ferment the edible flowers or fruits, and you have just invented something new in terms of texture and flavors.

The greater your knowledge of wild edibles in your area, the more creative freedom you will have. Five years ago, I would not have thought that I would be making cheeses with local acorns, walnuts, pinyon pine nuts, and various foraged seeds.

But realize that you don't even have to be a wildcrafter or forager to use this book. Many of the techniques and ideas are applicable to plants that can be found in your garden or the farmers market. You can make fermented soups, hot sauces, dehydrated soup stocks, fermented vegan cheeses, and so on without ever setting foot in the wilderness.

Enough rambling, let's get started!

STARTING SIMPLE: DANDIKRAUT

I create mixed ferments like DandiKraut all the time; they're wonderful for experimenting and learning how the flavors and texture of wildcrafted plants will change through the fermentation process. It's hard to go wrong, as the wild edibles are really used as an accent in the fermented cabbage, but sometimes you get surprises.

For the dandelion, you can substitute all kinds of different plants such as watercress (*Nasturtium officinale*), bur chervil or regular chervil, black mustard and all the other mustards, perennial pepperweed, stinging nettle, lamb's-quarter, chickweed, sow thistle (*Sonchus* spp.), and countless others.

One plant that didn't work for me was garden nasturtium (*Tropaeolum majus*). The flavor changed quite drastically during the fermentation, and I didn't like it. Also, too much stinging nettle will make your ferment smell like a cow pie (cow dung), and I didn't have the heart to even taste it. In small quantities nettles are awesome, though.

Of course, you can also experiment with regular plants bought at the store or the farmers market—parsley, cilantro, basil, dill, and so on. It's a fun way to bring a regular sauerkraut to a new level of yumminess. And if a ferment is really good, next time change the ratio and start experimenting with more plants mixed with the cabbage. That's how I discovered that perennial pepperweed is so good fermented that I can reduce the amount of cabbage.

The preferred knife technique is definitely the chiffonade (cutting in very thin strips), especially for dandelion, mustard, and pepperweed leaves, which can be quite tough once fermented. Plants like chervil or watercress are much better roughly chopped. Wild fennel fronds are quite stringy and should be minced.

Ingredients for a 1-quart jar (946 ml)

1 pound 10 ounces (737 g) cabbage
4 ounces (113 g) dandelion leaves
2 teaspoons (11 g) salt

Procedure

1. Remove the outer leaves of the cabbage and set a clean leaf aside to be used later for keeping the ingredients under the brine (fermentation method 1, page 16). Quarter the cabbage and slice it into thin strips. You may want to remove the core, but some people don't mind leaving it.
2. With both hands, twist your dandelion leaves and slice them very thinly (chiffonade). I don't use the hard stems, just the top green leaves.

Massage/squeeze the mixture forcefully with both hands until the cabbage becomes very watery.

3. Place all your ingredients in a bowl, add the salt, and massage/squeeze forcefully with both hands until the mixture becomes very watery. I like to do this in a couple of steps: I massage for 3 minutes, let everything rest for a few minutes, then do it one more time until it's quite juicy. It usually requires 5 to 10 minutes of massaging.

4. Place a canning funnel on top of the jar (optional) and pack the ingredients inside it. You can also use your hand or a wooden cabbage pounder. The goal is to eliminate air pockets, but also to have liquid covering the contents (important so you don't get mold). Try to leave at least 1½ inches (3.8 cm) headspace (space between the brine and the rim of the jar). When you're done, cover the top with the folded leaf you set aside at the beginning. I also like to place a pasteurized stone (boiled for 10 minutes) or similar weight on top, but if you have a commercial fermentation system such as Masontops or Easy Fermenter, use the fermentation weights provided.

5. Position the lid and close it, but not so tight that fermentation gases can't escape. Store the jar in a somewhat shaded area of the kitchen. It's a good idea to place a plate underneath. After the initial fermentation is complete and fermentation gases are almost nonexistent (7 to 10 days in Southern California), I screw the lid tight and place the jar in the fridge, where it will keep for months.

With experience, you can use other techniques; forget the leaf and stone on top and simply push down the contents with a clean fork; or even stir the contents at least once a day and burp as necessary—but for now, let's stick to the basic technique of keeping all the ingredients under the brine with a weight on top.

As you eat the contents, it's a good idea to transfer and pack the remain ferment into a smaller jar. The less airspace above your sauerkraut, the longer it will keep. I've eaten a sauerkraut that was 1 year old and still crunchy.

If you use an alternate commercial system such as those described on page 20, follow the manufacturer's instructions.

Place a canning funnel on top of the jar (optional) and pack the cabbage inside.

OTHER SIMILAR RECIPES

Locally we have so many wild mustards taking over the environment that I use them as often as possible. They're also quite delicious, but the flavor profile will range anywhere from broccoli to wasabi. The two mustards I use most often are the Mediterranean mustard and black mustard. Wild radish leaves will also work extremely well. The key is definitely to cut the leaves in very thin strips (chiffonade) so the end result isn't too "chewy."

Although it is very abundant in many states, I cannot find garlic mustard locally—it's something for you to experiment with if it grows in your region. I'm sure there are many other plants from the mustard family and others that can be used.

All the recipes that follow use the same preparation and fermentation method as DandiKraut. All these recipes have a ratio of around 80 percent cabbage to 20 percent greens (aside from the wild fennel version, which has very strong flavors). You can experiment with different ratios if you like the flavors. You're not stuck with wild ingredients, either; I've made mixed sauerkraut with cilantro, parsley, and countless other store-bought or garden herbs with great success.

Mediterranean Mustard Sauerkraut

A recipe pretty much identical to DandiKraut. Because the flavors of the black mustard are a bit more intense than those of dandelion, I use a bit less. If the mustard you use is quite pungent, try this recipe first.

Ingredients for a 1-pint jar (475 ml)

12 ounces (340 g) cabbage, finely grated
   or chopped
2 ounces (57 g) finely cut (chiffonade cut)
   mustard leaves, stems removed
2 teaspoons (11 g) salt

WaterKraut (Watercress Sauerkraut)

Watercress stays quite pungent during the fermentation process, so I tend to add it on the light side, but by all means, if you like this ferment, increase the ratio.

Ingredients for a 1-pint jar (475 ml)

13 ounces (360 g) cabbage, finely grated
   or chopped
1½–2 ounces (42–57 g) chopped watercress
   leaves, stems removed
2 teaspoons (11 g) salt

Black Mustard Sauerkraut

Ingredients for a 1-pint jar (475 ml)
13 ounces (360 g) cabbage, finely grated or chopped
1½ ounces (42 g) finely cut (chiffonade cut)
    mustard leaves, stems removed
2 teaspoons (11 g) salt

I often serve mixed ferments mixed with
fresh greens. I think they're a fantastic
base for salads. At my last workshop we
served a MustaKraut made with fresh
arugula, watercress, and regular salad
greens. I added a couple of tablespoons
of pickled mustard seeds and some
homemade seasoned vinegar.

Fennel Sauerkraut

Wild fennel isn't exactly the same as the kind you
purchase at the store. Unlike regular fennel, the
root is too tough to use in a ferment, so we are
more interested in the featherlike leaves (fronds).
The flavor is quite intense in the beginning, but
it will mellow up after a couple of weeks. You'll
need to chop the leaves very, very finely; otherwise, they end up as tough little strands that are a
distraction and will stay stuck between your
teeth. You can probably follow this recipe with
dill, but unless you're really in love with dill, I
would use half the amount; dill tends to keep
strong flavors during the fermentation process.

Ingredients for a 1-pint jar (475 ml)
12 ounces (340 g) cabbage, finely grated or chopped
2 tablespoons *very* finely chopped fennel leaves
    or finely chopped dill leaves
1½ teaspoons (8 g) salt

Spicy MustaKraut

Let's slowly go to the next level and start mixing in more ingredients. In this recipe the mustard leaves are fermented with mustard seeds. While still very simple, this recipe is a good example of using wildcrafted organic ingredients for their nutritional value as well as flavor additives. We're just getting started, though—nature is amazing, and as we go through this book, we'll journey much, much deeper into the no-man's-land of wildcrafted ferments. You can definitely create recipes similar to this one with various foraged ingredients and use organic mustard if you can't make your own, but you'll need to experiment a bit with the number of wild edibles you use. For example, black mustard or perennial pepperweed leaves are quite strong, so 2 ounces (56 g) for a pint jar (473 ml) is good enough, but for milder ingredients such as Mediterranean or garlic mustard, dandelion, lamb's-quarter, and so on, you can definitely up the amount and reduce the cabbage.

Ingredients for a 1-pint jar (475 ml)

2 ounces (56 g) black mustard leaves
   (or other savory wild greens)
12 ounces (340 g) cabbage
1½–2 teaspoons (9–11 g) salt
2 tablespoons (36 g) organic (or homemade)
   stone-ground mustard (I make my own
   mustard from black mustard seeds, elderberry wine, and mugwort beer vinegar;
   you can find directions on page 180 of my
   first book, *The New Wildcrafted Cuisine*)

Tip: Before serving, taste! I often mix the ferment with more mustard or add spices when I serve it. During my workshops, I place the MustaKraut on tacos with fresh wild herbs (watercress, chickweed, and so on). If you're not vegetarian or vegan, you can add pickled herring, lengua *(beef tongue)*, roasted chapulines *(grasshoppers)*, or crickets. Lots of creative tacos, sandwiches, or toasts can be made with this type of ferment as a base.

Procedure

1. Remove the stems from the black mustard leaves, then roll the leaves in your hand and cut finely (chiffonade). Slice/shred the cabbage and place it into a bowl (fermentation method 1, page 16). Add the leaves, then the salt.

2. Massage until you get enough brine. Place a canning funnel on top of the jar (optional) and pack the shredded cabbage inside it. Try to leave 1 to 1½ inches (2.5–3.8 cm) headspace When you're done, cover the top with a folded leaf. Place a pasteurized stone (boiled for at least 10 minutes) on top, or use a similar weight.

3. Position the lid and close it, but not so tight that fermentation gases can't escape. Store the jar in a somewhat shaded area of the kitchen. It's a good idea to place a plate underneath. An alternative is to close the jar and burp as necessary. For the first 4 to 5 days, open the jar at least once a day. Use a clean fork or spoon, push down the contents to release all the air bubbles and keep the ingredients under the brine.

4. After the initial fermentation is complete, screw the lid on tight and place the jar in the fridge, where it will keep for months. As you eat the contents, it's a good idea to transfer and pack the contents into a smaller jar. The less airspace above your sauerkraut, the longer it will keep.

Going a Bit Wilder: Fermented Cattail

Cattail (*Typha* spp.) can be found throughout the Northern Hemisphere. The plant loves water and grows in streams or wetland habitats. It's a very ancient food source: Remnants of preserved starch on prehistoric grinding stones indicates it was already eaten in Europe over 30,000 years ago.

Locally, I find cattail in streams, marshes, swamps, or very wet soil. It is usually 5 to 8 feet (1.5–2.4 m) tall once mature. It is easily recognizable with its stiff, flat leaf blades. In the center you will find an erect, rounded stem reaching up to 6 or 7 feet (around 2 m) in height. At the end of the stem, the flower head forms a cylinder densely packed with tiny male flowers in the top cluster, and tiny female flowers in the bottom cluster. When the male cluster is loaded with pollen, it looks bright yellow. The pollen is extremely easy to forage in large quantities.

For fermentation, I'm mostly interested in the tender inside of the shoot. Picked at the right time, the bottom of the stem can be eaten either raw or cooked. It is extremely important to make sure the water is not polluted; don't pick cattails where there is lot of human activity, horseback riding, or the like—there may be harmful bacteria or even parasites in the water.

The bottom end of the stem looks very much like a leek. There are two methods for foraging. One is to push aside the largest two leaves, then grab the inner part of the stem close to the ground or water and pull gently. It should come up easily. You can also use a knife, cutting the lower stem (the first 10–12 inches / 20–25 cm) and placing it in your foraging bag. Back home you should clean your stems thoroughly, then, using a knife, cut and remove the top layers until you get to the very tender part inside.

Due to its starchy and somewhat sweet contents, cattail is a perfect candidate for fermentation. I usually slice the tender shoot, then add it to sauerkraut, but you can also preserve large sections of the shoots in brine with spices. There is a recipe for cattail shoots in spicy brine later in this book.

CATTAILKRAUT

I really like this ferment, and you can add a bit of savory wild greens, too, if you want. Personally, I like to create with what I can find in the same environment where I collect my main ingredient. Very often you will find other savory plants—such as watercress—where cattail grows, and adding a small amount is a nice touch.

It's a very easy ferment to make. Most of the work is really about collecting some good-quality cattail shoots; you want them young and tender. It's okay to be picky and remove any outer layers that could be too fibrous.

I like a ratio of around 60 percent cabbage to 40 percent cattail. You can experiment with using more cattail, but due to its starch content, the ferment can become quite mucilaginous.

Ingredients for a 1-pint jar (475 ml)

8 ounces (227 g) shredded cabbage
5 ounces (141 g) tender cattail shoots, sliced
½–1 ounce (14–28 g) minced savory greens
 (optional), such as watercress, fennel,
 chickweed, or chervil
1½ teaspoons (9 g) salt

Procedure

Use the same method (fermentation method 1, page 16) as for making a DandiKraut or MustaKraut. The only difference is that you want to massage the cabbage separately first to get as much juice as possible. Basically, you're making a regular sauerkraut, then adding the cattail. If you used a bit of savory plants, you can definitely add them when massaging the cabbage. You'll need to slice the tender cattail shoots; the slice size is really up to you, but around ¼ inch (0.6 cm) works well for me.

The reason you don't want to massage the cattail is that it will break apart, and frankly, that cattail is so pretty that you want to keep it intact as much as possible. I like an aesthetic appeal in my ferment.

When the shredded cabbage is juicy and ready, add the cattail shoot slices and massage them *very* gently with the soggy cabbage. Let everything rest for 10 minutes, then place into a jar. If necessary, to keep the ingredients under the brine, add a bit of 2 percent brine (1 teaspoon salt per cup of water / 23 g salt per liter).

Going More Local: Fermenting Yucca Flowers and Lamb's-Quarter

Yucca is a local native plant in Southern California that can also be found in Arizona and Mexico. The plants have tons of uses, from being prepared as food to extracting fibers and even making soap with the leaves due to the saponin content. Yucca flowers are still eaten in Mexico, usually parboiled, then sautéed. When I attended a native Cahuilla cooking class in Palm Springs a few years ago, we prepared and ate the flowers and fruits.

Cooked, the flowers taste very much like Belgian endive and a bit like cabbage. It's easy to sustainably harvest a few flowers here and there without damaging the plants. It's also a plant worth planting/propagating, not just for food but also because it's quite beautiful and because a local moth (California yucca moth) has a symbiotic relationship with it (pollination). In some areas yuccas are protected, and if that is the case, you'll need to grow your own (I started planting some in the late 1990s) and be patient. From experience, the plant will flower every seven years or so before dying. Seeds are usually available at local native plant nurseries. Each year, just before the rainy season, I usually plant 10 to 20 yuccas by sprouting the seeds first at home, then planting the sprouts in the ground with a bit of water.

With the flowers tasting similar to cabbage when cooked, I thought they could be a good candidate mixed in a sauerkraut-type ferment, and they are, to the point that you can barely tell the difference between the flowers and the cabbage. I use the petals only. Because wild radish pods are abundant during the yucca flowering season, I like to incorporate some of them as well.

YUCCA FERMENT

This is really a basic recipe, and you can experiment from here by adding spices and other flavorful ingredients. I've also used yucca in some of my "wild" kimchis with great success. I've never tried to make a ferment with just yucca flowers (I'm not sure if they have enough sugar in them to ferment properly), but it's on my list of projects to do.

Ingredients for a 1-quart jar (946 ml)

11 ounces (311 g) regular cabbage
11 ounces (311 g) tender wild radish pods
6 ounces (170 g) yucca flowers
Salt

Procedure

I ended up with 1 pound 12 ounces of ingredients (798 g) and mixed it with 1 tablespoon (17 g) of salt. I used the exactly same method as for making a regular sauerkraut (fermentation method 1, page 16).

LAMB'S-QUARTER SOY FERMENT

Also called goosefoot, wild spinach, manure weed, and fat-hen, this plant is cultivated in some parts of the world such as India, but in Europe and North America it is considered a "weed." The plant's origin is a bit murky, but it is considered non-native and naturalized locally. We have a native goosefoot (*Chenopodium californicum*), but the plant contains too much saponin, so I don't use it for culinary purposes.

The flavor is very similar to spinach and the nutritional value is quite high, but the only problem is the fact that lamb's-quarter contains a decent amount of oxalic acid, as well, more than our regular spinach. Being genetically prone to kidney stones, I use the traditional method of boiling the plant first and changing the water, which helps remove some of the oxalic acid. Recent research seems to show that fermentation also helps with this issue.

The fermentation recipe is very much based on how I cook the plant. I use soy sauce, aromatic herbs, and garlic. The soy sauce serves as a substitute for salt.

I have little information about the flavors that develop over a longer aging period, but I have a jar in the fridge that I intend to taste after 6 months of fermentation. Who knows, this could be one of the extreme ferments that I age for a year or more!

Ingredients for a ½-pint jar (236 ml)

6 ounces (170 g) fresh lamb's-quarter leaves
2 garlic cloves, minced
2 teaspoons (6 g) roasted sesame seeds
2 tablespoons (10 ml) soy sauce
  (as a salt substitute)
½ teaspoon (0.5 g) dried thyme
¼ teaspoon (0.5 g) chili flakes
1 teaspoon (5 ml) maple syrup
  (food for lacto bacteria)
2 tablespoons (30 ml) Culture Starter

Procedure

1. First remove the lamb's-quarter leaves from the stems and blanch them in boiling water for 2 to 3 minutes. Remove the leaves place in cold water. Once cooled, place them in a colander for a couple of minutes to drain.
2. Using your (clean) hands, squeeze any excess liquid from the leaves. You can decide to chop the leaves a bit, but I don't mind leaving them whole. Next, place all the ingredients in a bowl and mix them gently for 20 seconds or so. It's that simple.
3. Transfer the contents to the jar; it will be quite full. If it's too much, eat some of the excess right there and then—it's already pretty tasty, though salty.
4. Use fermentation method 1 (page 16), making sure there is enough brine to cover the contents. However, my current method is simply to close the lid

tight and open the jar once or twice daily. Using a fork or spoon, I push the ingredients under the brine, then close the jar again. The fermentation gases are not excessive, and there should be no need for any additional burping, but do monitor the pressure just in case.

5. Ferment for 7 to 10 days at room temperature, and when the fermentation gases stop, place in the fridge for aging. I like to eat that ferment after a month, but it's also okay to eat it quite young.

Spicy Gingery Wild Greens

I really like the base recipe here; I went through trial and error while developing it, and it's now one of my top 10 favorite ferments. You can easily substitute other wild greens for the pepperweed or the dandelion tops, such as wild mustard or radish leaves, or even use store-bought or garden ingredients like kale, chopped arugula, and others.

The flavors are quite intense and a little goes a long way, but the ginger really shines through. I use these ferments sparingly as side condiments in some of my dishes. At my last fermentation workshop, I served pepperweed ferment on top of a fermented soft cashew cheese and cracker. It's fantastic paired with fish.

SPICY GINGERY
PERENNIAL PEPPERWEED

Enjoy this recipe whenever you want—the stuff will last for months—but I really like it after 3 weeks in the fridge. In case you're impatient, know that it doesn't taste fantastic during the initial fermentation. It's much better aged.

Ingredients for a 1-pint jar (475 ml)

8 ounces (226 g) perennial pepperweed leaves, finely cut (chiffonade cut)

7 ounces (199 g) cabbage, finely cut (chiffonade cut)

8 large garlic cloves, finely diced

1 tablespoon (7.5 g) chili flakes; I use smoked jalapeño flakes (*chile morita*)

¾ teaspoon (1 g) ground peppercorns

2½ tablespoons (37 ml) fresh lime juice

3½ tablespoons (48 g) freshly grated gingerroot

Salt

Procedure

The total weight was around 1 pound 3 ounces (540 g). I used around 2 teaspoons (11 g) of salt.

1. Use fermentation method 1 (page 16). Place the pepperweed and cabbage into a bowl; add the garlic, chili flakes, peppercorns, lime juice, ginger, and salt. With your clean fingers, mix everything together with tenderness and love until it's nice and juicy. I usually mix for 10 seconds, let it rest for a few minutes, then repeat the gentle massaging.

2. Transfer everything into a jar and with a clean spoon or fork, push down the ingredients to remove any air pockets. There should be some liquid on top, but it's not a must.

3. Close the lid, but not so tight that fermentation gases can't escape. At least twice daily, unscrew the lid and stir the ingredients with a clean fork for 3 or 4 seconds, then push down to make sure you don't have any air pockets. Screw back the lid (not too tight).

   Another method, which I use often, is to screw the lid tight and check the pressure on top to gauge how active my fermentation is. Burp the jar as necessary to release fermentation gases, and stir the contents once or twice a day.

4. Ferment for around 10 days; when the initial fermentation is complete (no more visible gas bubble activity), place in the fridge.

SPICY GINGERY DANDELION TOPS

This is very similar to the perennial pepperweed recipe, but because dandelion is so bitter, I changed the ratio and added more cabbage to balance the flavors. Also, I use the dandelion's green leafy parts and not the stems.

The end result is quite spicy, and you can cut the amount of chili flakes in half if you prefer a milder ferment.

Ingredients for a 1-pint jar (475 ml) (should fill around 60 percent of the jar)

2½ ounces (71 g) dandelion, finely cut (chiffonade cut)

5¼ ounces (142 g) cabbage, finely cut

8 garlic cloves, diced thinly

¾ teaspoon (1 g) ground peppercorns

1–2 tablespoons (6–12 g) chili flakes; I use smoked jalapeño (chile morita)

1½ tablespoons (9 g) ginger powder

2 tablespoons (29 ml) lime juice (basically 1 lime) (I haven't done it, but you could try this with lemon juice)

Salt

Procedure

The total weight was around 11 ounces (310 g). I used around 1½ teaspoons (8 g) of salt. If you want to use this ferment as a salty alternative or additive, such as mixed in salad, in soup, or as a topping on fish, you can use 2 teaspoons (11 g) salt.

Use the same method as the perennial pepperweed recipe. The flavors are much better after 3 weeks of fermentation.

As you use the ferment, transfer the remainder to a smaller jar as soon as possible for better storage.

Salsa

I like making wild food salsas and fermenting them, too. The recipes change all the time based on what I can find locally. They are a great representation of the seasons and changes in the environment. Of course, early spring is always the best time, but here in Southern California I can make salsas all year long.

WILD FOOD SALSA

This recipe is a good example of a spring salsa. There's nothing very complicated about it: You basically make a regular salsa, but instead of using just cilantro you can add savory wild greens such as chickweed, wild chervil (or carrot tops), miner's lettuce (*Claytonia* spp.), and so on. This is a concept recipe that you can use with your local wild greens.

You don't even need to add a starter, since the ingredients are already loaded with lacto bacteria. All you will need is salt.

Note that if you ferment a salsa, it's better to make it quite chunky. If the ingredients are diced too small, the fermentation process results in a mushy sauce. There are no rules as to when you can eat it. I usually do so within 3 to 5 days at the most—it's a great source of probiotics. Although the fermentation process will make the contents sour, I still like to add lime juice when I serve it, or even some of my homemade vinegar.

Ingredients for a 1-quart jar (946 ml) (around 80 percent full)

9 ounces (255 g) tomatoes, diced
2 ounces (57 g) white or red onion, diced
1 small garlic clove, minced
4 ounces (113 g) bell peppers, diced
1 jalapeño pepper, diced, around 1½ ounces (42 g)—
    remove seeds if you want
¼ ounce (7 g) chopped cilantro
¾ ounce (21 g) chopped savory wild greens
    (chickweed, chervil, and the like)
Salt

Procedure

The total weight was more than 1 pound (453 g). I used 1½ teaspoons (8 g) of salt. It's a bit too salty at first, but will end up tasting all right after the fermentation.

1. Use fermentation method 3 (page 28). Place the contents in a quart jar; it should loosely fill around 80 percent of the volume at first, but the next day the contents will become juicier and will decrease in volume.

2. Close the lid and shake the contents two or three times daily. Burp as necessary to release fermentation gases. Sometimes I place the jar upside down, with the lid firmly closed for a couple of hours. As the contents become acidic, food preservation is guaranteed. You also have the option of not closing the lid too tightly so that fermentation gases can escape and stirring the contents instead of shaking the jar.

3. If you want to age the salsa, when the initial fermentation is done, with no more fermentation gases (around 10 days), store the jar in the fridge. But as I said, I really like to eat it as a young ferment. I often let my salsa ferment for 3 days, then store it in the fridge—which slows down the fermentation process—and eat it within the next 48 hours.

   For storage, it's best to transfer the contents to a pint jar. By this time, the fermented salsa should fit in a jar of that size.

CHAPTER 3

Exploring Local and Ethnic Flavors

There are many ways you can bring your ferments to the next level by wildcrafting aromatic plants such as sages, making your own spice blends, and mixing wild and regular savory herbs, berries, and seeds to explore local or ethnic flavors. Let's look at some possibilities.

Fermenting with Spice Blends

A few years back I had no idea how to make my own spice blend. Like most people I would purchase my favorite ones at the store, but it never occurred to me that the process was quite simple.

I mean, it's not that obvious: You basically purchase some colored powder or odd mix of herby bits and it makes food taste great. It's quite magical! Somehow I had the (mis)conception that creating this magic powder was a very esoteric process requiring some sort of obscure knowledge, huge amounts of herbal enlightenment, possibly incantations and a master's degree from the Hogwarts School of Witchcraft and Wizardry.

It wasn't until I started researching and making my own spice blends using local wild herbs and aromatic seeds that I understood how simple the process can be. I also learned that, with a bit of practice and experimentation, you can create blends much more delicious than whatever you can purchase at the store. The reason is quite simple: By making your own blends, you can adjust the ingredients to your own taste buds, and with practice it becomes a highly intuitive endeavor based on your savory preferences.

I'm not saying that you *must* absolutely make your own blends. There are quite a few wonderful commercial blends out there! Some are so delicious that I'm still trying to deconstruct them, which isn't always an easy task. (Maybe they do use incantations!)

Being active in several online fermenting groups, I think not enough fermenters are taking advantage of the possibilities. A good blend can really elevate your regular ferments to new levels—sauerkrauts, kimchis, or even mixed vegetables. It doesn't have to be complicated at all: Last week I made a sort of kimchi using a barbecue spice blend as flavoring instead of the regular chili powder, garlic, and ginger. As a result the smoky/sweet flavors made the ferment incredibly tasty, and I'm not even sure if I can still call it a kimchi.

Mixing spice blends with fermented wild edibles is even more exciting. Not only are you experimenting with new savory ingredients in the first place, but by flavoring them with various blends, you can multiply the creative culinary possibilities indefinitely. A new world of tasty fermented condiments waits to be explored.

Don't hesitate to experiment with regular ingredients. I could probably write a whole book on just fermenting cabbage with various spice blends and aromatic herbs.

But let's start with a simple blend using spices that can already be found in your kitchen or the local supermarket. We'll deal with more complex stuff later on. The method is really not elaborate, and in this case we're not even using dried herbs, tough roots, or seeds. All the ingredients can be purchased in the form of powders or granules (sugar).

If you have to deal with ingredients requiring grinding, you can easily use a coffee grinder, a Vitamix (for larger quantities), or—like me—a stone grinder. There is something primal and feral in stone-ground spices; it seems to be ingrained in our DNA. I can imagine one of my ancestors doing exactly the same thing to flavor a dish thousands of years ago. Doing it by hand, you also have more control over the "roughness" of the final product.

Sometimes I want components such as bits of leaves or herbs to be part of the aesthetic. My Dandharissa (fermented hot dandelion paste) is rough and slightly stringy. It's unlike anything you can possibly purchase at the store; it's more akin to the types of textures you find in nature—rough, muddy, and coarse. Texture and appearance can carry some powerful messages. The best examples will be found in my chapter about fermented wild cheeses and creating savory crusts.

Never take an existing recipe as the last word, by the way: A spice blend should be your own personal creation. You can move stuff around, find substitutes, and add other things that you like or think would work. If it wasn't a good idea, you just learned something. Cherish the mistakes; with time and experience you can become a spice Jedi and—who knows?—maybe make a fortune selling your own "secret" blend.

BARBECUE SPICE BLEND

I'm sure you already have some of the ingredients for this at home. Go open the cabinet; if you like cooking, you should already have some chili flakes, brown sugar, garlic granules, and peppercorns. Take note of what you're missing, and the next time you go to the store (which should be right now), purchase the rest. By the way, ethnic markets are the best locations to find more spices than you'll ever be able to make savory blends with. The selection in a regular all-American supermarket is pretty slim and, dare I say, boring. I'm lucky to have Middle Eastern, Indian, and Hispanic stores nearby. One of them has a full aisle dedicated to spices. Some are so obscure, I don't even know what they are and what to do with them. Purchasing online is another good option.

Ingredients for 2½ tablespoons (about 20 g)

1 tablespoon (6 g) paprika

1 teaspoon (3 g) chile morita powder (smoked jalapeños) or smoked chipotle powder

½ teaspoon (1.5 g) ground peppercorns

½ teaspoon (1.5 g) garlic granules or powder

½ teaspoon (1.5 g) onion powder

½ teaspoon (1.5 g) ginger powder

1 teaspoon (4 g) brown sugar

Procedure

All you need to do is mix everything together in a bowl with a fork or spoon. I like to use a wooden grinder to really mix the ingredients. Simple, isn't it? We'll use this blend in the next recipe. The recipe doesn't include salt; you'll add that when you're mixing the ingredients to be fermented.

Interested in personalizing the blend? Instead of smoked chipotle powder, you could use a regular chili powder or flakes, but add smoked paprika powder instead of regular paprika powder. That way, you'll keep the wonderful smoky flavors that many barbecue blends have. Heck, you can even skip any smoked powders but add a bit of liquid smoke in the ferment itself. If you love garlic or ginger, by all means double the amount.

WILD RADISH PODS FERMENTED
IN BARBECUE SPICE BLEND

Super easy to make, and the final result is fantastic in salads, sandwiches, tacos, or even added to soups. You can also try the same recipe with regular ingredients such as diced daikon, sliced carrots, and mixed vegetables.

Ingredients for a ½-pint jar (236 ml)

7 ounces (226 g) wild radish pods
2 garlic cloves, finely chopped
⅕ small red onion (¾ ounce / 21 g), finely diced
1 teaspoon (5.5 g) salt used for fermentation
Barbecue Spice Blend

Procedure

For this recipe, use the whole amount of spice blend from the previous recipe; it's close to 2½ tablespoons (around 20 g).

The method used is a variant of fermentation method 3 (page 28); you'll just add a bit of brine at the end because you don't get much "juice" from radish pods.

1. First mix the wild radish pods, garlic, onion, and salt, then massage tenderly for 2 to 3 minutes. Let everything rest for 20 minutes, massage it again, and let it rest again for 15 minutes. You want the salt to start extracting moisture. The mix should be quite wet, with the pods soft and tender, which makes it easier to pack them in the jar.
2. When the pods are ready, add the Barbecue Spice Blend and massage again for 2 to 3 minutes, then pack everything into the jar. No need to pack too tightly. Mix ¼ teaspoon (1.5 g) salt with ¼ cup (59 ml) water and pour it into the jar.

   The ingredients won't be under the brine, so the method used is to simply close the jar tightly and shake two to three times (or more) a day for a few seconds, then unscrew the jar a tiny bit so fermentation gases can escape. The goal of the small amount of brine is really to distribute the acidity occurring during the fermentation process to all the ingredients during the shaking—good insurance that all the pods will ferment properly.
3. Ferment for 7 to 10 days, and when the initial fermentation is complete, place in the fridge.

WILD FOOD KIMCHI

Well, sorta wild . . . basically I use locally foraged mustard and wild radish leaves fermented with chili flakes/powder and garlic, but you also use some regular sugary ingredients like bok choy, napa cabbage, or regular cabbage. In this version I also add some sliced wild turnip (a variant of *Brassica rapa*) roots.

Because of seasonality and location, you can't really make the same recipe twice, so this is again a concept recipe. If I were in Belgium, I could do something similar, but with different wild plants. You are looking at a ratio of around 30 percent wildcrafted ingredients and 70 percent regular stuff. Of course, you can experiment and decide to use many more wild edibles.

Ingredients for a 1-quart jar (946 ml)

12 ounces (300 g) bok choy leaves

4 ounces (110 g) regular cabbage, shredded

Salt

4 ounces (110 g) mustard and radish leaves

1 ounce (30 g) curly dock leaves

2 ounces (60 g) wild turnip roots

6 garlic cloves

2–4 tablespoons (15–30 g) mild chili flakes

1 teaspoon (3 g) spicy chili flakes

⅓ cup (78 ml) water

Procedure

The total weight ended up at a bit more than 1 pound 11 ounces (765 g). I used 3½ teaspoons (20 g) of salt.

1. I use a method similar to that for making sauerkraut (fermentation method 1, page 16). First, I place the bok choy and cabbage in a bowl, add the salt, and massage the ingredients tenderly for 10 minutes. I let the contents rest for 10 minutes then repeat twice until it is tender. I end up with a decent amount of brine.
2. Meanwhile I cut all my wild greens leaves in thin strips (chiffonade cut), thinly slice the turnip roots, mince the garlic, and get all my other ingredients ready.
3. Place everything into the bowl including the spices, then add the water and with your hands (wear gloves) massage the contents one more time for 3 to 4 minutes until "juicy."
4. Transfer the "kimchi" to a jar to ferment for 3 to 4 days at room temperature. Burp as necessary and stir the contents at least once a day. Then place your jar in the fridge to age and continue fermenting slowly. It will last for months.

Serve it as a condiment or mixed in a wild food salad. Heck, I've been known to blend it into a paste and use it as a kind of hot sauce.

This recipe is super good for the environment, too, since all the wild plants I used are non-native and invasive.

CURRY BLEND

Curry is a type of spice blend you're familiar with if you like Indian food. The different ingredients used in the blend can be quite variable, but the main flavors are usually created with coriander, turmeric, fenugreek, cumin, and chili powder. Some blends can be very hot or even slightly sweet. Once you start making curry blends, you realize there is a substantial amount of freedom in terms of ingredients. This is a good example of a blend that can easily be adapted to your taste buds. I'm not too fond of cumin in large amounts, for instance, so I tend to tone down the amount used. I also add a tad of sugar and even salt (not usually part of curry blends). For local flavors, I incorporate ingredients from my native garden: 2 leaves of white sage, a small amount of California bay (½ small leaf), and 1 teaspoon (1.5 g) of dried rabbit tobacco (*Pseudognaphalium californicum*), which already smells and taste like a curry blend.

Ingredients for around ⅓ cup (32 g)

1½ tablespoons (8 g) ground coriander *or* 2 tablespoons (8 g) coriander seeds

1½ tablespoons (9 g) ground turmeric

1½ teaspoons (3 g) ginger powder

1 teaspoon (4 g) black mustard seeds (or yellow mustard)

½ teaspoon (1 g) cardamom powder *or* 1 teaspoon (1.5 g) cardamom seeds

1½ teaspoons (4 g) chili powder of your choice (mild, hot, sweet, or smoked)

1 teaspoon (2 g) cumin powder

½ teaspoon (1.5 g) ground peppercorns

½ teaspoon (2.5 g) salt

1 teaspoon (5 g) brown sugar

Procedure

Recipes online often include additional ingredients such as cinnamon, cloves, allspice, nutmeg, and more. So you really have some room to adjust the recipe to your liking.

If I use whole seeds, I roast them in a pan to get more flavors from them. You can use a coffee grinder or Vitamix to reduce everything to a powder. I use my stone grinder (molcajete) for more control over the texture. For ferments, I like the powder a bit on the coarser side, but that's just a personal preference.

FERMENTED CATTAIL SHOOT HEARTS IN SPICY SAUCE

I had the most interesting experience collecting cattail shoots. I didn't know rattlesnakes could swim in shallow water. I was minding my own business standing in the water when I saw a beautiful snake coming down the stream toward me. There was no time to do anything, so I just froze. The snake passed by dangerously close without paying much attention. Scared the hell out of me, but it's all good! The snake and I shook hands (metaphorically speaking) and we're friends now.

That morning I collected around 12 young, tender cattail shoots in a pristine stream. Once home, I soaked them for an hour or so in two or three changes of water. (The original stream was pretty pure, but I'm a nut about food safety.) If you do this, you may need a weight to keep the shoots under the water, as they tend to float.

Next, remove the stringy outside layers to get to the tender heart. Cut them to a bit less than the height of a pint jar and set aside.

I like to ferment sizable shoots so I can cut them later on to whatever size I want; I use them with some of my wild food salads and various other dishes.

This time I fermented them in a very spicy hot sauce. To make the sauce, mix the ingredients in your blender. You can make a thin or rough paste.

Ingredients for a pint jar (475 ml)

8–10 garlic cloves, chopped
2–4 habanero peppers (4 if you like the heat)
1 medium red bell pepper, chopped
½ cup (118 ml) water
½ teaspoon (1.5 g) minced shallot or red onion
About 12 cattail shoots
2 tablespoons (12 g) mild red pepper powder
1 teaspoon (2.5 g) smoked jalapeño powder (chile morita or chipotle)
½ teaspoon (1 g) ginger powder
½ teaspoon (1 g) curry powder or Curry Blend
Salt

Procedure

Process the garlic, habaneros, bell pepper, water, and shallot in a blender. Remove the mixture to a bowl and mix with the cattail shoots. Add the spices, massage gently for a few seconds, then transfer everything into a pint jar. I ended up with 10 ounces (283 g) and used 2¼ teaspoons (12.5 g) of salt, so the end result was superhot and salty, too. The heat of the sauce will go down a bit with fermentation, but it will still hurt. If you really don't like a sauce that's too hot, just use 1 habanero.

The cattail shoots will be fairly loose in the jar and not under the brine, so use fermentation method 5 (page 33). Close the lid but not too tight; you want fermentation gases to escape. Around three times a day, close the lid tight, shake the jar gently, then unscrew the

lid a bit. Another option is to close the jar, shake daily, and burp as necessary. When the initial fermentation is complete (around 10 days), place the jar in the fridge for further aging.

This type of ferment and recipe can also be used with mustard stems, wild asparagus, ramps, stems, and tender roots as well as regular ingredients like carrot strips, daikon slices, cauliflower, and sliced beets.

FERMENTED AND CURRIED WILDKRAUT (WILD RADISH AND MUSTARD LEAVES, WILD RADISH PODS)

This recipe works well with our local wild mustards (Mediterranean or black mustard leaves), but would also work with a lot of other very common "weeds" such as perennial pepperweed, dandelion, watercress, lamb's-quarter, and so on. You can also experiment with store-bought or garden herbs such as parsley, carrot or beet tops, chard, kale, and countless others. I made the actual ferment with weeds I foraged one morning, mostly wild radish and Mediterranean leaves, a bit of lamb's-quarter, and 30 or so radish pods.

Ingredients for a 1-quart jar (946 ml)
1 pound 6 ounces (624 g) cabbage
2½ ounces (71 g) wild edible leaves and greens
30 radish pods
2 tablespoons (13 g) curry powder or Curry Blend
1 tablespoon (17 g) salt

Procedure
1. The method used here is similar to that for making sauerkraut (fermentation method 1, page 16). Remove the outer leaves of the cabbage and set aside a clean leaf to be used later for keeping the ingredients under the brine. Quarter the cabbage and slice it into thin strips. Twist and slice very thinly (chiffonade) your wild edible leaves.
2. Place all your ingredients in a bowl and massage/squeeze forcefully with both hands until the mixture becomes very watery.
3. Position a canning funnel on top of the jar (optional) and pack the ingredients inside it. You can use your hand or a wooden cabbage pounder. The goal is to eliminate air pockets, but also to have liquid covering the contents (important so you don't get mold). Try to leave at least 1½ inches (3.8 cm) headspace (space between the brine and the rim of the jar). When you're done, cover the top with the folded leaf you set aside at the beginning and place a pasteurized stone (boiled for 10 minutes) on top, or a similar weight.

4. Position the lid and close it, but not so tight that fermentation gases can't escape. Store the jar in a somewhat shaded area of the kitchen. It's a good idea to place a plate under the jar.
5. For the first 3 to 4 days, open the jar daily (once, twice, or even more frequently) and use a clean fork or spoon to push down the contents to release all the air bubbles and keep the ingredients under the brine.

   Another option is to close the lid, then open the jar daily and, using a clean fork or spoon, push down the contents. Burp as necessary.
6. After the initial fermentation is complete and fermentation gases are almost nonexistent (7 to 10 days in Southern California), screw the lid on tight and place the jar in the fridge, where it will keep for months. As you eat the contents, it's a good idea to transfer and pack the remaining ferment into a smaller jar.

SIMPLE SPICE BLENDS

If you want to incorporate more spice blends into your ferments, here are a few basic ones. By all means, do your own research, too—you'll find hundreds of possibilities and variations online! To make the blend you can use a coffee grinder, a high-speed blender such as a Vitamix, or a good old stone grinder (molcajete).

Mexican-Style Spice Blend

This basic spice blend features a lot of the flavors used in Mexican cuisine, and you'll find many recipes close to this one used for sauces or tacos. It's a fun blend to play with; you can add some of it to various ferments such as hot sauces, root brines, and raw soups. I haven't tried it, but I would think that even a simple sauerkraut-type ferment would work, too.

Ingredients for around 1½ ounces (40 g)
2 tablespoons (6 g) garlic powder (or granules)
2 tablespoons (15 g) chili powder of your choice
    (can be super spicy or mild; you can also try
    smoked chili powder)
1 tablespoon (6 g) ground cumin
2 teaspoons (4 g) onion powder
1 teaspoon (2 g) ginger powder
½ teaspoon (2.5 g) salt
1 teaspoon (2 g) smoked paprika powder
1 teaspoon (1.5 g) dried oregano
¼ teaspoon (0.5 g) dried epazote (optional—
    it's a plant I can forage locally)
¼ teaspoon (0.5 g) cinnamon powder (optional)

Garam Masala

A classic Indian spice blend: sweet, hot, and bitter at the same time. I've used this one successfully with fermented radish pods or cattail shoots with added salt and water. It would work nicely with regular ferments such as green beans or yellow beets.

Ingredients for ¾ ounce (21 g)
1 tablespoon (6 g) ground cumin
2 teaspoons (4 g) ground coriander
2 teaspoons (4 g) ground cardamom
1 teaspoon (2.5 g) ground peppercorns
½ teaspoon (1 g) cinnamon powder
½ teaspoon (1 g) ground cloves
½ teaspoon (1 g) ground or freshly grated nutmeg
½ teaspoon (1.5 g) chili powder
Pinch of crushed bay leaf (optional)

Cajun Spice Blend

Smoky, hot, and spicy! This is a blend I love to use with some of my fermented cheeses, but it also works well with many of the spicy ferments using the shaking method. I can see roasted carrots or diced daikon fermented in a Cajun brine.

Ingredients for around 1⅕ ounces (32.5 g)

1 tablespoon (7 g) smoked paprika powder
1 teaspoon (2.5 g) chipotle powder, chile morita (smoked jalapeño powder), or hot chili flakes
1 teaspoon (5.5 g) salt (take this amount into account when fermenting)
1 tablespoon (6 g) ground coriander
1½ teaspoons (3 g) ground cumin
2 teaspoons (3 g) dried oregano
1 teaspoon (3 g) garlic powder
1 teaspoon (2.5 g) ground peppercorns

Thai Spice Blend

One of my favorites for making fermented roots, preparing salad dressings, or imbuing Asian flavors into some of my basic ferments.

Ingredients for around 2⅖ ounces (67 g)

1 teaspoon (2 g) ground cumin
1½ teaspoons (7 g) salt
   (take into account when fermenting)
2 teaspoons (5 g) freshly ground black peppercorns
1 tablespoon (7.5 g) chili powder of your choice
   (this blend is supposed to be hot!)
1 tablespoon (6 g) dried lemongrass powder
1 tablespoon (6 g) dried lime zest
1 tablespoon (9 g) garlic powder
½ teaspoon (1.5 g) onion powder
1 tablespoon (7 g) ginger powder
1 tablespoon (4 g) dried mint
   (I love using my foraged water mint)
1 tablespoon (12 g) brown sugar

HERB BLENDS

The diversity of herb blends you can make is limitless, but there are a few classics I've used over the years with great results.

Herbes de Provence

This is the blend I grew up with. I use it in my fermented cheeses (both inside and as part of the crust), but you can also add a bit of the blend to very basic ferments such as a sauerkraut. All the herbs in this blend are dehydrated.

Ingredients for 1⅕ ounces (34 g)

1 tablespoon (4 g) rosemary
1 teaspoon (1.5 g) fennel seeds
1 tablespoon (4 g) savory (or substitute mint)
1 tablespoon (5 g) thyme
1 tablespoon (4 g) basil
1 tablespoon (4 g) marjoram
2 teaspoons (2.5 g) lavender flowers
1 tablespoon (3.5 g) parsley
1½ teaspoons (2 g) oregano
1 teaspoon (2 g) tarragon
1 bay leaf
1 teaspoon (1.5 g) culinary sage

Italian Herbs

Same uses as Herbes de Provence. This is also the blend I use on my fermented cheese pizza.

Ingredients for 1⅕ ounces (34 g)

2 tablespoons (8 g) dried basil
2 tablespoons (8 g) dried cilantro
2 tablespoons (9 g) dried thyme
1 tablespoon (4 g) dried oregano
1 tablespoon (4 g) dried rosemary
1 teaspoon (1 g) dried marjoram

Other common inclusions such as garlic, onion, and salt are usually added when you're cooking with the herbs.

Creating Spices from Ferments

Some of my best spices are made by dehydrating my fermented concoctions and grinding them into powder, which I then sprinkle on food or mix into soups. Depending on the ingredients used in the fermentation, the flavor range can be quite wide. For example, dehydrated Spicy MustaKraut (mustard and cabbage) has some nice balance of bitterness and saltiness.

Maybe it's because I love kimchi, but my personal favorite spice is made from dehydrated Wild Food Kimchi powders. It's sweet, sour, spicy, salty, and perfect for fish and various dishes with an Asian influence. I like to make a lot of dashi soup stocks, too, and sprinkling some kimchi powder into the final soup really takes it to the next level.

You can even create ferments with the sole intention of using them as spice once dehydrated. By using specific wild ingredients in the original ferment, you can create precise flavors. I can add some lemon flavor hints by using curly dock, for instance, or bitterness by using plants like dandelion or thistle.

If you experiment a lot with fermentation, you'll discover that dehydration can sometimes be a tool to recycle ferments that didn't work well or are getting too old (sour). Recently one of my ferments was way too salty, probably a mistake on my part in the first place, but through the dehydration process it ended up making an incredible flavoring salt. There is still so much experimentation to do, and the flavor combinations are really infinite. The process is rather simple.

1. Make a regular ferment like a kimchi, or use one you already have on hand.
2. Once the fermentation is done, place the contents on a silicone rubber pad. If you don't have one, you could use a large plate or parchment paper on a tray.
3. Dehydrate until the ferment is thoroughly dry and crispy. This will take several hours or a whole day depending on the temperature. I usually use a temperature setting around 135°F (57°C) in my dehydrator, but have gone as high as 170°F (77°C) in a regular oven. Dehydrating outside is not a good idea—flies seems to love some ferments—but if you can protect your concoction from flying critters, go ahead.

Interesting Spice Blends to Check Online

- Ras el hanout (North Africa)
- Shichimi togarashi (Japan)
- Adobo (Latin America)
- Za'atar (Middle East)

The dried ferment may not be a pretty sight, but trust me, the flavors are in there. I dehydrate the contents until everything is really dried.

Remove from the dehydrator or oven and let it cool for a while. If you've made a large quantity, you can store what you won't use in tightly closed containers such as canning jars.

4. Using a molcajete (stone grinder) or coffee grinder, grind the dried ferment into powder.

If you plan to use an electric grinder such as one used to grind coffee, make sure to remove any pieces that are too hard, such as tough, dehydrated stems. I think going primitive and grinding by hand or using a hand-crank grinder is the way to go.

FERMENTED COOKED WILD GREENS

Cooked greens are a childhood memory for me. I remember vividly having them for dinner on a sourdough toast with butter that came from the neighborhood farm. My mom cooked the greens with milk and a bunch of chopped garlic, and served them with a decent layer of ground peppercorns. If we were lucky, a bit of cooked mushrooms was mixed in the concoction. Add to that a good soup and it was heaven. Savory pleasures can be simple like that.

By the way, cooking greens is really a preservation technique. We sometimes had surplus salad greens from the garden, and after a few days in the basement (the original fridge), some of them didn't look so good. From a food safety perspective, we may have had some interesting bacteria growing in there, but from our elders' perspective, wasting valuable food was not an option. The solution was to cook the greens that may not have been too fresh to "pasteurize" them and at the same time turn them into rustic gourmet food.

But your greens don't have to get old before you make this recipe. It's fantastic with fresh greens, and the technique is perfect for flavorful wild edibles such as chickweed, arugula, watercress, dandelion, sow thistle, lamb's-quarter, and countless others.

The recipe is simplicity itself. Note that the end product can be quite sour depending on the plants you cook, but if you include some members of the Brassicaceae family as part of the recipe, it should work well. My favorite is a mix of arugula (40 percent), dandelion (10 percent), watercress (10 percent), and regular salad greens (40 percent). If you're not a forager, use a mix of store-bought or garden arugula, watercress, and salad greens. Don't use too much nettle—maybe no more than 10 percent—and the same goes for dandelion greens, which, in large quantities, make the dish too bitter.

At the conclusion of a recent fermentation workshop, we held a tasting of over 15 different ferments. This one came up as the most liked.

For fermentation purposes, I don't use milk but regular store-bought springwater. Instead of salt, I opt for soy sauce, which really adds a new layer of flavor (umami).

Ingredients for a 1-pint jar (475 ml)

1 pound (454 g) mixed wild greens (dandelion, watercress, chickweed, sow thistle, et cetera) or store-bought arugula, spinach, and salad greens

1¼ cups (236–296 ml) water

7 garlic cloves, coarsely chopped

5 tablespoons (74 ml) soy sauce

1 teaspoon (2.5 g) ground peppercorns

2½ teaspoons (4 g) herb blend (Italian Herbs or Herbes de Provence)

2 tablespoons (30 ml) Culture Starter

Procedure

1. Chop the greens if necessary. Dandelion will need to be sliced thin (chiffonade), while other greens such as arugula or watercress can be chopped coarsely. Regular salad greens or spinach can be very coarsely chopped, if at all.
2. Place 1¼ cup (296 ml) of the water in a pan, add as many greens as you can, then cover.
3. Bring the liquid to a boil, then set the burner to medium. You may need to add the greens at various stages, cooking the first batch for a couple of minutes until the volume is reduced, then adding more fresh ones until all the greens are in the pan.

   Continue simmering the greens, covered, for around 10 minutes. You want them to be thoroughly cooked. You'll need to stir the contents a few times during that period. When the greens are done, remove the lid so the liquid can start evaporating.
4. At this stage, add your garlic, soy sauce, ground pepper, and 2 teaspoons of the herb blend. Mix everything together and continue simmering. Stir the contents every 3 to 4 minutes or so, until most of the liquid is evaporated, but not all of it. This may take another 5 minutes.
5. Transfer the contents into a bowl and place the bowl in a sink containing cold water. It may take 15 minutes of so for your greens to cool off. You can stir the contents and change the cold water to speed up the process.
6. When the mixture has cooled, add the starter along with the remaining ½ teaspoon of the herb blend. Transfer everything into a jar.
7. Use fermentation method 4 (page 32). Close the lid, but not too tight so fermentation gases can escape. At least once a day, stir the contents with a clean fork or spoon and push down the ingredients to remove air bubbles. When the initial fermentation is complete (7 to 10 days), place the jar in the fridge for further aging. Personally, I like this ferment after 3 weeks.

When you serve the greens, if you think they're a bit too sour, you can add some fresh soy sauce to balance the flavors, or add cooked mushrooms for their sweetness. I usually serve the greens on toast.

If you want your cooked greens to be chewier and more "whole," you can use a smaller amount of water and cook them for a shorter amount of time, but don't skimp on the soy sauce—you need it as a salt replacement for fermentation.

Achar and Chutney

In essence, achars are a type of Indian pickles. India is such a huge subcontinent that recipes vary quite a lot based on the region, but to make things simple, I'm talking about ingredients such as fruits and vegetables preserved in vinegar, brine, or specific types of vegetable oils such as mustard oil or sesame. Some recipes ask for the ingredients to be dehydrated in the sun first. Achars are usually heavily mixed with various Indian spices. I had an authentic salted mango achar once and I must say that it was an acquired taste for my European palate; nevertheless I loved it.

Achars blend various methods of food preservation including dehydration, salting, use of specific spices to inhibit bacteria growth, vinegar pickling, and/or oil preservation. Some achars use a fermentation process whereby the vessel containing the ingredients and spices is exposed to the sun for a couple of weeks. The lacto bacteria present in the ingredients initiate the fermentation, thus making the food acidic enough to ensure food safety.

Chutney is defined by Merriam-Webster as "a thick sauce of Indian origin that contains fruits, vinegar, sugar, and spices and is used as a condiment." The difference between achars and chutneys can be a bit confusing if you're not Indian, probably because some of the recipes could be interpreted as both, but to make things simple, chutneys are more saucelike while achars usually feature a specific "solid" ingredient pickled with spices.

I think I'm correct in defining some of my fermented concoctions as more akin to achars than chutneys—they usually feature one main ingredient such as daikon or similar root vegetables fermented with oil and spices. The recipes are probably far from traditional, because I use local wild edibles in addition to specific Indian spices and oil. Sometimes I dehydrate the root vegetables before fermenting them, but not always.

The spices I use are a good representation of basic Indian flavors. They are:

Turmeric	Coriander	Cloves
Curry	Mustard	Chili
(store-bought	Fenugreek	Fennel
or homemade)	Cumin	Cardamom

Although it's not discussed in this book due to size limitations, you can lacto-ferment fruits (dehydrated or not) using the same methods explained in the next few pages. Heck, I even made a fermented mushroom achar.

I must give some credit to authors and fermentation experts Kirsten K. Shockey and Christopher Shockey. I probably would not have thought of making acharlike fermented concoctions if I had not read their wonderful book *Fiery Ferments*. It's a must-buy for any serious fermentation fan.

MIXED WILD GREENS AND DAIKON ACHAR

This ferment is one of my favorites and will work well with many store-bought or wild greens such as watercress, lamb's-quarter, dandelion, chickweed, miner's lettuce, various mustard leaves, wild radish leaves, and countless others. You can replace daikon with other large radishes (Korean radish, cherry radish, et cetera) or experiment with beets, turnips, and similar root vegetables. Carrots would probably work well, too. In early spring I incorporate tender wild turnip roots. During the winter I may add a bit of herb powder—mallow, nettles, chickweed, and so on. So really take a look at this recipe as a base to create from.

Warning! The following recipe will make you cry—probably in an awesome way, with tears of joy. But seriously, it's quite spicy; it's meant to be used sparingly to boost flavors. My main use is in salads; I mix in some achar with my greens to add some zing. But it's quite good as a side condiment or topping for fish and meat, too.

Ingredients for a 1-pint jar (475 ml) (around 70 percent full)

8 ounces (226 g) daikon (you can also use any other large radish roots)

5 garlic cloves, *or* 1½ teaspoons (5 g) garlic powder

1 ounce (28 g) dandelion (green leaves) or other wild greens, chiffonade cut

1 teaspoon (2 g) turmeric powder

½ teaspoon (1 g) curry powder or Curry Blend

1–2 tablespoons (7.5–15 g) chile morita or other chili flakes, mild or not

½–1 teaspoon (1–2 g) ground peppercorns

½ teaspoon (1 g) ginger powder

1 teaspoon (3 g) coriander seeds

½ teaspoon (2 g) fenugreek seeds

1 teaspoon (4 g) black mustard seeds

½ teaspoon (2 g) fennel seeds

1½ teaspoons (8 g) salt

2 tablespoons (30 ml) Culture Starter (this may not be necessary, but I use it anyway)

Procedure

1. Trim one side of your daikon (or other radish) root and turn it to lie flat. Take your time and cut the root lengthwise into ¼-inch (0.6 cm) slices, then carefully slice again into large matchsticks. Think small French fries. Cut the dandelion and place everything into a bowl.

2. Mince the garlic gloves and add them to the bowl with the turmeric, curry, chili flakes, peppercorns, and ginger.

3. Roasting the seeds takes a couple of minutes. I warm a cast-iron pan on high heat and place the bigger seeds in first (coriander and fenugreek). After a minute, I add the smaller seeds (mustard and fennel). Keep the seeds moving using a wooden spatula (or regular spoon). Judge doneness by smell: With high heat it should not take more than a couple of minutes. Watch out for the mustard seeds, which have a tendency to pop a bit.

4. When your seeds are roasted, add them to the bowl as well. Add the salt and, using gloves, massage everything for a couple of minutes. Let it rest for 5 minutes,

Left: Watercress and radish achar.
Right: Dandelion achar.

then massage again for another couple of minutes. You want the contents to be quite juicy. Repeat if necessary. Next, add the culture starter (active sauerkraut juice), then pack everything into a pint jar. I use the stir or shake method (fermentation method 3, page 28).

5. Place the lid on top and close it, but not so tight that fermentation gases can't escape. At least twice a day, open the jar and stir the contents with a clean spoon or fork. Most of the time I actually leave the lid closed tight to monitor the fermentation; I will burp as necessary while stirring or shaking only once a day. Both methods work well. Ferment for 7 to 10 days, and when the initial fermentation is complete (no more gases), place in the fridge. Enjoy whenever you want; the stuff will last for months. The ferment should end up quite salty on purpose.

WATERCRESS-RADISH ACHAR

You can also use dandelion, lamb's-quarter, garlic mustard, black mustard, and countless other greens with this recipe. The main difference with this technique is the fact that we'll cut the roots into squares and dehydrate them first, which creates a denser texture. In Southern California it took me half a day in the sun to get the best results. Tested in the oven, it took around 7 hours at 170°F (77°C).

Ingredients for a 1-pint jar (475 ml)

1 pound 8 ounces (680 g) cubed fresh
    Korean radish, daikon, or beets
½ ounce (14 g) chopped watercress *or*
    1 ounce (28 g) dandelion, curly dock,
    or similar wild greens (chiffonade cut)
2 teaspoons (6 g) pan-roasted
    sesame seeds
2 teaspoons (6 g) pan-roasted
    coriander seeds
½ teaspoon (1.5 g) fenugreek seeds, cracked
½ teaspoon (1 g) ground peppercorns
½ teaspoon (1 g) Curry Blend
1–2 teaspoons (2.5–5 g) chili flakes—
    mild or spicy
2 tablespoons (30 ml) Culture Starter
1½ teaspoons (7.5 ml) toasted sesame oil
1½ teaspoons (8 g) salt

Procedure

Cube the radish, daikon, or beets into small squares, a bit larger than ½ inch (1.3 cm), and dehydrate them in the sun, or in a dehydrator or oven set at low temperature. The cubes should end up somewhat spongy and not fully dried—kind of a middle ground between fresh and dehydrated. Place all the ingredients into a bowl, massage, then transfer into a pint jar. Use fermentation method 3 (page 28), just as you would for the Mixed Wild Greens and Daikon Achar.

The ferment may look a bit dry, but more liquid will be extracted by the next day.

Fermenting Mushrooms

Fermented mushrooms make a great salad addition or side condiment. You can balance any sourness by adding some maple syrup or seasoned rice vinegar.

Fermenting mushrooms can be a bit controversial. If you do some research, you'll find recipes for raw, dehydrated, and cooked mushrooms. Some health experts such as Dr. Andrew Weil suggest that mushrooms are indigestible if eaten raw because of their tough cell walls and advise people to cook them to release their nutrients. We also need to be aware that some mushrooms can be toxic if not cooked properly. As a wildcrafter, the rule I learned from my elders is to avoid eating wild mushrooms raw, and I follow that rule for fermentation. I usually slice the mushrooms, but if they are small enough, like baby bella or shimeji, I use them whole.

So far I have fermented shiitake, baby bella, shimeji, portobello, enoki, button, and oyster mushrooms (commercial and foraged). Before using any wild mushrooms, exercise caution and do some research on edibility and cooking time. Because the mushrooms are cooked, I assume there are no live bacteria and I use a lacto bacteria starter in my ferments (see Culture Starter, page 44).

Some Russian recipes ask you to boil the mushrooms, cool the solution, then add a brine of water, salt, and spices with the addition of a leaf on top to keep everything under the brine. Whey is usually used as a starter, and it's common to add sugar to kick the fermentation into high gear. I haven't used this method, but it seems valid as long as the mushrooms are properly cooked. I also add maple syrup or another source of sugar in my mushroom ferments.

I like to steam the mushrooms instead of cooking them in a pan; even small ones keep their shape when steamed. There's nothing complicated about it: Just use a steamer basket or pot, the same one you steam vegetables with. Place your mushrooms in the steamer basket over water and turn the heat to high. Steam, covered, until quite tender, about 10 to 15 minutes for small or delicate mushrooms and up to 20 minutes (baby bella) or more depending on the size. My simple rule is to make sure they are thoroughly cooked.

Remove and place the mushrooms in a colander. Let them cool off for 20 minutes, and you're ready to ferment them.

A Note on Mushrooms

If you use button or cremini mushrooms, purchase "babies" or young ones. You want them small. The larger ones will tend to become too mushy once aged, unless you like that sort of thing; or, they could be used to make a fermented paste (see "Mushrooms Too Mushy?" on page 98).

MUSHROOM ACHAR

The idea of fermenting mushrooms came from my dandelion and Korean radish achar. I was completely in love with the taste and thought it could be a perfect flavor pairing with diced king oyster mushroom stems. I wasn't wrong; I think it's an excellent ferment, very popular with people attending my wild food tasting events, and I have done it many times since with various types of mushrooms.

This recipe for mushroom achar uses ingredients that you can purchase at the store but, as you'll see from the recipes that follow, you can also truly go wild!

Ingredients for a 1-pint jar (475 ml)

10 ounces (283 g) mushrooms (such as shimeji, baby button mushrooms, or diced king oyster mushroom stems)

2 tablespoons (18 g) sesame seeds

2 teaspoons (6 g) coriander seeds

8 garlic cloves

½ ounce (14 g) watercress, mustard, arugula, or dandelion greens (you can also mix the various greens)

Around 1 tablespoon (7 g) dried cranberries or raisins

2½ teaspoons (14 g) salt (it's supposed to be a somewhat salty condiment)

5 tablespoons (75 ml) Culture Starter

2 teaspoons (10 ml) maple syrup (you could also use sugar or honey)

2 teaspoons (6 g) chia seeds

1 teaspoon (2 g) turmeric powder

1 teaspoon (2 g) curry powder or Curry Blend

1 tablespoon (7.5 g) chili flakes, mild or hot (smoked is fantastic if you can find it)

2 teaspoons (5 g) mild chili powder or flakes

1 teaspoon (2.5 g) ground peppercorns

½ teaspoon (1 g) ginger powder

3 tablespoons (44 ml) toasted sesame oil

Procedure

1. For this type of ferment, I use fermentation method 3 (page 28). First, steam your mushrooms, making sure they're thoroughly cooked, then place them in a colander to cool off. Once they're cooled, transfer them into a bowl.

2. For better flavors, you want to toast the coriander and sesame seeds. In a dry, heavy skillet, place the seeds over medium heat for 2 or 3 minutes until they become golden brown and give off a rich aroma. Stir frequently with a wooden spoon or paddle for even toasting.

   Transfer the toasted seeds from the skillet into a separate small cup or bowl to cool for a few minutes.

3. Chop the garlic cloves into small pieces and thinly cut (chiffonade) the greens you're using.

4. With that done, place the toasted seeds, garlic, greens, and remaing ingredients (except for the sesame oil) into the bowl containing the mushrooms and, with clean hands, massage everything gently for 10 seconds or so. I usually add the sesame oil at the end and massage the ingredients one more time for a few seconds, then let everything rest for a couple of minutes.

5. Pour all the contents into a clean pint jar. A canning funnel is very helpful. With a clean spoon

Mushrooms Too Mushy? Make a Fermented Paste!

When I experimented with fermenting different types of mushrooms, sometimes I would end up with less-than-satisfactory results. The mushrooms ended up too soft and mushy.

Still, failures can become wonderful opportunities. Try blending your fermented concoctions and make a savory paste. Add a bit of acorn (or regular) flour as a thickening agent. You can even add more spices, vinegar, and so on.

Pastes are wonderful for plating or to add little flavoring touches on a dish. The last time I had a fermentation I wasn't happy with, I ended up mixing it with my homemade vinegar, added a tad of honey and salt, some savory herbs, and voilà—I transformed my failure into an awesome salad dressing.

(or finger), push down the ingredients to remove any air pockets.

6. Place the lid on top and close it, but not so tight that fermentation gases can't escape. At least twice a day, open the jar and, with a clean spoon or fork, stir the contents very gently. Gentleness is extremely important if you're dealing with small, pretty mushrooms such as shimeji (beech mushrooms).

Most of the time, I leave the lid closed tight to monitor the fermentation and will burp as necessary while stirring twice a day. Both methods work: The idea is to work with your ferments and supervise them. I also like to turn the jar upside down for a couple of hours each day.

Probably due to the starter and the mushrooms, this is a very active fermentation for the first 2 to 4 days; then it slows down considerably. I place the jar in the fridge when the fermentation gases are not very noticeable (which is where the closed lid helps), usually after 6 to 7 days.

I have a little secret, though . . . most of the time, I eat the stuff after 3 to 4 days of fermentation. It's so good, I can't resist! Aging it doesn't help the flavors; it's not bad, but not as good as a young ferment. Basically, the rule is . . . when it tastes good for you, eat it!

WILDCRAFTED MUSHROOM
AND WILD SEED ACHAR

This is my wild version using local seeds, aromatic herbs, and locally foraged ingredients. You can't really make this one if you don't live in Southern California, but I've included it in this book to give you some ideas. With a bit of education and knowledge, you can make a version that will represent your local terroir.

Ingredients for a very full ½-pint jar (236 ml)

½ ounce (14 g) various wild greens, such as chickweed, dandelion, wild mustard, or radish leaves (chiffonade cut)

5¼ ounces (150 g) steamed mushrooms (I used foraged oyster mushrooms)

1½ teaspoons (4 g) dried red currants

1 teaspoon (5 ml) maple syrup (you could also use sugar or honey)

Seeds

1 teaspoon (4 g) black mustard seeds, lightly pan-roasted

½ teaspoon (2 g) Chinese mustard seeds, lightly pan-roasted

2 teaspoons (6 g) sesame seeds, lightly pan-roasted

1 teaspoon (3 g) coriander seeds, lightly pan-roasted

½ teaspoon (1.5 g) black sage seeds, lightly pan-roasted

½ teaspoon (1.5 g) white sage seeds, lightly pan-roasted

¼ teaspoon (1 g) clarkia seeds

½ teaspoon (1.5 g) broadleaf plantain seeds

¼ teaspoon (1 g) longleaf plantain seeds

¼ teaspoon (1 g) nettle seeds

Spices

½ teaspoon (2 g) turmeric

½ teaspoon (2 g) Curry Blend

4 garlic cloves, chopped

½ tablespoon (4 g) chile morita (smoked jalapeño flakes)

1 teaspoon (2.5 g) Korean chili flakes

½ teaspoon (1.5 g) ground peppercorns

½ teaspoon (2 g) ginger powder

1½ tablespoons (22 ml) toasted sesame oil

2 tablespoons (30 ml) Culture Starter

Salt

Procedure

The total weight was around 8 ounces (227 g). I added 1½ teaspoons (8 g) of salt. I used fermentation method 3 (page 28), as for the Mushroom Achar.

FERMENTED (BABY) CREMINI MUSHROOMS

This is a super-simple recipe, and you can really personalize it by adding different spices. Works well with shiitake, baby bella, shimeji, portobello, enoki, button, and oyster mushrooms (commercial and foraged).

Ingredients for a 1-quart jar (946 ml) (around 80 percent full)

14 ounces (397 g) baby cremini mushrooms

1 garlic clove, chopped
  (or 2 if you really like garlic)

2 teaspoons (1 g) herb blend of your choice;
  I use a mix of Herbes de Provence and
  local wild aromatics (sages, California
  bay, California sagebrush, et cetera)

1 teaspoon (2.5 g) chili flakes (mild or hot;
  I used smoked jalapeño flakes)

1 teaspoon (2.5 g) ground peppercorns

2 teaspoons (11 g) salt

2 teaspoons (10 ml) maple syrup
  (you can also use sugar or honey)

½ cup (118 ml) water

3 tablespoons (44 ml) Culture Starter

Procedure

1. Steam the mushrooms for 20 minutes, then place them in a colander to cool off for 30 minutes or so. Transfer them into a bowl and add the remaining ingredients. Mix everything thoroughly, then pack it into a quart jar. The jar should end up around 80 percent full.

2. We'll use fermentation method 3 (page 28). The ingredients won't be under the brine, so simply close the jar tightly and shake it for a few seconds two or three times daily, then unscrew the jar a tiny bit so fermentation gas can escape. The goal of the small amount of brine is really to distribute acidity to all the ingredients during the shaking, to ensure that all the mushrooms will ferment properly. More brine will be created by the mushrooms during fermentation. Most of the time, I leave the lid closed tight to monitor the fermentation, shake the contents two or three times daily, and burp as necessary.

3. Ferment for 7 to 10 days, and when the initial fermentation is complete (no more gases), place in the fridge. The fermentation is usually quite active within 24 hours. I usually eat this after a week or so, but you can try aging it a bit and see if you like the flavors. To "Americanize" the ferment, I often marinate it for a few hours in a small amount of seasoned rice vinegar and dried herbs before I serve it. Another idea is to serve with pan-roasted sesame seeds and sesame oil. It's not complicated; do it by taste.

KIMSHROOM (OR SHROOMCHI)

I'm not sure what to call this, so you can pick the name you prefer. It's simply mushrooms fermented in brine with chili flakes and garlic, akin to some kimchis, though you may argue that anything that has garlic and chili flakes/powder will have a similar flavor profile.

It's a delicious, tangy, sour, and spicy ferment with regular (baby) button mushrooms, but it also works well with shimeji (beech) or oyster mushrooms.

Ingredients for a 1-quart jar (946 ml) (around 80 percent full)

Around 14 ounces (397 g) mushrooms

3 tablespoons (22 g) Korean chili flakes (quite mild); you can add some spicy chili powder or flakes as well

½ teaspoon (1.5 g) smoked jalapeño chili powder (optional)

2 teaspoons (11 g) salt

5 garlic cloves, chopped

1 cup (236 ml) water

1 teaspoon (2.5 g) freshly grated gingerroot

3 tablespoons (44 ml) Culture Starter

2 teaspoons (10 ml) maple syrup (you can also use sugar or honey)

Procedure

1. Steam the mushrooms for 20 minutes, then place them in a colander to cool off for 20 minutes or so. Transfer them to a bowl and add the remaining ingredients. Mix everything thoroughly, then pack it into a quart jar. The jar should end up around 80 percent full.

2. Use fermentation method 3 (page 28), as for the Fermented (Baby) Cremini Mushrooms. The only difference is that I like this ferment aged.

SPICY GARLICKY SHIMEJI

This is a tasty and spicy condiment. You can add a splash of seasoned rice vinegar when serving, but it's really not a must. The ferment ages very well, too.

The recipe is nearly identical to that for Kimshroom (mushroom kimchi), but spicier. A mushroom lover will cry tears of happiness and pain. Feel free to use milder chili powder if you are not a fan of spicy food. Because of the habaneros, the heat will be unbearable when the ferment is young but will subside (a little) after a couple of months. You can totally skip the habaneros and use milder fresh red peppers if you want, or simply omit the fresh peppers.

Ingredients for a ½-pint jar (236 ml)

Around 5½ ounces (158 g) shimeji or
    similar mushrooms
1–3 fresh habanero peppers (optional—
    3 is *very* spicy)
4 garlic cloves, minced
1½ teaspoons (12 g) Korean chili powder or similar
    mild chili powder
1½ teaspoons (4 g) chile morita or chipotle
    (you could use smoked paprika powder, too)
1 teaspoon (5.5 g) salt
½ teaspoon (2 g) ginger powder
1 teaspoon (5 ml) maple syrup
    (you can also use sugar or honey)
2 tablespoons (30 ml) Culture Starter

Procedure

1. Steam the mushrooms for 15 minutes, then transfer to a colander to cool for 30 minutes or so.
2. While the mushrooms are steaming, if you choose to use fresh habaneros or other red peppers, mince them or grind them into a paste using a mortar and pestle.
3. Transfer the cooled mushrooms into a bowl and add the habanero paste along with the remaining ingredients. Mix everything thoroughly, then pack into a ½-pint jar.
4. The ingredients won't be under the brine, so the technique used (fermentation method 3, page 28) is to close the jar tightly and shake for a few seconds at least three times a day, then unscrew the lid a tiny bit so fermentation gases can escape; or, if you close the lid tight, burp as necessary.

The goal of shaking the jar and formed brine is really to distribute acidity to all the ingredients, which ensures that all the mushrooms will ferment properly and the contents will be acidic enough. More brine will be created by the mushrooms during fermentation. Sometimes I place the jar upside down with the lid closed tight for a few hours so all mushrooms marinate in the acidic brine, but it's not a must if you shake the stuff daily.
5. Ferment and shake for 7 to 10 days, and when the initial fermentation is complete (no more gases), place the jar in the fridge. I like to start eating them after 3 weeks and consume them all within a couple of months. I've never aged them for a longer time, but I don't think it would be a problem to do so. The ferment can also be eaten very young, as soon as a week after fermentation has started.

THAI-INSPIRED
FERMENTED MUSHROOMS

This is one of my favorite mushroom ferments, but due to the amount of garlic used, it's better if you age it for at least a month or two. If you want to use it young, I suggest using half the amount of fresh garlic; it's a bit overwhelming in the beginning, but the flavors will mellow over time.

Ingredients for a ½-pint jar (236 ml)

Around 5½ ounces (158 g) shimeji or similar mushrooms

4 garlic cloves, chopped

1 teaspoon (5 ml) maple syrup (you can also use sugar or honey)

¼ teaspoon (0.5 g) ground peppercorns

2 tablespoons (30 ml) Culture Starter

½ teaspoon (2 g) ginger powder

1 teaspoon (5.5 g) salt

Procedure

Use the same overall method as for Spicy Garlicy Shimeji.

Serve with the addition of fresh ingredients. I like to squeeze in a bit of lime juice, adding a tad of salt to taste along with sliced red onions, fresh cilantro (chickweed or wild chervil works well, too), and a small amount of sliced chili peppers. It really takes it to the next level.

You could add a touch of vinegar, but if you are a fermentation purist, it's completely okay to leave it alone.

If your diet is not plant-based, adding a bit of fish sauce is also an option.

A Note on Shimeji

Also known as beech mushrooms, shimeji can be purchased commercially and are used frequently in Asian cuisine. They're always available at my local Asian markets.

FERMENTED MUSHROOM SPAGHETTI

Mushroom spaghetti is made using large king oyster stems. These mushrooms can be found easily in Asian markets. It's possible that a forager could use large boletes for this recipe. I mostly use soy sauce instead of salt in this ferment.

Ingredients for a ½-pint jar (236 ml) (around 90 percent full)

1 pound (453 g) sliced king oyster mushroom stems

2½ tablespoons (37 ml) soy sauce

2 teaspoons (10 ml) maple syrup (you can also use sugar or honey)

6 tablespoons (90 ml) Culture Starter

1½–2 teaspoons (3–4 g) garlic powder *or* 3 garlic cloves, finely diced

¼ teaspoon (2 g) salt

Procedure

1. Cut the mushroom stems lengthwise in thin slices, then steam them for 20 minutes. Once they've cooled off, slice them in thin strips using the julienne cut. You should end up with around 10½ ounces (300 g) of mushroom strips due to water evaporation.
2. In a bowl, combine the julienned stems with the remaining ingredients; mix and then transfer to a ½-pint jar. The jar will be around 90 percent full.
3. Use fermentation method 3 (page 28). The ingredients won't be under the brine, so simply close the jar tightly and shake or stir the contents for a few seconds two or three times daily, then unscrew the jar a tiny bit so fermentation gases can escape. I leave the lid closed tight to monitor the fermentation, shake the contents two or three times daily, and burp as necessary.
4. Ferment until the initial fermentation (around 10 days) is done and place in the fridge. You can eat the ferment after a couple of months, but it will age very well, too. The flavors are a mix of sour and sweet with a nice texture—quite delicious.

Serve with fresh salsa or tomato sauce like regular spaghetti. I like the salsa better, as it is a nice complement to the sourness of the fermented mushrooms. You can even make the salsa spicy or sweet.

FOREST MEDLEY

This ferment is very similar to the previous recipe, but it shows that you can really mix all kinds of ingredients together. It does take a bit of skill and experience; just blending stuff randomly doesn't guarantee success in terms of flavors at the end. I like to have a main "base" to start from and add savory components that work well with it. In this case, the base is composed of mushrooms and Chinese cabbage (bok choy).

From there, I added wild roots, roasted seeds, spices, mustard leaves, and so on. Such medleys are always a representation of a time and place. During the winter mushrooms are the main component, but in spring I'll start playing with mustard shoots, roots, and leaves, wild radish pods, and very savory greens such as chickweed and chervil.

Don't be afraid to try things and make mistakes. I made some terrible dishes when I started exploring wild food fermentation, but I've learned so much in the process. Over time you learn to evaluate the savory components and create fermented masterpieces.

Ingredients for a 1-quart jar (946 ml)

14 garlic cloves

½ cup (118 ml) springwater

⅛ red onion (chopped)

5–6 tablespoons (35–42 g) Korean chili powder

6 ounces (170 g) shredded green cabbage

3 ounces (80 g) bok choy (cut the leaves if they're too big)

1½ ounces (40 g) wild mustard and radish green leaves (chiffonade cut)

1 ounce (28 g) tender field mustard (*Brassica rapa*) roots sliced thin and julienned burdock roots

½ ounce (14 g) various wild components, such as unripe mustard flowers, watercress, cattail shoots, and so on

8½ ounces (240 g) sliced oyster mushrooms

Around ½ ounce (24 g) whole splitgill mushroom

Salt

Procedure

1. Using a stone grinder (molcajete), make a paste with the garlic, springwater, chopped onion, and Korean chili powder.
2. Place the cabbage, bok choy, greens, roots, and whatever wild components you're using into a bowl.
3. Steam the oyster and splitgill mushrooms for 15 minutes, then place them in a strainer until cool.
4. Transfer the paste, greens, roots, wild components, and mushrooms into a second bowl and weigh the contents. My total weight was around 1 pound 11 ounces (765 g); I added a bit more than 1 tablespoon (19 g) of salt. If you think about it, it's really a mix of around 40 percent mushrooms and 60 percent greens from the Brassica family (cabbage, bok choy, radish leaves, plus roots) with some spices added.
5. Mix and massage your components with the salt for a few minutes and transfer everything into a quart jar. The jar will be quite full.
6. Use fermentation method 3 (page 28). The ingredients won't be under the brine, so simply close the jar

Forest Medley being served
after 3 months of fermentation.

tightly and shake or stir the contents for a few seconds two or three times daily, then unscrew the jar a
tiny bit so fermentation gases can escape. Or you
can leave the lid closed tight to monitor the fermentation, shake the contents two or three times daily,
and burp as necessary.

7. Ferment until the initial fermentation is done
(around 10 days) and place in the fridge.

OYSTER AND SPLITGILL MUSHROOMS
FERMENTED WITH BOK CHOY

I made this ferment once I came back from a wildcrafting expedition with a huge amount of oyster and splitgill (*Schizophyllum commune*) mushrooms. If there is one thing I like about lacto-fermentation, it's the fact that it's a very easy food preservation technique. In one morning I was able to ferment 7 pounds (3.2 kg) of mushrooms, which I used throughout the year. It you don't like chewy texture, you can skip the splitgill mushrooms.

The recipe is quite basic, a sort of mix between regular ferments and kimchi composed of bok choy, roasted wild seeds, wild radish leaves, foraged mushrooms, chili peppers/flakes, and garlic. You could add curry and other spices, too. No need for Culture Starter. You can replace the wild seeds with regular seeds like sesame or flaxseeds, and the radish leaves with many other wild greens.

Ingredients for a 1-quart jar (946 ml)

1 pound (453 g) bok choy
6 garlic cloves, minced
1 ounce (28 g) shredded wild radish leaves
Salt
9 ounces (255 g) oyster mushrooms, sliced thick
1 ounce (28 g) splitgill mushrooms
2 teaspoons (4 g) pan-roasted wild seeds such as black sage, white sage, sesame, sedge, et cetera
1–2 Thai chili peppers, diced
5–8 tablespoons (36–60 g) Korean chili flakes (medium heat)

Procedure

I ended up with close to 2 pounds (900 g) of ingredients and I used 4 teaspoons salt (around 22 g).

1. Massage/squeeze the bok choy, garlic, and radish leaves with salt for 2 to 3 minutes. Let them rest for 10 minutes, and massage again slowly until they're really juicy. Meanwhile, steam the mushrooms for 15 minutes, then transfer to a colander to cool.

2. Once the mushrooms have cooled, place everything into a bowl along with the roasted seeds, Thai chili, and chili flakes, and massage again for a minute or so. (Use gloves to do this.) You want the contents to be somewhat juicy. Transfer into a quart jar.

3. Use fermentation method 3 (page 28). The ingredients won't be under the brine, so simply close the jar tightly and shake or stir the contents for a few seconds two or three times daily, then unscrew the lid a tiny bit so fermentation gases can escape. For my part, I leave the lid closed tight to monitor the fermentation, shake the contents two or three times daily, and burp as necessary.

4. Ferment until the initial fermentation is done (around 10 days) and place in the fridge.

ROASTED AND FERMENTED OYSTER MUSHROOMS

I was still going through the huge amount of oyster mushrooms that I foraged last winter and using fermentation to preserve the harvest, but I was getting a bit bored with the regular ferments. Then I had a bright idea.

I think this ferment is pretty cool, but we all have our favorite cooked mushroom recipe. My own is super simple: basically sliced oyster mushrooms pan-roasted with olive oil, garlic powder, salt, ground peppercorns, and my special blend of local aromatic herbs (but Herbes de Provence or Italian Herbs work fantastic, too).

I'm not going into the recipe for cooking the mushrooms, since it's basic and similar recipes can be found in books and online. But my bright idea was this: Why not ferment cooked mushrooms? If you can make achar ferments with sesame or mustard oil, I concluded that regular olive oil should work. And it did! Just don't use butter if you plan to ferment—I'm not sure it would work.

In this experiment I followed my favorite recipe for cooked mushrooms. Once they were nicely pan-roasted, the fermentation fun began.

Ingredients for a 1-pint jar (475 ml)

10 ounces (283 g) pan-roasted mushrooms with olive oil, garlic, spices—already cooked according to your favorite recipe

2 garlic cloves, finely chopped (additional to the amount used in the cooked mushroom recipe)

¾ cup (177 ml) Culture Starter

½ teaspoon (0.3 g) additional herb blend like Herbes de Provence or Italian Herbs

2–3 teaspoons (10–15 ml) maple syrup (sugar source for the lacto bacteria)

Salt

Procedure

1. Mix all the ingredients in a bowl. The total weight should be a bit more than 12 ounces; I used 1 teaspoon (5.5 g) of salt. Massage the ingredients for a bit, then placed them in a pint jar. (The mushrooms are already salted from the original roasting, so take that salt amount into account.)

2. Use fermentation method 3 (page 28). The ingredients won't be under the brine, so simply close the jar tightly and shake or stir the contents for a few seconds two or three times daily, then unscrew the jar a tiny bit so fermentation gases can escape; or leave the lid closed tight to monitor the fermentation, shake the contents two or three times daily, and burp as necessary. To ensure food safety, I checked the acidity (pH); it was perfect at around 3.4.

3. Ferment until the initial fermentation is done (around 10 days) and place in the fridge. I don't age this ferment very much; I like to eat it within a month, and I haven't experimented with aging it much longer than that.

POTATOES FERMENTED
WITH LOCAL FLAVORS

Sometimes the taste of a "wild" ferment is not determined by the main ingredients being fermented but by the flavoring added. You can use very common ingredients and still, through the use of wildcrafted spices, explore true local flavors. Even simple ingredients such as potatoes can be used. I love potatoes because they're quite neutral. In my first book, *The New Wildcrafted Cuisine*, I cooked them in "forest floor," wrapped them in clay with aromatic herbs, and played with them in countless other ways. They're incredibly versatile, but what about fermenting them?

Here's a little trick that some Belgian and French chefs use to add extra flavor to fries or roasted potatoes: Ferment them in a brine with a bit of crushed garlic for 2 to 3 days. My mom used to place potatoes (sliced lengthwise) in salted water for a couple of days. I don't think she knew it was a fermentation process, but it made the fries taste better. The potatoes get a nice little sour taste that's very subtle and quite pleasant, like a dash of umami. You would not know why those potatoes taste better than regular ones, but they do.

This was somewhat experimental on my part, but I simply added my favorite spice blend, made with herbs from my native garden (black sage, sagebrush, white sage, peppercorns, salt, California bay, garlic powder, smoked chili, and a small amount of foraged oyster mushroom). The idea was to infuse even more flavors into the potatoes during the fermentation process, then roast them with olive oil and more of the same spice blend.

It worked beautifully. I had to adjust the amount of spices used and the fermentation time; 2 to 3 days of fermentation ended up being ideal. You can also do this type of ferment with a French or Italian herb mix. In fact, why not play around with other flavors, like a bit of Curry Blend?

The same method can be applied to French fries, but make sure you leave some skin on the cut fries or use some Culture Starter to encourage fermentation.

Don't limit yourself to fermenting potatoes. I made a similar ferment using sunchokes, which I aged for weeks in the fridge.

Ingredients for a 1-quart jar (946 ml)

Salt

12½ ounces (354 g) potatoes, quartered

1 teaspoon (0.5 g) wild spice blend or herb blend (Italian/French herb mix)

3 garlic cloves, crushed

½ bay leaf (I use California bay)

1 dried chili (optional)

Procedure

1. Make a brine composed of 1½ teaspoons (8.5 g) salt per cup (236 ml) of water (a 3 percent brine); you'll need around 2 cups of water for this ferment. Place all the ingredients in a quart jar and add the brine. Leave a headspace of 1 inch (2.5 cm). Use fermentation method 2 (page 23); close the lid, but not too tight, so fermentation gases can escape. Shake a couple of times daily. If you decide to leave the lid closed, burp as necessary.
2. Ferment for 2 to 3 days—longer fermentation will give you off flavors. Strain and dry the potatoes a bit with a paper towel, then rub with olive oil and spices of your liking.
3. Roast in a preheated oven at 450°F (250°C) for 20 to 25 minutes. Stir the potatoes a couple of times during the roasting process. Just for kicks, I even added oyster mushrooms, jalapeños, and onions.

BLACK MUSTARD LEAVES
FERMENTED IN THEIR OWN SEEDS

I like this simple ferment: It's quite unusual in that it really represents a full circle, from spring to fall. The mustard leaves, which taste a bit like wasabi, were wildcrafted in March when the mustard is at its prime, and the seeds were collected in October the prior year.

The mustard sauce was homemade by grinding the seeds and mixing them with elderberry wine, mugwort beer vinegar, and homemade sea salt (from seawater). You can't purchase flavors like that in the store, but you can still use a good-quality organic stone-ground mustard if you don't make your own.

Ingredients for a ½-pint jar (236 ml)

7 ounces (198 g) whole mustard leaves
½ teaspoon (2.5 g) sea salt
1 tablespoon (15 g) stone-ground prepared mustard

Procedure

1. Use young, tender mustard leaves if possible, and remove the center stems on any older leaves. Place the leaves in a bowl, add the salt, and gently massage them for 30 seconds or so. Let them rest for a couple of minutes, then repeat until they're quite wilted and juicy.
2. Add the prepared mustard and mix it with the wilted leaves, then transfer the contents into a ½-pint jar.
3. Use fermentation method 4 (page 32). Close the lid and, at least once a day, stir the contents a bit with a clean fork and push the ingredients down under the formed brine. They may not stay under the brine, but that's okay. If you stir or push down the contents daily, the ferment will become acidic and you won't develop any problems. When the initial fermentation is complete, usually 7 to 10 days, place the jar in the refrigerator.

You can eat this ferment quite young or aged. I had some that was 6 months old and it was quite delicious. It's a chewy ferment. If you don't like that, simply chop the contents a bit prior to consumption.

Taste and use this ferment as a creative base. You can still add spices, more fresh mustard sauce, lemon juice, vinegar, chili flakes, and so on.

Fermentation Without Salt

Making gundruk or not . . . That is the question!

Quite a few fermentation books talk about an interesting non-salt fermentation technique used in Nepal and the resulting product called *gundruk*. For local Nepalis, it's one way to deal with the excess of mustard and radish leaves after the fall harvest. Over 2,000 tons of gundruk are produced every year.

The basic method I've seen described in books or online is quite simple. You take the leaves of vegetables from the Brassica family (mustard, radish, kale, and others), let them wilt in the sun for a day or two, shred or chop them, and finally pound them with a wooden vegetable pounder or stomper into a closed container to ferment for around 10 days. There are some slight method variations here and there; for example, some people add a bit of water to keep the vegetables under the brine. Instead of pounding to extract the juice, you can squeeze/massage the leaves quite forcefully with your hands to extract the juice, then pound them into the container. It usually takes me around 10 minutes to extract the juice from the wilted leaves. Some recipes keep the stems, mostly if the gundruk is intended to make soup, but I like to remove them because my wild ingredients can have tougher stems than regular commercial greens.

The chopped leaves are then fermented for 10 days (up to 2 weeks in some books), then removed and dried in the sun. Once they're thoroughly dried, you can store them in a jar or other airtight container.

This sounded awesome to me because I have so many wild plants from the Brassica family around, such as Mediterranean hoary mustard, wild radish, black mustard, perennial pepperweed, and many others.

My main worry, though, was the issue of food safety and the possibility for botulism. Botulism is not something to scoff at—it's a severe and sometimes deadly food poisoning caused by the ingestion of toxins produced by the bacterium *Clostridium botulinum* due to improper food preservation techniques. For example, using the wrong canning method with low-acid foods or preserving in oil ingredients with a pH above 4.6.

When I completed the Master Food Preserver program at the University of California, I learned that *C. botulinum* will not grow in acidic conditions (pH less than 4.6), and therefore the toxin will not be formed in acidic foods.

But mustard and radish leaves are not very acidic; in fact, when I juiced some wild radish leaves and tested the juice, it had a pH close to 6, which is quite high. Because botulism can thrive in a low-oxygen / low-acid environment, you can see how a non-salt fermentation in a closed container and the possibility of high pH in my "fermented" ingredients would make me nervous.

On the good side, some online research showed me that the final after-fermentation pH of gundruk is supposed to fall between 3.8 and 4, which makes it safe for consumption. On the bad side, I'm dealing with wild ingredients that, although they are from the Brassica family, are probably not the same as used in Nepal.

For my first experiment, I made my gundruk with the leaves of black mustard and Mediterranean hoary mustard, using the traditional method explained above and with no salt added. The fermentation went well, but when I took a reading after 10 days the pH of the hoary mustard was just above 4.6, while the black mustard one was around 4.5. Not good enough in my book. The stuff smelled really nice and sour, though.

Can it be used? Probably, but you will need to add different layers of food safety. The botulism toxin is heat-labile and can be destroyed by high temperatures. That's a very good thing. I remember my mom water-canning green beans, which are high pH, and I'm probably alive today because they were cooked before serving.

In a document titled "Preventing Foodborne Illness: *Clostridium botulinum*," released by the University of Florida IFAS (Institute of Food and Agricultural Sciences) Extension, the following is clearly stated: "Heating food to a typical cooking temperature of 176°F (80°C) for 30 minutes or 212°F (100°C) for 10 minutes before consumption can greatly reduce the risk of foodborne illness."

Thus, you could do two things:

1. Dehydrate your wild gundruk at a temperature of at least 176°F (80°C) for more than 30 minutes. I did 40 minutes of dehydration at that temperature in my stove, then finished it in the sun.
2. If you make soup with it, boil it for at least 15 minutes. I boil for more than 10 minutes because water boils at different temperatures

due to altitude. At sea level, water boils at 212°F (100°C). With each 500-foot (150 m) increase in elevation, the boiling point of water is lowered by just under 1°F (0.5°C). For example, at 7,500 feet (2,286 m) water boils at about 198°F (92°C). I currently live at an altitude of 3,600 feet (1,097 m), so my water boils at 205°F (96°C).

But guess what? I still don't advise it. In my opinion, it's not necessary to make a gundruk without a tad of salt. I do think the recipes in other books are safe, it's probably because I deal with wild plants. I've made wild gundruk with these two layers of food safety added at the end and I've also made some by adding a bit of salt, some shredded cabbage, a bit of garlic, and some chili powder. The flavors were pretty much identical, and I even think the latest one tasted better. So why not play it safe?

With this recipe I ended up with a pH of 4 after 10 days.

Step 1

Step 2

Step 3

Step 4

WILD GUNDRUK

Ingredients for a 1-pint jar (475 ml)

2 pounds (907 g) fresh leaves,
   which gives me 12 ounces (340 g)
   wilted ones after a few hours in the sun
3 ounces (85 g) cabbage, sliced in thin strips
Salt
7 garlic cloves, minced
2 teaspoons (5 g) smoked jalapeño
   chili powder (chile morita) or
   regular chili flakes

Step 5

Step 6

Procedure

The final weight of the ingredients was 1 pound (453 g), and I used 1 teaspoon (5.5 g) salt (half the regular amount).

1. Forage, clean, and remove the stems from the leaves if the former are too tough. The reason I remove the stems is that many of our wild stems are too fibrous and tough for culinary uses, unless you want to grind the final gundruk into powder to make a spice.
2. On a clean surface (I use a plastic tabletop), place the leaves outside in the sun until well wilted, which can take a day or two depending on where you live. Here in Southern California, if the weather is too hot, I just place them in the sun for maybe an hour, then continue the process in the shade. Don't over-complicate things; you just want them wilted, not fully dehydrated.
3. Chop the wilted leaves and place them in a bowl. Add the cabbage, salt, minced garlic, and chili.
4. Massage until the ingredients are juicy. This may take 5 minutes or so. Wear gloves if you used spicy chili flakes.
5. Chopping quite well is important for tougher leaves, like those of our local Mediterranean mustard. I like to finely shred/cut (chiffonade) all the ingredients after I've massaged them. It's easier.
6. Pack the leaves into a jar using a wooden vegetable pounder or stomper to remove any air pockets between the shredded leaves. Try to get some of the juice to the surface so that the greens are covered. Eventually the greens will absorb the juice; it's not necessary for them to stay under the brine in this method.
7. Leave a little bit of headspace, ½ to 1 inch. Seal the jar and ferment for 10 to 15 days. Some recipes call for the jar to be placed in a sunny location, but I can't do that here in Los Angeles; it would simply cook the greens and kill all the bacteria in the jar. If I have the time, I leave the jar in the sun for maybe 30 minutes at the end of the day when the sun is going down and it's not too hot, but otherwise I place my

jar in a well-lighted location or outside in a shaded area. The reason for placing the jar in the sunlight is to help reduce the possibility of mold.

You will need to monitor the pressure inside the jar and burp the jar if necessary. The smell should be quite sour but pleasant.

8. When the ferment is done, remove the contents from the jar and place in the sun to dehydrate. You can also use your dehydrator or oven at low temperature. Sometimes I mix the greens with more chili flakes and garlic powder before placing them in the sun. Once they're dried, they make fantastic little snacks, but let's be honest . . . not everybody will like them.

There are a lot of different things you can do with your final wild gundruk. It's probably better if you do some research online, where you'll find various recipes for soups and stews. For my part, I also like to coarsely grind my dehydrated gundruk to use as a spice. If your diet is not plant-based, the sour/spicy accent is nice with fish or lamb.

Step 7

Step 8

SIMPLE WILD GUNDRUK STEW

This makes for an interesting bitter, sour, and spicy soup. It's probably an acquired taste to some, but I like it very much. Like many soups, it's always better the next day. If you are not vegan, it's quite interesting to add some fish sauce instead of salt for a flavor twist.

The first time I made this soup, I realized how important it is to chop the leaves into small pieces: Many of our wild greens are tougher than similar greens such as kale or mustard leaves. In my first attempt at making this soup, the gundruk ended up quite chewy.

Ingredients for around 1 cup (236 ml)

1⅕ ounces (35 g) Wild Gundruk
2½ cups (591 ml) water
¾ medium-sized red onion, chopped
1 bell pepper, chopped
   (if you like it spicy, you can also add 1 or 2 green jalapeños, diced)
1 teaspoon (2 g) turmeric powder
1 teaspoon (2 g) ginger powder
¼ teaspoon (0.5 g) cumin powder
Juice of 1 lime
Salt to taste
Cilantro or parsley plus sliced red onion as garnish

Procedure

1. Place the gundruk in 2 cups (473 ml) of the water for 15 minutes or so. Sauté the red onion, bell pepper, and jalapeños until they are fully cooked. Place in a blender and add the remaining ½ cup (118 ml) of water. Blend until smooth.

2. Transfer the contents to a pot, then add the gundruk with its water, the spices, and the lime juice. Bring to a boil, then simmer for 15 to 20 minutes. Season to taste with salt.

3. Garnish with a few leaves of cilantro or parsley (for those who don't like cilantro) and a few slices of red onion. The last time I made this dish, I added chickpeas (already cooked), but you can also add other interesting ingredients—cooked lentils or beans, seeds, and so on . . .

Fermented Leaf Chips

Snacking on kale chips is one of my favorite pastimes and so, of course, I had to explore some possibilities with similar wildcrafted leaves. I tried all kinds; some were quite good, and some were so-so, but there are numerous culinary possibilities with wild food.

Locally, my favorite chips were made using mallow (*Malva neglecta*). They're not only beautiful (albeit quite thin) but also have some nice flavors: salty—bitter—sour—spicy. Mustard leaves worked well, too, but are a bit bitter, which is usual—the results reminded me of gundruk. There are tons of other leaves I haven't experimented with yet, such as lamb's-quarters, nettles, and so on. I'm sure you can have fun with your local wild edibles.

FERMENTED MALLOW LEAF CHIPS

Proceed carefully: Mallow leaves are quite beautiful, but you want to leave them intact as much as possible in the ferment. You'll need to carefully lay the leaves flat so you can easily remove them to make your chips. You want them to look good, right?

Ingredients for a ½-pint jar (236 ml)

7 ounces (198 g) mallow leaves
1 teaspoon (5.5 g) salt
2 garlic cloves, chopped
1½ teaspoons (4 g) chili flakes, spicy or not
½ teaspoon (1 g) Curry Blend
2 tablespoons (30 ml) Culture Starter

Procedure

1. Work slowly and gently so you don't damage the leaves. Massage the leaves and salt tenderly in a bowl for maybe 10 seconds, leave them alone for 15 minutes, and restart the process. I want the salt to do the work and tenderize the leaves slowly. Repeat the process as necessary until the leaves are ready. They should look kind of wet, soft, and limp.

2. Add the rest of the ingredients and massage again tenderly for a few seconds, then place the leaves carefully one by one in the jar. This will take a bit of time, but when you remove them later on to make the chips, they'll look great.

3. Use fermentation method 4 (page 32). Close the lid, then once a day, open the jar and use a clean finger or a spoon to press the leaves under the brine. There won't be much brine, but it should be enough. Burp as necessary. When the initial fermentation is complete, usually 7 to 10 days, place the jar in the refrigerator.

4. Those chips are a delicate gourmet snack; they take work. When you're ready, spray them lightly with olive oil, layer the leaves on a dish, and leave them alone for 20 minutes or so. You can add a bit of garlic powder if you want, or nutritional yeast, or more chili, but don't add salt. I think it's not necessary.

5. Place the leaves gently on parchment paper (I use a silicone rubber pad). Flatten them carefully if you want beautiful leaves, or they can be a bit more crumbled and messier; it's all good.

6. Preheat the oven to 350°F (177°C) and place the tray inside the oven. It's all about timing: 10 minutes worked perfectly for me and I had crunchy yummy leaves; 14 minutes and I had not-so-yummy carbonized leaves and ashes. So watch your timing. Serve right away or store in a closed (dry) container, as they tend to go soft very fast if you leave them out.

Try this with some of your other wild leaves—there are interesting culinary experiments to do!

Dehydrated and Fermented Dock Leaves

Curly dock, also called yellow dock, is a plant native to Europe and western Asia that can now be found commonly in North America; it's quite plentiful in the Los Angeles area. In a nearby park, I have access to several acres of beautiful plants during spring and early summer.

Note that all kinds of other docks look similar. Not all of them are edible per se: The ones I find in Vermont or Belgium are extremely bitter and tannic. The locals call them by the common name bitter dock, and they're probably dealing with *Rumex obtusifolius*. Curly dock has narrow leaves that curl along the edges and the flavor is usually sour and lemony, a bit similar to rhubarb.

You'll find all kinds of recipes for curly dock. Every parts of the plant has a use, either for cooking or in traditional herbalism. People have made crackers with the seeds, and they've used the young leaves in salads and other culinary applications including soups and sauces, chopped and sautéed with onions, as part of ferments, and so on. Note that the plant, like spinach, contains a decent amount of oxalic acid and therefore should not be overindulged in. Some recent articles seem to suggest that the fermentation process does reduce that issue somewhat, but I have to do more research on it.

Not many people forage dock locally. The only people I've seen doing so are from Armenia and often in their 70s or older. It's interesting that the older generation is still in touch with the land and its bounty.

Their preparation technique is quite intriguing, too. Once the leaves are gathered, they are taken home and braided together in long strings about 3 feet (1 m) long, which are hung up to dry in a dark location with a good airflow. Once dried, the strings can be stored for months and used as the main ingredient in a traditional soup. The Armenian name for the sorrel is *ave-luk*; I can even find it sold at a local Middle Eastern supermarket under the name "mountain sorrel." If you do some research online, you'll find videos and various recipes for aveluk soup.

The reason I've included it in this book is that, a few years ago, I made aveluk. My approach was to simply dehydrate the leaves at room temperature instead of braiding them, but the smell and flavors of the dried leaves were completely different from the "mountain sorrel" I purchased at the store and used as a reference.

I tried again and braided the leaves, then left the rather fat string hanging in my open garage until they were fully dried. The smell and flavors were identical to the store-bought product, and I finally understood what I was dealing with. Because of the large braiding size and the time it takes to dehydrate, the leaves will ferment and smell a bit like tobacco. I was dealing with two preservation methods: dehydration and fermentation due to the lacto bacteria present on the leaves. The end result is quite sour and tangy, similar to gundruk.

I'm not going to include a recipe, because you can easily find some traditional Armenian dishes online by simply searching for "aveluk recipes," but the method is worth noting. If you live in North America or Europe, you probably have this plant available locally. It took me a while to learn how to braid it, but with experience, it's not that difficult. I'm sure you can even find videos of the braiding process on the internet.

Curly dock (*Rumex crispus*).

CHAPTER 4

Delving Deeper into Local Ingredients

R oots are so interesting: Some are fibrous while others have one main taproot, but they're all so unique and come in all shapes and colors. Some seem young and full of life while others like the burdock we collected in Vermont looked like gnarly old snakes reaching for the center of the earth.

Aside from extracting nutrients for the plant, roots also serve as its anchor, and in my fertile imagination I fancy that the plant's soul resides there, connected to a deep and hidden spiritual network where plants talk to one another and share sacred wisdom.

I don't have that many edible roots locally, but quite a few can be found in North America or Europe, such as wild carrots / Queen Anne's lace (*Daucus carota*), burdock, prairie turnip (*Pediomelum esculentum*), purple poppy mallow (*Callirhoe involucrata*), creeping bellflower (*Campanula rapunculoides*), and many others. The book *Incredible Wild Edibles* by Samuel Thayer is a great resource to learn more about them.

If a root is tender like a regular carrot or daikon, then—as you'll see later—you can simply ferment it in a brine.

But living in Southern California, I'm not so lucky. The local roots that I can forage easily, such as wild mustard or radish roots, can be extremely tough in terms of texture. For the longest time, I didn't know what to do with them. When I was learning about local wild edibles and attending classes with various instructors, such roots were considered inedible, too tough, and not worth the effort.

And yet if you take a knife and scrape a black mustard or Mediterranean mustard root, you definitely know there is a whole universe of pungent, spicy deliciousness in there, a bit like horseradish or wasabi. But

Wild mustard roots, cleaned and about to get crushed.

I didn't know how to fully extract those wonderful flavors until I learned about fermentation.

Fermentation became the key to unlocking their inner distinctive taste and using them as the main flavoring agent to create interesting dishes and condiments such as soups, spicy sauces, vinegar blends, and so on.

The secret to extracting flavors from such tough roots is to clean them thoroughly (I use a toothbrush), cut them with a pruning shear or crush them in a stone grinder (molcajete), then place them in a spicy/pasty brine to ferment. You can submerge the ingredients and keep them under the brine, but it's not even a necessity; sometimes my "thick" brine fills only half the jar.

The brine you put together can be extremely creative. You can make all kinds of spice blends or even submerge the crushed roots (to be strained later) in a fermenting hot sauce.

All you need to do is shake your concoction several times daily and burp as necessary. When the initial fermentation is done, after about 10 days, you can strain the contents and use them. You can also age them.

I've made some nice soups by using such brines, too, but one of my favorite uses is to add some of my own raw homemade vinegar and various spices to make delicious salad dressings.

If you think about it, it's a new way to look at the wild edibles you already know. Examine the roots, scrape them with a knife, and smell or chew on them a bit. Do some research on edibility before making any elaborate ferments.

FERMENTED SPICY MUSTARD ROOTS

This is how you can turn something "inedible" into gourmet stuff. The technique will work well with roots that have interesting flavors but are tough and "inedible" due to their texture. I use the same technique with wild radish roots, but I would think that pretty much anything in the mustard family (Brassicaceae) has a good flavor potential, such as garlic mustard or hairy bittercress (*Cardamine hirsuta*). Next spring, I plan to experiment with filaree (*Erodium cicutarium*), which has some radishlike qualities and is pretty much everywhere here.

Ingredients for a 1-quart jar (946 ml)

6 ounces (170 g) mustard or radish roots (you can experiment with other edible roots, too)

12–15 garlic cloves

½ medium-sized red onion, diced

2–3 tablespoons (15–23 g) chili flakes, spicy or not

1–1¼ cups (236–355 ml) water (not tap water, which contains chlorine)

1½–2 teaspoons (8–11 g) salt

Shake the jar several times daily. As the brine becomes acidic, it will ensure a safe fermentation.

Procedure

1. Using a stone grinder (molcajete), crush the roots by pounding them hard, then set them aside in a separate bowl. If you don't have a stone grinder, a hammer or stone on a hard surface should work.

2. In the now empty molcajete, place the garlic cloves, diced onion, and chili flakes, then add ¼ cup (59 ml) of the water. Make a rough paste of everything. You could also use a blender for this step.

3. When you're done, if you want, you can even put back the roots and pound everything together to make a splendid mess. Place everything into a quart jar.

4. Make a brine of ¾ to 1 cup (177–236 ml) of the remaining water and the salt; pour this into the jar. The liquid (brine) will go only halfway up the jar. It's okay; I do that on purpose to concentrate the flavors in the brine, which is what I use for making soups or salad dressings.

5. Use fermentation method 5 (page 33). Close the lid tight and shake, shake, shake for a few seconds, then unscrew the lid a little so fermentation gases can escape. Doing so really stirs all the ingredients, and as the solution becomes acidic through the fermentation process, you won't have an issue with possible mold or rotting. But you need to have the discipline to shake two or three times daily. I usually leave the lid closed and burp as necessary in between.

6. When the initial fermentation is done (around 10 days), place it in the fridge, where it will keep for months—but from experience, I can tell you that the flavors are best in the first 2 to 3 weeks. If it's too old, the brine can get a bit too sour. I still like to shake the contents maybe once every few days when it's in the fridge, but it's not a must.

To make a salad dressing, strain the brine, then add vinegar and more spices (thyme, tarragon, more garlic powder) to your liking. I often add some sliced red onion as well. Another favorite use is to make a dashi soup stock (see chapter 6) mixed with some brine (around 20 percent). It's really delicious.

FERMENTED WILD RADISH ROOTS

My first experience with fermenting tough roots was so much fun (and delicious!) that I decided to play with the concept. This ferment uses a similar technique for dealing with tough roots, but with very different ingredients.

In this case I used some wild radish roots but, based on taste, it's very obvious mustard roots would work as well. The brine is a sort of *sauce verte*—a green sauce made with savory and aromatic greens. Pretty much every country has its own take on it. In Belgium we use ingredients such as parsley, mint, tarragon, chives, shallots, garlic, green chilies, and lemon juice. In Southern California it is usually called *salsa verde*—very common in Mexican cuisine—and uses cilantro, habaneros, lime juice, onions, garlic, and tomatillos. A similar Thai version sometimes also includes ginger. The only difference is that I ferment it instead of using it fresh.

You can use this brine for cooking. I have cooked potatoes in it, but I can see how the sour lemony and spicy flavors would be perfect for fish as well.

Ingredients for a 1-quart jar (946 ml)

4 ounces (113 g) wild radish or mustard roots (you can experiment with other edible roots, too)

10 garlic cloves

4 ounces (113 g) jalapeño peppers, diced

1 small shallot, sliced

⅔ ounce (17 g) cilantro, chopped

1½ tablespoons (7.5 g) freshly grated gingerroot

Juice of 2 limes

1½ cups (354 ml) water, to make the brine

2 teaspoons salt (11 g), to make the brine

Variation: No stone grinder? No problem! Use a cleaver knife or pruning shears to chop or cut the roots into smaller pieces, then set them aside. Blend all the other ingredients including the salt and water, then pour the resulting liquid into your jar and add the chopped roots.

Procedure

1. First crush the roots in your stone grinder (molcajete) by pounding them hard, then set them aside in a separate bowl. In the now empty molcajete, place the garlic, jalapeños, shallot, cilantro, and ginger, then add the lime juice. Make a rough paste of everything.
2. When you're done, if you want to, you can put back the roots and pound everything together. Place all your ingredients into a quart jar. Make a brine by mixing the water and salt, then pour it into the jar as well.
3. Use fermentation method 5 (page 33). The liquid (brine) only go approximately halfway up the jar, which is perfect to concentrate the flavors in the brine. Three to five times a day, close the lid tight and shake, shake, shake for a few seconds, then unscrew the lid a little so fermentation gases can escape. As you do so, the ingredients become acidic and ensure a safe fermentation (no mold or rotting). But you need to have the discipline to shake daily.
4. When the initial fermentation is done (around 10 days), place in the fridge where it will keep for months. I like to use it within a month. I still like to shake the contents maybe once every few days when it's in the fridge, but it's not a must.

Cooking in Fermented Root Brine

While working on this book and figuring out how to use my local (wild) resources to the maximum, I had a deep paradigm shift related to the culinary uses of brines.

As I've mentioned, quite a few wild ingredients are edible but not very palatable due to their texture or toughness. However, if you look deeper, many seeds, roots, leaves, stems, and branches can be used to infuse flavors. In specific cases, such as fermented mustard or radish roots, the brine is the medium into which flavors are extracted, and it becomes itself the main ingredient.

If you start thinking that way, you can create ferments specifically to create tasty brines and use components that, in the first place, you probably would have never thought about. These brines can be transformed into light or chunky additives for soups or further processed in a blender, with or without the addition of more ingredients, to make smooth sauces.

I often add tasty brines to my homemade vinegars to make some pleasant salad dressings.

Fermented brines can also become a very interesting medium for cooking vegetables, fish, or meat. Shellfish such as mussels or clams often make a nice pairing with the deep salty, sour, and spicy savory complexities of some intentional brines. Of course, you can add other spices and aromatics to the brine when cooking with it as well. No rules!

Any plant that can be cooked via boiling would work nicely, from roots and tubers such as celeriac, beets, turnips, carrots, or sunchokes to vegetables like cauliflower, broccoli, and even mushrooms.

As you'll see later in this book, as a source of lacto bacteria and as flavoring agents, brines are a perfect base for fermented plant-based or vegan cheeses, and on many occasions I've created delicious brines specifically for making these cheeses.

The photo of potatoes cooked in brine is a good simple example of how a tasty brine can be used with a humble ingredient. In this example, I used some of the brine and components from my Fermented Wild Radish Roots. You can add some water, but it's not a must if you have enough brine. The ratio was about 70 percent brine, 30 percent water, and salt to taste.

Using a fork, poke a few holes in the potatoes, then place them in the jar with the brine to ferment overnight. The next day, transfer everything into a pot, bring the liquid to a boil, and simmer until done. This took me a bit more than 15 minutes.

The result was quite nice, not too sour at all. I was actually expecting much more "punch," but it ended up quite mild. The cooked potatoes were served with fermented acorn cheese and sprinkled with smoked chili powder.

Imagine all the creative possibilities if you look at brine as a main ingredient! Roots, leaves, barks—anything that is safe to use and can imbue flavors is fair game.

FERMENTED BURDOCK ROOT

I don't find a lot of burdock in my area, but this past year I managed to locate a couple of plants. Locally, I can also purchase fresh roots at local Korean stores, but it's not as much fun as collecting them yourself. You'll need to use the same method as for julienning a carrot; make thin strips, as the texture can be tough. Think tiny French fries. As you make them, place the strips in water so they don't oxidize and turn brown. Another option is to slice the roots into thin rounds.

This ferment will be chewy, but in a good way. I like to serve it with a touch of seasoned rice vinegar.

Ingredients for a 1-pint jar (475 ml)

10 ounces (283 g) julienned burdock root

4 garlic cloves, diced finely

1½ teaspoons (4 g) smoked jalapeño flakes (chile morita) or regular chili flakes

2 teaspoons (10 ml) fresh lemon or lime juice

2 teaspoons (3.5 g) freshly grated gingerroot

½ teaspoon (1.5 g) ground peppercorn

¼ teaspoon (1 g) ground coriander seeds

Salt

2 tablespoons (30 ml) Culture Starter

Procedure

The total weight should be a bit more than 11 ounces (311 g). The roots are slightly bitter, and I ended up adding more salt than usual. I used 2 teaspoons (11 g) of salt.

1. Place all your ingredients (except the culture starter) into a bowl and massage gently for a couple of minutes; let rest 3 minutes and repeat that cycle a couple more times. When you're done, add the starter. Transfer the contents into a pint jar.

2. Use fermentation method 3 (page 28). The ingredients won't be under the brine, so simply close the jar tightly and shake or stir the contents for a few seconds two or three times daily, then unscrew the jar a tiny bit so fermentation gases can escape; or leave the lid closed tight to monitor the fermentation, shake the contents two or three times daily, and burp as necessary. Ferment until the initial fermentation is done (around 10 days) and place in the fridge.

FERMENTED WILD TURNIP ROOTS

Locally, we have an interesting mustard called field mustard or wild turnip. Compared with other local wild mustards such as black or Mediterranean mustard, the roots are much more tender. They are called "wild turnip" because it seems that in some locations the root looks like an actual turnip. Locally, while I have properly identified the plant, the root is more like a carrot, but foraged before the plant is flowering it's quite tender. Could it be that there is some crossbreeding of all the various local mustards? Either way, it's good to go.

Slicing the roots is the best approach, and you can ferment them with all kinds of delicious spices. In this case I also added a bit of shredded cabbage, but it's not a must, and I also decided to give the ferment some curry flavors. Feel free to create with this basic recipe if you have similar wild roots.

Ingredients for a 1-pint jar (475 ml) (around 80 percent full)

6 ounces (170 g) sliced roots
4 garlic cloves, minced
3 ounces (85 g) shredded cabbage
   (shred very thin)
½ cup (118 ml) water
2 teaspoons (4 g) curry powder
   or Curry Blend
2 teaspoons (5 g) Korean chili flakes
1 teaspoon (2 g) ground coriander
½ teaspoon (1.5 g) hot chili flakes (optional)
1½ teaspoons (3 g) ginger powder
Salt

Procedure

The total weight was around 12 ounces (340 g), including the water. I used 1½ teaspoons (8 g) of salt.

The jar should be around 80 percent full. Use the same method as for the Fermented Burdock Root. However, there's no need to use a Culture Starter for this one.

I like this one as is, but you could also serve it with a dash of lime juice or seasoned rice vinegar. Because I make my own vinegar, often I use my favorite elderberry wine vinegar.

Fermenting Tender Stems

When wildcrafting and preparing food, stems are often forgotten. It's too bad, because some stems are quite delicious and crunchy if foraged at the right time. Some, like dandelion stems, can be quite challenging (I'm not a fan), but I love using the tender stems of our local mustards, which taste like broccoli once cooked. Watercress has interesting stems, too; when cooked they are very tender, and if you make WaterKraut (Watercress Sauerkraut) with the leaves, you can save the stems and ferment them, too.

FERMENTED WATERCRESS STEMS

This recipe is really a take on a Korean recipe (*namul*). The stems are placed in boiling water for about 30 seconds, then put in ice water. Remove and drain in a colander, then squeeze the watercress with your hands to remove excess water and cut it in 1-to-2-inch (2.5–5 cm) pieces. It's served with garlic, soy sauce, roasted sesame seeds, and sesame oil.

But if you think about it, all the ingredients for a ferment are there, and the soy sauce can replace the salt. All that's missing is the lacto bacteria, which have been destroyed during the boiling process. It's easy enough to add some active sauerkraut juice (Culture Starter), though.

Ingredients for a ½-pint jar (236 ml) (around 80 percent full)

6 ounces (170 g) watercress stems, cooked

2–3 garlic cloves, crudely chopped

1 tablespoon (15 ml) soy sauce

½ teaspoon (2.5 ml) toasted sesame oil

1½ tablespoons (22 ml) Culture Starter

½ teaspoon (1 g) chili flakes, spicy or not
    (optional: you can also sprinkle some on
    when you serve)

Procedure

1. Cook the stems as explained above. Place everything into a bowl and mix with your hands for a few seconds, then transfer the contents to a ½-pint jar. The jar will be around 80 percent full.

2. Use fermentation method 3 (page 28). Close the lid and monitor the pressure by pressing the top. Burp as necessary. Shake the jar two or three times a day. As the ingredients ferment and become acidic, the shaking ensures that everything is fermenting properly and you won't get mold. Ferment for 7 to 10 days; when the fermentation gases stop, place in the fridge for aging. I like to eat this ferment quite young.

MALLOW STEM RELISH

Most people I know just use mallow leaves in soups or as wraps, but picked up at the right time, the stems are quite tender and can be cooked as well. They're a bit fibrous, but it's not excessive. In my opinion the best technique for fermentation is to chop them up somewhat crudely and ferment them in a sort of relish. Before serving, you can sweeten that relish by adding honey or maple syrup and an acidic note such as lemon or lime juice. Vinegar works as well, but the relish will stand on its own, too; it's quite delicious.

Use the stems when they're very fresh. They tend to harden if you store them too long, and this could be true of other stems, too.

Ingredients for a ½-pint jar (236 ml) (around 80 percent full)

7 ounces (198 g) tender mallow stems
¼ ounce (6 g) red onion
2 garlic cloves
Salt
2 teaspoons (1 g) Herbes de Provence, Italian Herbs, or your favorite mix
¼ teaspoon (1 g) spiced chili flakes (I use chile morita—smoked jalapeños)
¼ teaspoon (0.5 g) Curry Blend
1 small Thai pepper, chopped (optional)

Procedure

The total weight was a bit less than 8 ounces. I used 1 teaspoon (5.5 g) of salt.

1. Chop the stems and onion, and mince the garlic. Add the salt, herbs, spices, and optional pepper. Mix thoroughly in a bowl, then let it rest for around 30 minutes. I like to mix the contents every 10 minutes or so, and even press lightly with a fork. If you didn't make things too spicy, you can massage the contents a bit with your fingers (use gloves) to extract some of the juice contained in the stems. Transfer everything into a ½-pint jar; it should be 80 percent full.
2. Use fermentation method 3 (page 28). Close the lid and monitor the pressure by pressing the top. Burp as necessary. Shake the jar two or three times a day. As the ingredients ferment and become acidic, the shaking will ensure that everything is fermenting properly and you won't get mold. Ferment for 7 to 10 days; when the fermentation gases stop, place in the fridge. You can definitely age it, but it won't be as crunchy as a young ferment. As explained above, you can add some maple syrup or honey to make it a sweet relish, and vinegar works well, too.

A Note on Stems

I would think that many stems from edible plants could potentially be used for fermentation. It's really a matter of using the right knife technique based on the texture of the stem you're working with. Some are more fibrous or tough, but chopping, slicing, or even the chiffonade cut can work wonders. So far, I have made ferments with various large stems such as mustard, mallow, cattail, and wild radish, but a friend of mine has made fermented relish with dandelion stems (probably quite bitter) and purslane.

Experiment with different knife techniques and use spices that will mellow or complement the original flavors. A dandelion stem ferment would probably need a bit of sweetness to balance the bitterness.

FERMENTED MUSTARD STEMS

Black mustard stems are great for fermentation, spicy and with hints of wasabi. I'm sure other types of mustard would work, too, but I haven't tried them yet. I usually forage the growing tops, and may end up with 10 inches (25 cm) of tender stem or more. The skin on the stems can be a bit fibrous; the secret is to slice them quite thinly to break the fibers. The inside is sweet and crunchy. There are tons of possibilities with the addition of various spices, and the resulting ferment is delicious as a small side dish, condiment, or addition to salads. I like to add seasoned vinegar after only 3 to 4 days of fermentation, then serve it fresh and crunchy.

Ingredients for a ½-pint jar (236 ml) (about 80 percent full)

7 ounces (198 g) mustard stems
1 garlic clove
1 tablespoon (12 g) sesame seeds
1 teaspoon (5 ml) toasted sesame oil
2 teaspoons (5 g) coriander seeds, ground coarsely
1–2 teaspoons (2.5–5 g) chili flakes of your choice (spicy or not)
1½ teaspoons (8 g) salt

Procedure

1. Slice the stems and mince the garlic. Using a pan, slightly roast the sesame seeds on the stove over medium heat while stirring them with a wooden spoon. It should not take long; stop when you begin to experience that wonderful roasted smell.
2. Place the stems, garlic, and sesame seeds into a small bowl, then add the remaining ingredients. Mix thoroughly for a few seconds and let the contents rest for around 10 minutes. Repeat the procedure twice. If you didn't make it too spicy, you can massage the contents a bit with your fingers to extract some of the juice contained in the stems.
3. Transfer everything into a ½-pint jar; it should be 80 percent full. Use fermentation method 3 (page 28). Close the lid and monitor the pressure by pressing the top. Burp as necessary. Shake the jar two or three times a day. Ferment for 7 to 10 days, and when the fermentation gases stop, place in the fridge. As with the mallow stems, you can definitely age this, but it won't be as crunchy as a very young ferment.

Fermenting in Wilder Brine

This is another interesting way to introduce flavors from your local environment into regular ingredients by using the brine as the savory medium. There is a lot of creative experimentation possible with this method: Locally I have made various blends using mustard and wild radish leaves, chickweed, wild chervil, watercress, and other tasty plants, but you could also use store-bought or garden ingredients such as celery, basil, or cilantro. Be aware that flavors can change during the fermentation process; not all herbs will work, and you should probably experiment with a small quantity (light brine) and see how the final ferment will taste. I didn't have much luck with stinging nettles, for instance, and fermenting mustard stems in mustard leaf brine had too much of a sour greenish tang. These days I like to use this type of brine to ferment regular root vegetables such as daikon, beets, radishes, and so on.

It's a very basic concept: You just create a brine by blending herbs and spices with water, then add some salt. If the brine tastes good, then the end product will probably taste great. With experience, you can create some complex artistic blends and truly delicious ferments.

YELLOW BEETS FERMENTED
IN MUSTARD BRINE

Ingredients for a 1-quart jar (946 ml)

2½ cups (591 ml) water

6 ounces (170 g) mustard leaves

1 small red onion, diced
   (around 1½ ounces / 42 g)

4 garlic cloves

1 tablespoon (20 g) stone-ground mustard
   or store-bought organic Dijon mustard

1 tablespoon (17 g) salt

12 ounces (340 g) yellow beets, julienned

Procedure

1. Blend everything together (except the beets); you should end up with around 3 cups (710 ml) of brine. Strain the liquid into a quart jar, then add the yellow beets.

2. Use fermentation method 2 (page 23). I just close the jar and shake the contents two or three times a day. Sometimes I'll even place the jar upside down for a few hours. Burp as necessary.

3. Ferment until the initial fermentation is complete, around 10 days, then place in the fridge to age. It should keep for several months. The original flavor of the brine is quite bitter but will mellow while aging.

FOREST FLOOR BRINE FERMENT

With this ferment, I wanted to infuse some forest flavors into a somewhat tasteless ingredient such as daikon. It's a simple process: Just make a juice with savory edible plants and water, add some salt to make it a brine, and ferment your ingredients in it. You don't have to go "wild" with this technique; you can also make a brine with standard ingredients such as bell peppers, celery, cilantro, parsley, and all that good stuff.

I made a mix of tasty wild greens that are abundant in my local forest—chickweed, chervil, mustard sprouts, miner's lettuce, cleavers, and even a bit of forest grass (young foxtail). Note that not all wild plants will work flavor-wise. For instance, I'm not a fan of nettles in large amounts.

Ingredients for a 1-quart jar (946 ml)

4 ounces (113 g) savory wild edibles (chickweed, chervil, et cetera)

¼ red onion

4 garlic cloves

12 ounces (340 g) daikon, julienned

2½ cups (591 ml) water

1 tablespoon (17 g) salt

¾ teaspoon (2 g) ground peppercorns

Small (10 g) piece roasted oak bark (optional)

3 tablespoons (44 ml) Culture Starter

Procedure

1. Place everything (except the peppercorns, optional roasted oak bark, and culture starter) in the blender, blend into a smooth liquid, then strain. Voilà! Wild brine.

2. Transfer the ingredients to a jar along with the peppercorns, bark (if you used it), and culture starter. The latter probably isn't necessary, but I haven't tried the recipe yet without adding some.

3. Use fermentation method 2 (page 23). These days, I just close the jar and shake the contents two or three times a day. Sometimes I'll even place the jar upside down for a few hours. Burp as necessary.

4. Ferment until the initial fermentation is complete, around 10 days, then place in the fridge to age. It should keep for several months.

Fermenting Berries and Fruits

Berries and other fruits can be quite delicious fermented, but it's somewhat of a challenge, too. A lot of berries contain natural yeast. It's sometimes very noticeable by the appearance of a white bloom; this is composed mostly of wax but also of yeast. Thus, your fermentation could go two ways: yeast-based fermentation (alcohol) or, with some help, lacto-fermentation.

You can ferment berries similarly to common ferments such as sauerkraut by adding 2 percent salt by weight. As I was writing this book, *The Noma Guide to Fermentation* was published; there the authors use that technique for lacto-fermenting blueberries, tomatoes, plums, and gooseberries. There's nothing wrong with that technique, and it may work for aging ferments much longer than I do. You simply need to mix the berries with 2 percent salt (by weight): Thus, 1 pound would require around ⅓ ounce of salt (20 g salt per kilogram). Transfer the salted berries into a jar, close the lid, and shake the contents two or three times daily. Burp as necessary. When the initial fermentation is complete, store the jar in the fridge. You can also puree the berries and use the paste for various culinary purposes.

I use a different technique that doesn't include salt aside from what is present in the Culture Starter. The idea is to place the berries in a jar, add some sugar if the berries aren't too sweet in the first place, then pour in a bit of brine from an active sauerkraut ferment, usually 3 to 5 days old. You know it's very active because it's bubbly and a decent amount of fermentation gases occur. The lacto bacteria present in the starter will start digesting the sugar right away and make the contents acidic, ensuring food safety and preservation.

A problem can occur when berries contain a lot of wild yeast, such as blueberries, huckleberries, or grapes. If the amount of wild yeast is excessive, you risk ending up with an alcoholic fermentation instead of a lacto-ferment, because the yeast takes over. My solution is to quickly blanch the berries in boiling water; that way you kill the wild yeast present on the surface of the berries, so they don't compete with the lacto bacteria. Most of my berry ferments are also meant to be eaten quite young, usually within a week. They're a good source of probiotics, but the fermentation process can give them a delicious complexity.

Aside from using the active brine of a sauerkraut, you can probably also use whey or live culture probiotics (which can be purchased as capsules at regular supermarkets or health food stores) but, to be honest, I haven't made berry ferments with them. So you'll need to experiment on your own, making sure you check the pH as you go along. I don't foresee any problems, though; it should work well.

One problem I've encountered with berries, even organic ones, is the fact that store-bought berries can sometimes be completely tasteless compared with wild berries. Recently I purchased a bunch of organic blueberries for a ferment, and they pretty much had no flavor at all. The difference was as dramatic as that between drinking a fine wine and a cup of water. The savory qualities and freshness of your berries are crucial if you want a delicious end product. If you use tasteless berries, you'll end up with a tasteless ferment.

As with any other ferments, there is a lot of creativity possible by adding savory herbs or spices. For example, you can add some orange zest or cinnamon to a cranberry ferment to give it a holiday touch. I like to use a bit of mugwort leaves and pinyon pine or white fir needles. Instead of using regular sugar, I'll add molasses, honey, or maple syrup.

Be aware that raw honey contains a lot of wild yeast. Honey you buy at the store is usually fine (it's really pasteurized), but if you get raw honey from someone who has bees, you'll need to pasteurize it. Otherwise you risk wild yeast taking over and giving you boozy berries.

As a final note, using an active sauerkraut brine will not add off flavors in your final ferment.

LACTO-FERMENTED BLUEBERRIES
WITH LOCAL AROMATICS

This is very easy ferment, and it tastes amazing after a few days. I like to taste as I go along and add maple syrup if necessary. I mix the berries in my morning cereal, but they're awesome with pancakes, too, or to make sauces. You can add savory herbs as well. In this case I added a bit of black sage and a couple of mugwort leaves.

I don't use salt at all aside from the small amount found in the Culture Starter (active sauerkraut juice). The lacto bacteria will start digesting the sugar and make the contents acidic. Blueberries are loaded with wild yeast, but you have the option of blanching the berries in boiling water for a few seconds to make sure the wild yeast doesn't take over the fermentation.

Ingredients for a 1-quart jar (946 ml) (around 60 to 70 percent full)

1 pound (453 g) blueberries
6 tablespoons (90 ml) maple syrup
1 sprig (top) black sage with stem (optional)
2–3 mugwort leaves (optional)
⅓ cup (70 ml) Culture Starter

Procedure

1. Wash the berries quickly. You can blanch them in boiling water for a few seconds if you want. Place all the ingredients (except the starter) in a bowl and mix well. Transfer to a clean jar and add the starter. The jar should be 60 to 70 percent full, but you could increase the number of berries.
2. Use fermentation method 5 (page 33). I just close the jar, shake the contents at least three times a day, and burp as necessary. I ferment it until day 4 or 5, then place it in the fridge to slow down the fermentation and age.

I like to use this ferment young, within a week, when it's still nice and sweet. If you didn't blanch the berries, your ferment will probably become alcoholic. Lacto-fermentations of berries without salt are much better when not aged very long.

CRANBERRIES, MUGWORT, AND CALIFORNIA SAGEBRUSH

This is another version of the fermented blueberries recipe, but with cranberries and different flavoring herbs. I used this ferment instead of the usual cranberry sauce we serve for Thanksgiving. I know it's fermented, but you can use it raw or cooked; ferments can be about flavors and not just probiotics. I really like the taste of our local sagebrush with cranberries. It provides some complex savory accents, and the bitterness is well balanced. Make sure you do some research before using any sagebrush-type plants for culinary uses, however: They may smell wonderful, but based on my own research, quite a few are not recommended due to somewhat toxic terpenes (aromatic chemical compounds).

Ingredients for a 1-quart jar (946 ml)

1½ pounds (680 g) fresh cranberries
5 tablespoons (75 ml) maple syrup
4–5 mugwort leaves
1 small sprig fresh California sagebrush
¼ cup (59 ml) Culture Starter

Procedure

1. Wash the berries quickly. You can blanch them in boiling water for a few seconds if you want. Place all the ingredients (except the starter) in a bowl and mix well. Transfer to a clean jar and add the starter. This jar will be quite full—maybe too full, depending on the size of the berries. Try to leave at least 1 inch (2.5 cm) headspace.
2. Use fermentation method 5 (page 33). I just close the jar, shake the contents at least three times a day, and burp as necessary. I ferment it until day 4 or 5, then place it in the fridge to slow down the fermentation and age.

This ferment is much better eaten within a week and doesn't age very well (too sour). I really liked it at around day 5 and used it right there and then. If your diet is not plant-based, it makes quite a nice sauce with the traditional Thanksgiving turkey.

LACTO-FERMENTED DEHYDRATED (WILD) BERRIES

I love collecting berries during the summer, but come fall, all I have are dehydrated berries to play with. You can easily ferment dehydrated berries; just make sure that you add enough liquid, which will be mostly absorbed by the fruits when they rehydrate. Of course, you can create a simple ferment with just dehydrated blueberries or wild currants, but it's much more fun to make interesting blends by mixing dry berries and even some aromatic herbs.

In this example my ferment was a mix of blueberries, red and black currants, elderberries, raspberries, and feral grapes. I also added a bit of local mugwort for flavoring.

Ingredients for a 1-pint jar (475 ml)

3½ ounces (99 g) dried berries (mixed or not)
2 tablespoons (30 ml) maple syrup
½ cup (118 ml) Culture Starter
½ cup (118 ml) water
2 mugwort leaves (fresh mint or similar herbs would work, too)

Procedure

The sugar in the berries I used wasn't excessive, so I added some maple syrup. If you work with dried grapes, for example, you might not need to add maple syrup due to their higher sugar content, so you'll need to make a bit of judgment call. Overall, the mix should taste quite sugary as a rule. You can also taste the ferment as you go along and add maple syrup if necessary. It's a good idea to blanch the berries, too, as some of them, such as dried grapes, can be loaded with yeast.

Use fermentation method 5 (page 33). I just close the jar, shake the contents at least three times a day, and burp as necessary. I ferment it until day 4 or 5, then place it in the fridge to slow down the fermentation and to age.

As with my other berry ferments, I use the contents within a week. It is quite good with pancakes, cereals, or waffles, or to make galettes.

APPLES AND PEARS IN FOREST AROMATICS

These ferments are easy and they're great for making desserts. The fermentation time will vary greatly, mostly based on the texture of the fruits you're using. Pears become a bit too mushy if you ferment them too long, while other fruits like apples can withstand longer aging.

What I really like about this ferment is the flavors you can achieve by adding savory and aromatic plants. It's another way to explore the essence of your local (wild) terroir.

In this recipe my wild aromatics are from Southern California, but you can easily replace them with your local ingredients or store-bought and garden aromatics such as tarragon, thyme, mint, rosemary, fennel . . . whatever mix you want to create. Just think of it as a concept.

Ingredients for a 1-quart jar (946 ml) (around 90 percent full)

Pears (2–3) or apples (roughly 4, depending on size), sliced in halves or quartered

3–4 mugwort leaves (a mix of young and old)

1 sprig California sagebrush

1 sprig pearly everlasting (*Pseudognaphalium californicum*)

1 small top yerba santa (*Eriodictyon californicum*)

1 sprig black sage

⅓ cup (71 ml) maple syrup

⅓ cup (71 ml) Culture Starter

Procedure

1. Mix all the ingredients in a bowl and transfer to a clean jar. Add water until the jar is around 90 percent full.
2. Use fermentation method 3 (page 28). Fermentation should really kick in around day 3. Once it's active, let it ferment for 3 to 4 days and taste. I just close the jar, gently shake the contents at least twice a day, and burp as necessary. I ferment it until day 4 or 5, then put it in the fridge to slow down the fermentation and age.

Based on my experience, pears are perfect at around day 5 while apples can be fermented and aged for at least 10 days (I've never tried more time than that.) Note that some pear varieties can probably withstand more fermentation time. Just do as I do—taste as you go along and take notes.

I usually serve the fruits with a bit of my mountain syrup (pine-infused syrup) and crunchy lerps sugar (insect honeydew found on eucalyptus leaves).

MOUNTAIN CRANBERRY FERMENT

Sometimes you don't have to reinvent the wheel and instead can start with an awesome recipe as a base and add local flavors. I'm extremely happy with the results of this recipe, a perfect balance of sweet and sour with just hints of salt.

It was an interesting fermentation, too. For the first 3 days, nothing happened, and I was a bit worried. On day 4 I was pretty much gone all day teaching at a local college, and when I came back, the lid was about to explode. I could not unscrew it and had to poke a few holes on top to release some of the pressure (place a bowl upside down and on top while you do this!); then I finally managed to unscrew it. There was still a substantial amount of pressure inside, which means that I had to clean the whole kitchen and my face. Lesson learned: Always open a jar like this outside if you can. On the good side, I only lost 10 percent of the contents. Be sure to supervise this ferment.

The base recipe comes from the book *Nourishing Traditions* by Sally Fallon. I can see this recipe working well with all kinds of berries—blueberries, huckleberries, lingonberries, and so on. Feel free to experiment. Just my humble opinion, but I think this ferment, like the other berry ferments, is *much* better when consumed very young, like 7 to 10 days. That's because, over time, you'll get a mix of lacto- and alcoholic fermentation. You can also do the unthinkable (for a fermentation extremist) and bring the contents to a light boil for a couple of minutes, then cool them down again. Taste and add honey or maple syrup if you want. Boiling will kill any probiotics in the ferment and change the flavor a bit but will stop the fermentation. Remove the pine and fir branches first, since boiled pine/fir doesn't taste very good.

Ingredients for a 1-quart jar (946 ml)

11 ounces (310 g) fresh (organic) cranberries

½ cup (118 ml) raw honey

1 teaspoon (5.5 g) salt

⅓ cup (78 ml) whey (although I use Culture Starter instead)

½ cup (118 ml) apple or other juice (I use elderberry juice)

½ teaspoon (2 g) cinnamon powder (the original recipe calls for 1 teaspoon, but I'm not a fan of cinnamon)

Juice of 1 orange (a lemon or lime is okay, too)

1 teaspoon (2 g) grated orange zest (optional; I skipped this one when I made the ferment)

1 tablespoon (8 g) freshly grated gingerroot (my addition to this recipe)

Procedure

As you can see, the amount of salt is minimal. Place all your ingredients in a blender and make a rough paste. Use fermentation method 3 (page 28). I just close the jar, shake the contents at least three times a day, and burp as necessary. I ferment it until day 4 or 5, then place it in the fridge to slow down the fermentation and age.

Christmas Cranberries Variation

I made this ferment for a special dinner during the holidays, so I decided to add specific local Christmassy flavors: a bit of pinyon pine branches (they smell and taste like candy), white fir (bitter tangerine), mugwort (bitter and highly aromatic), and manzanita powder (apple). The manzanita powder I made by grinding the berries in my stone grinder (molcajete). To the original recipe I added the following in my ferment:

1 ounce (28 g) cracked pinyon pine branches

1 small (⅕ ounce / 6 g) white fir branch with needle tops cut off so flavors can be extracted

Top of a mugwort plant (¹⁄₁₀ ounce / 3 g)

1½ tablespoons (10 g) manzanita powder

Add the ingredients to the paste when you transfer it into the jar.

Of course, you should use your own local flavors. If I were in Vermont (for example), I would use white pine and spruce needles, possibly some cracked yellow birch branches, and a bit of dried apples.

Drinks Representing Your Terroir

I could write a whole book about lacto-fermented drinks with local flavors, and I certainly approached the subject with *The Wildcrafting Brewer*, although that book was mostly about using wild yeast and making unusual boozy concoctions. But a lot of the recipes there can be created with lacto-fermentation, which keeps things interesting because the flavors won't be exactly the same, and the drinks certainly not as intoxicating. And that's a good thing: A lot of the wild drinks I brew are more about enjoying the natural flavors of the land than getting drunk. If you're not inclined to drink alcoholic beverages, you can still experience the beautiful savory components nature offers and get some healthy probiotics in the process.

If you are interested to delve deeper into this subject, I would suggest you get hold of *The Wildcrafting Brewer* and see what ideas you can come up with. If you already have it, look at the recipes from the perspective of using lacto-fermentation instead of wild yeast fermentation, and you will have a brand-new book in your hands. How cool is that!

Making drinks that represent a whole environment (terroir)—such as a local forest, the mountains, chaparral, desert, and so on—is extremely rewarding, but it requires some good understanding of more esoteric plants and their culinary or medicinal uses. If wildcrafting is new to you, I suggest you do a search online and find a local teacher or guide to learn more. It could be an herbalist, forager, or someone who has experience collecting wild edibles. You can also find many groups on social media that are dedicated to sharing this knowledge.

A lot of the plants used traditionally to make ancient beers as well as other types of drinks are reviewed in my brewing book. Nevertheless, I thought it would be cool to include at least one example of what is possible here, along with the simple methods behind it.

The procedure is similar to that used for making ancient brews, but with a lacto bacteria starter instead of yeast. All you need are flavors, water, sugar, and a lacto bacteria starter.

The flavors can come from savory plants, mushrooms, roots, berries, bark, and the like. If you want a drink that has more "beery" qualities, choose herbs that were traditionally used for such concoctions and that have bitter aromatic qualities—mugwort, hops, yarrow, horehound, wormwood, ground ivy, or dandelion roots. For a soda-type drink, fruit and berries as well as tasty roots like sarsaparilla or ginger can make delicious libations. You can even create healing drinks using medicinal mushrooms and medicinal plants.

Creatively, there aren't many rules. I mix ingredients all the time. The blueberry-and-mugwort soda, for instance, is a mix of bitter, sweet, aromatic, and fruity flavors. Just make sure your drink is not unhealthy and actually tastes okay. Some ingredients such as mugwort, yarrow, some pine needles, and so on should not be consumed if you are pregnant. You need to do your own educated research for the ingredients used in your drinks.

The water you use should be quite pure. I don't use tap water, because it contains chlorine, but filtered water or natural springwater bought at the store works well.

You don't need salt for this type of fermentation unless you're a fan of salty drinks. (I'm definitely not!) The lacto bacteria will eat the sugar present in the drink and create lactic acid, making the contents acidic enough so that the ferment won't spoil. My sugar sources vary immensely, ranging from honey, molasses, organic cane sugar, and maple syrup to palm sugar or even insect honeydew (lerps), and I'm not shy about mixing them together.

Be aware that pure raw honey contains a lot of wild yeast, which can take over the fermentation process. If I use honey, I usually mix it with the water first and bring it to a boil to pasteurize it and kill the existing yeast. That way, the lacto bacteria have a chance to take over and you don't end up with an alcoholic drink.

For my wild beers I use around 1¼ pounds of sugar per gallon (149 g per liter) of water. This is enough to end up with more than 5 percent alcohol. A lot of the wild yeasts won't go further than that, although there are exceptions such as the wild yeast I find on our local elderberries.

I like to drink lacto-fermented sodas within a week of making them. To be honest, I've never tried aging one much longer than that.

I've had a couple of bottles over the last 3 years that didn't want to ferment properly. I'm not sure why this happened. In one case I used limes, and experience has taught me that limes can sometimes be tricky in lacto-fermentation. If I don't get any fermentation after 4 or 5 days, I just toss the liquid and start over again.

Your fermentation time may change a bit with different factors such as temperature. That's why it's important to check the pressure inside the bottle. During the summer, these ferments usually take off in 2 to 3 days, but in the winter it may take 3 to 4 days. Excessive carbonation in a swing-top bottle can result in an explosion. If you've never done this kind of fermentation before, it might be a good idea to use a recycled plastic soda bottle first, switching to a swing-top bottle after you have some experience.

For lacto-fermentation, that much sweetness is overkill. You'll end up with a supersweet drink, though in all honesty, I've never tried to age such beverages to see what happens. The lacto-fermented brews I create are closer to sodas and use much less sugar—approximately 7 to 10 ounces of sugar, maple syrup, or honey per gallon (52–75 g per liter). But you can add more if you want a sweeter drink. You get to create a recipe specific to your taste buds.

Don't worry too much if the drink tastes too sugary for you when you start; you need to remember that the sugar isn't just for you but is mostly food for the bacteria. The end product will be less sweet. Take notes as you make your recipe and you'll find the right amount to use for your liking.

To extract the flavors from ingredients, you can boil them first or simply place them freshly foraged in the sugary liquid. Not all ingredients need to be boiled; there is a bit of an art to it, which comes with experience. When

Lacto-Fermented Forest Brew with horehound, forest grass, mugwort, sycamore and willow bark, black sage, California sagebrush, turkey tail mushrooms, lemon juice, and manzanita berries.

I make a complex lacto-fermented drink from a specific environment, I usually mix methods and use a hot-and-cold process. Some ingredients such as mugwort, barks, dried berries, and mushrooms are much better boiled, while others—mint, pinyon pine branches, sages, or similar plants—taste much better if they are simply placed in the beverage and fermented cold. You basically use the method that works best for the ingredients you have collected. The idea is to boil or simmer some ingredients, cool down the solution, then add fresh ones, mixing in some lacto starter and fermenting your concoction.

As in many of my wild brews, I tend to add some acidic ingredients in my beverage recipes such as lemon or lime juice, which help lower the pH from the start and prevent possible spoilage. In my experience, too much acidity isn't a good thing, either, and it can impede the lacto-fermentation process. The juice of two lemons or limes per gallon seems about right and works pretty well. Add to that acidic sauerkraut juice as a starter and you should not experience any problems. For 1 gallon, I'll use around 1 cup of Culture Starter (62.5 ml per liter). That amount won't alter the flavors much.

Lacto-Fermented Forest Brew, which is detailed here in photos and a recipe, is a good example of a recent lacto-fermented beverage I made. A mix of barks, berries, mushrooms, and fresh aromatic herbs, it's very similar to some of the recipes you'll find in my brewing book, but with less sugar. All the herbs and other ingredients were collected from a private property owned by friends of mine in the Angeles National Forest.

The recipe and the results change all the time—true reflections of the environment. Even a single plant such as mugwort will have a wide range of flavors throughout the year. In springtime the taste is lemony and grassy and the aromatics are more young and light, while during wintertime the flavors are more mature and noble. It is as if you can taste the wisdom and experience accumulated by each plant during its short lifetime.

Unlike a yeast-based fermentation, which can start overnight, 3 to 4 days seems to be the magical amount of time for a lacto-fermented drink to start fermenting actively. You have various options in terms of fermentation vessels. I generally do my initial fermentation in a jar or similar container, then strain the ingredients once the fermentation is active and transfer the drink into swing-top or recycled soda bottles.

If you're new to this kind of fermentation, it's better to start with recycled soda bottles so you can better feel the pressure and sense whether it's excessive. With experience, you'll learn to be more comfortable and maybe switch to swing-top bottles. You can even ferment directly into a bottle.

The guidelines here are a bit vague, but there should be enough to help you think through the process and get started creatively.

Gather all the ingredients you'll need to create your fermented drinks. Some need to be boiled to extract the flavors, but others are much better raw.

Boil or simmer your ingredients for the amount of time specified in the recipe. Usually 20 to 25 minutes of boiling is a good starting point if you're trying a new recipe.

After boiling or simmering the ingredients, you'll need to cool down the solution in order to add the lacto bacteria later on. Put the lid on and place the pot in a sink with cold water for 10 minutes. You may need to change the cold water a couple of times.

When the liquid has cooled down, strain the contents. I compost the leftovers.

Add the lacto bacteria. In this case I used a Culture Starter, but you could also use whey or probiotics capsules. You can add savory herbs and berries to the bottle at this stage.

Close the bottle and supervise the ferment closely. Usually the fermentation will start producing a lot of gases after 3 to 4 days, but monitor the activity and burp as necessary. When you're happy with the carbonation, place the bottle in the fridge. I still burp as needed and usually drink the beverage within a week.

Here is my forest brew being fermented in a closed container, in this case a swing-top bottle. The contents will later be strained and transferred to a new bottle.

LACTO-FERMENTED FOREST BREW

This beverage is a mix of raw and simmered ingredients. I used some herbs that were traditionally used to make ancient beers, including mugwort, horehound, and willow bark, but also added some true local flavors like California sagebrush, local wild berries, yerba santa, grass (young foxtail barley), and so on. The result is pretty much identical to some of my seasonal wild beers, but using a lacto-fermentation starter instead of wild yeast.

This is a complex ferment, but it can give you some ideas on how to create mixed drinks.

Ingredients for a 32-ounce swing-top bottle (1 L)

3 cups (700 ml) water

Around ½ ounce (10 g) sycamore bark

¹⁄₁₀ ounce (3 g) willow bark

1 ounce (30 g) turkey tail mushrooms

4 large mugwort leaves (bitter and aromatic)

1 horehound leaf (super bitter)

2 black sage tops (around 6 leaves), bruised (highly aromatic)

¹⁄₁₀ ounce (3 g) California sagebrush, slightly bruised (bitter and highly aromatic)

3–4 willow leaves (bitter)

¼ ounce (8 g) of forest grass (young foxtail in this case)

20 manzanita berries (tastes like dried apple)

4 young and sweet yerba santa leaves

2 flower tops of pearly everlasting (highly aromatic)

2¾ cups water (650 ml) (don't use tap water, which contains chlorine)

⅓ cup (78 ml) maple syrup

Juice of ½ lemon

3 tablespoons (45 ml) Culture Starter

Procedure

1. In a pot on the stove, bring the water, sycamore and willow bark, and mushrooms to a boil, turn down the heat, and very slowly simmer until 1 cup (236 ml) is left. This took me around 3 hours. Add 2 of the mugwort leaves in the last 30 minutes of the process; with experience you can time the simmering period of ingredients for optimal flavors. Strain the liquid and set it aside to cool down.

2. Hand-bruise the 2 remaining mugwort leaves. Place them in a bottle, jar, or similar container along with the remaining plants and berries.

3. Add the cooled liquid and the remaining liquid ingredients, close or cover your bottle or jar, then ferment for around 3 days at room temperature. You'll need to burp as necessary. I usually check on day 2. Another technique is to cover a jar or similar container with a clean towel and stir or shake the contents a couple of times daily. When the fermentation is active, you'll see some bubbling and slight foaming.

4. When the fermentation is going well, strain the contents into a new swing-top or recycled soda bottle and leave at room temperature for a few hours, or longer if necessary. Open (burp) carefully; if you have a good carbonation, place the bottle in the fridge and age for a couple of days.

5. Check the pressure carefully before serving. If you need a bit more carbonation, bring the bottle to room temperature for a few hours. I don't age this kind of ferment for very long; I like to drink it within 4 or 5 days at the most.

LACTO-FERMENTED MUGWORT BEER

This beverage is based on my popular mugwort beer recipe and quite easy to brew. In this case I simply substitute a lacto starter for the yeast and end up with a nonalcoholic brew. You can replace the mugwort with other bitter and aromatic plants that have been used traditionally to make archaic beers, such as yarrow, horehound, hops, wormwood, and so on. Locally I also use California sagebrush.

Ingredients for a 32-ounce swing-top bottle (1 L)

6 cups (1.4 L) water (will reduce during simmering)

⅓ cup (120 ml) maple syrup or honey *or* 4 ounces (115 g) brown sugar

1 lemon

4–5 dried mugwort leaves

¼ cup (59 ml) Culture Starter (you could also use whey or 2 probiotics capsules)

Procedure

1. Place all your ingredients (except the culture starter) in a pot. You can cut the lemon in half, squeeze out the juice by hand, and place the halves in the liquid with the rest of the ingredients. Bring the water to a boil, then simmer for 25 minutes. The liquid should reduce to around 4 cups (946 ml). Remove the pot from the heat, put the lid on, and set it into cold water to cool down the brew. You may need to change the cold water a couple of times to accelerate the cooling.

2. When it's lukewarm or colder, strain the liquid into your swing-top bottle, then add the starter. You want the contents to reach up to the bottom of the bottle's neck, but no higher. If you need more liquid, it's okay to add some water. Ferment for 2 to 4 days at room temperature and check the carbonation. If it's decent, place the bottle in the fridge. Every couple of days, check the bottle and burp it if necessary.

This type of brew is best enjoyed within 2 weeks (my opinion), but feel free to experiment with aging it a bit longer. If you do so, make sure to keep an eye on the pressure inside the bottle and burp it as needed. It will continue fermenting in the fridge.

LACTO-FERMENTED RAW SODA

This is a very simple raw soda. You can replace my local herbs with all kinds of aromatic and tasty herbs of your choice, foraged or not, such as mint, anise hyssop, sages, or elderflowers.

I've made similar ferments with herbs such as mugwort, California sagebrush, various wild mints, yarrow, elderflowers, pinyon pine branches, white fir (*Abies concolor*), spruce tips, and others.

Ingredients for a 32-ounce swing-top bottle (1 L)

1 sprig black sage
1 sprig yerba santa
¾ ounce (21 g) fresh gingerroot
1 lemon
3¼ cups (769 ml) water
⅓ cup (79 ml) maple syrup
¼ cup (59 ml) Culture Starter

Procedure

1. There's not much to do here. Place the fresh herbs in your bottle or jar; I like to bruise them gently with my fingers, just enough to facilitate flavor extraction. My next steps are to dice the ginger such that the pieces can go through the opening and then juice my lemon.
2. Pour the water into the bottle, add the ginger pieces, lemon juice, maple syrup, and culture starter. You want the contents to reach up to the bottom of the bottle's neck but no higher. Close the top.
3. Ferment for 2 to 4 days at room temperature and check the carbonation by opening the top slightly. Usually I get enough carbonation on day 3 or 4.

If I decide to drink the soda at this point, there is no need to strain the contents, but if I'd like to keep it in the fridge for a few more days, I first strain the liquid into a new bottle and leave it at room temperature for another day. This is usually enough to get some decent carbonation going again. Then I place the bottle in the fridge. Every couple of days, I still check the bottle and burp it if necessary.

CHAGA AND TURKEY MUSHROOM MEDICINAL BREW

This is a medicinal lacto-fermented brew good for the flu season. It's mostly composed of mushrooms (turkey tail, splitgill, and chaga), which are known to boost the immune system and are used in Chinese medicine for their anti-cancer properties. I also added a bit of willow leaves and bark (willow bark acts a lot like aspirin, so it's used for pain and fever), horehound (good for lung and breathing problems), and mugwort.

Ingredients for a 32-ounce swing-top bottle (1 L)

Around 8½ cups (2 L) water
   (will reduce during simmering)
1¹/₅ ounces (35 g) turkey tail mushrooms
1 ounce (30 g) chaga mushrooms
Around ²/₅ ounce (10 g) splitgill mushrooms
Piece of willow bark (½ by 4 inches /
   1.3 by 10 cm) and a few leaves
1–2 horehound leaves
Juice of 1 lemon
½ cup (118 ml) molasses or 3½ ounces
   (100 g) brown sugar
3–4 mugwort leaves
⅓ cup (78 ml) Culture Starter

Procedure

1. Place all your ingredients (except the mugwort leaves and culture starter) in a pot. Bring to a boil, then simmer for 3 to 4 hours. The volume of water should reduce to around half the original amount. Add the mugwort leaves 30 minutes before you end the simmering. Remove the pot from the heat, put on the lid, and set the pot into cold water to cool down the brew. You may need to change the cold water a couple of times to accelerate the cooling.

2. When it's lukewarm or colder, strain the mixture into your swing-top bottle, then add the starter. You want the contents to reach up to the bottom of the bottle's neck, but no higher. If you need more liquid, it's okay to add some water. Ferment for 2 to 4 days at room temperature and check the carbonation. If it's decent, place the bottle in the fridge. Every couple of days, check the bottle and burp if necessary.

This type of brew is best enjoyed within 2 weeks (in my opinion), but feel free to experiment with aging it a bit longer. If you do so, make sure to keep an eye on the pressure inside the bottle and burp it as needed. It will continue fermenting in the fridge.

CHAPTER 5

Fermenting with the Environment

Spring is beautiful in California. Around March and April all the local mountains and forests turn a lush green. Each location is unique, but my favorite place is my friend's property in the Angeles National Forest. For whatever reason, pretty much 90 percent of the plants covering the area are delicious edible greens.

This foraging site nicely illustrates how conscious foraging can help the environment. Every single one of those edible greens, aside from miner's lettuce (*Claytonia perfoliata*), is non-native. Over the years, by removing many of those delicious plants, I've noticed a remarkable comeback of the native ones. For a wildcrafter, it's an interesting dilemma: Most of us have great affinity for all plants, and quite a lot of the really flavorful ones are considered invasive. So sometimes, as a nature lover and steward of the forest, your role is to supervise and keep in check some of the most aggressive plants so you can still enjoy them without fully destroying them, which often requires the use of herbicides.

Forest Floor Fermentation

One of my most enjoyable foraging projects involves picking a large amount of herbs and other plants randomly from a specific locale, then simply adding salt and spices to create a "forest floor" mix. I use these blends for all kinds of fermentation purposes ranging from creating soup stocks to incorporating them into wild food salsas, hot sauces, or pastes. After they've been fermented and dehydrated, the herbs can also be used to flavor soups or ground like a spice. I'm sure there are tons of other creative ways to use a forest floor; I'm only scratching the surface. I can't wait to hear what you do with the concept.

A typical handful of plants picked up in one fell swoop from my own forest floor might include the following:

Chickweed (*Stellaria media*), an edible and nutritious plant native to Europe, often used raw in salads. Also used by herbalists, mostly for skin conditions.

Bur chervil (*Anthriscus caucalis*), native to Europe and Asia. A truly delicious herb. To me it tastes like a mix of parsley, carrot, cilantro, and anise. I use it often in salads, soups, or as a flavorful garnish. In folk medicine it's also considered a digestive. When young the plant can look very similar to poison hemlock, so proper identification is extremely important.

Sow thistle (*Sonchus oleraceus*), a plant native to Europe and western Asia and related to dandelion. Often used in raw salads or cooked. It tastes very similar to dandelion, but when it's young the bitterness is pretty much nonexistent.

Cleavers (*Galium aparine*), a native of Europe, some parts of Africa, and Asia, but also found all over North America. Considered a noxious weed in many places. Due to the hooked hairs present on the plants, it's more often cooked than eaten raw. Mild flavors.

Young foxtail grass (*Hordeum murinum*). I've juiced the young grass like wheatgrass with other ingredients. It tastes a bit like wheatgrass, too, albeit less sugary and with nice herbaceous notes.

Miner's lettuce (*Claytonia perfoliata*), native to most of the western and coastal regions of North America and part of Central America. Most often used raw in salad but can be cooked as well. Extremely abundant locally. Thanks to my removal of mostly non-native plants on my foraging site, I would say that the population of this native plant has quadrupled in the last two years.

By the way, you can very much do similar fermentation projects with herbs from your garden or those sold at your local supermarket or farmers market. Think parsley, cilantro, carrot tops, basil, fennel, chives, and countless others.

Gather your edible and flavorful ingredients from the forest floor, being sure to carefully identify each one.

Gather, prepare (cut, slice), and salt the ingredients you want to ferment in the forest floor and set aside.

Mix your forest floor with salt, minced garlic, and spices. Massage with both hands until it's very juicy. Wear gloves if you use hot spices.

Place a layer of forest floor at the bottom of a jar and pack it nicely with your fist or a wooden stomper/pounder.

Add a layer of the regular ingredients in the center, another layer of forest floor, a bit more ingredients, and one final layer of forest floor on top. Pack it tight, trying to leave as little air as possible.

By the next day you should be able to see brine nearly reaching the top. Once or twice a day, with clean hands, churn/stir the top layer. Burp the jar as necessary.

FERMENTING IN FOREST FLOOR

This ferment is a good example of exploring the unique flavors that nature can provide. The result is salty, sour, tangy, spicy, and you can definitely experience some of the green/herby flavors of a whole environment. You can't go more local than this. My original concept was to find a way to infuse forest flavors into regular ingredients such as radishes, daikons, and so on by wrapping them in fermenting herbs collected on the ground. It worked very nicely.

You don't have to be a master wildcrafter to do this; you can start picking from the ground the herbs you can identify with a small amount of experience. Just chickweed, a bit of wood sorrel, some fresh grass, and chervil would give you excellent results. Nothing will get wasted in this ferment—in the end even the fermented forest floor itself will be used.

Ingredients for a ½-gallon jar (1.9 L)

2 pounds (907 g) forest floor, comprising approximately:

- 20 percent grass (young foxtail barley in this case—not all grasses are edible)
- 77 percent wild chervil, chickweed, cleavers, thistle, miner's lettuce (use more of the very tasty and aromatic plants such as chervil or chickweed)
- 3 percent miscellaneous—oak leaves, bark, twigs (tannin will help keep ferments crunchy)

2½ tablespoons (42.5 g) salt
Around 2 pounds (907 g) ingredients that you want to ferment (I used beets, green onions with medium bulbs, and regular radishes)
¼ cup (39 g) garlic powder
15 garlic cloves, minced
½ cup (60 g) Korean chili powder
2 tablespoons (15 g) smoked jalapeño flakes (chile morita) or chipotle powder (optional)

Procedure

The total weight of the ingredients was around 4 pounds (1.8 kg). I used 2½ tablespoons (42.5 g) of salt.

1. First, in a bowl, mix the forest floor with 1½ tablespoons (25.5 g) of the salt and massage it for 5 minutes, leave it alone for 10 minutes, and do it again for 5 minutes until everything is quite juicy.
2. The next step is to cut and slice the regular ingredients. Cut beets into thick slices; leave some of the small radishes whole while cutting the bigger ones in half. Slice the green onions in two, leaving some of the leaves attached for aesthetics and for plating later on. After the fermentation is done, you'll still have the opportunity to cut the beets thinner (julienne) if you wish.
3. In a separate bowl, sprinkle the remaining 1 tablespoon (17 g) of salt on the cut beets, onions, and radishes. Massage them a bit, then leave them alone for 10 minutes or so.
4. When the bowl with the forest floor is juicy and ready, add the garlic powder, minced garlic, and chili powders, massaging everything for 2 to 3 minutes.
5. Then, in a clean jar, placed a juicy chunk of forest floor at the bottom, add a layer of regular ingredients in the center, another layer of forest floor, then a bit more ingredients, and one final layer of forest

Creating Your Own Forest Floor Mix

You can use the Forest Floor Fermentation technique with "weeds" or herbs found in your garden, or those purchased at the supermarket or your local farmers market. You can even mix wild herbs such as chickweed, dandelion, or sorrel with non-wild ones like watercress, fennel, or arugula. Experiment a bit, maybe with smaller amounts and pint/quart jars to start with until you find your favorite mix. There are countless creative mixes you can assemble, and your imagination is really the only limit. Some mixes may end up "meh" but you'll learn in the process. Very soon you can be a forest floor or garden floor fermentation expert.

The basic concept is to make a flavorful blend with herbs, then add salt and spices. Mix everything together, then place in the center some ingredients you want to ferment and infuse with your blend. To give you some ideas about possible ingredients, you could use:

Herb blends: Arugula, alfalfa, watercress, dill, cilantro, regular chervil, chives, fennel, tarragon, oregano, thyme, rosemary, wheatgrass, parsley, watercress, shiso, mustard greens, licorice, lemongrass, celery, basil (various types), mint (various types), carrot tops, dandelion, various salad greens, spinach, rhubarb, and so on.

Spices: Various types of chili flakes/powder, cinnamon, bay leaves, juniper berries, star anise, allspice, peppercorns, cloves, coffee, coriander, mustard seeds, garlic (fresh or powder), onion (fresh or powder), tamarind, saffron, nutmeg, lemon or lime zest, dried lime powder, sumac, za'atar, cumin, mushroom powders, and countless others. I made another of my favorite forest floor ferments with a homemade curry spice blend that included coriander, turmeric, cumin, mustard powder, cayenne, and cardamom.

Roots: Ginger, turmeric, horseradish, galangal. I've even used crushed wild chervil, black mustard, or radish roots to add flavors.

Ingredients you can ferment in the herbs and spices: Carrots, parsnips, radishes, cucumbers, beets, peppers, cherry tomatoes, turnips, rutabagas, cauliflower, various types of hot peppers, green beans, asparagus, leeks, bok choy . . . gosh . . . so many things!

And don't forget that you can also add fruit juices to your blend such as lime or lemon.

I use stinging nettles sparingly, though— too much can give you off flavors. But that's my opinion based on my personal taste.

floor on top. Using a clean hand or a wooden stomper/pounder, pack it tight to remove air pockets.

6. Twelve hours later, everything should be super juicy, and the fermentation should already have started. Churn and stir the top layer twice a day to avoid mold, then pack it tight again with your hand or a wooden stomper. Supervise and burp the jar as necessary. Ferment until the initial fermentation is complete (around 10 days), then place in the fridge. The flavors will get better with time. I like to use the contents within a month or two, but this ferment will keep much longer.

DRINK THE FERMENTED FOREST

Nothing goes to waste. When I made my first forest floor ferment, I fell completely in love with the flavors from my blend of wild herbs and spices. After 4 months of fermentation, the complexity was quite astounding. Originally my intention was to throw away the forest floor and eat the regular ingredients fermented inside, but instead I decided to dehydrate it and store it in jars until I figured out what to do. Two months later, as I was making some wildcrafted dashi with local kelp and mushrooms, I had my eureka moment.

Dashi—a soup and cooking stock used often in Japanese cuisine—is a simple broth usually made with kombu (kelp) and bonito (fermented skipjack tuna), though you'll find all kinds of interesting variations. I usually use local kelp from Northern California and shiitake mushrooms to make a plant-based version.

Anyhow, my dashi was ready, and I was thinking about which flavorful ingredients I could place in it to create a nutritious and yummy soup. I often use a bit of sliced red or green onions, a tad of minced garlic, some chili flakes, and some shredded or thinly sliced greens such as watercress, dandelion, or regular salad greens. As I was contemplating my next creative culinary move, the idea popped up in my mind: Why not infuse some of the dehydrated fermented forest floor in it?

And so I did! I infused some of the forest floor for a few minutes, and the results were amazing. Since then, I've used dashi as a base broth for all kinds of soups with fermented ingredients, but my favorite is still the forest floor soup. So much so that I ran out of my dehydrated stock within a month, but I can't wait to make more next spring. I even made a version with smoked forest floor, which was heavenly.

Ingredients for 2½ cups (591 ml) forest dashi

1 ounce (28 g) kombu (dried kelp), cut in squares (1–2 inches / 2.5–5 cm)
½ ounce (14 g) small dried foraged oyster mushrooms or shiitake mushrooms
3 cups (710 ml) cold water
½ ounce (14 g) dehydrated forest floor (smoking the herbs is an option)

Procedure

Place the kombu and mushrooms in a pot with the cold water and bring to a boil. Simmer on low for 5 to 10 minutes, then strain the kombu and mushrooms. (I like to eat them, too.)

As an option, while the dashi was simmering, I smoked the dehydrated forest floor with mesquite wood for a couple of minutes. Just enough to get some nice smoky flavors.

My next step was to place the smoked forest floor into a ceramic strainer and soup bowl (thank you,

Sheldon Ceramics). I poured in some of the hot dashi stock, placed a clean cotton cloth on top to keep everything warm, and after 3 minutes removed the top strainer. Voilà! My forest floor soup was ready to drink.

It was extremely delicious. I think next spring I'll ferment forest floor just to make soups, then dehydrate and keep the herbs in jars all year long. The salt, spicy heat, and smokiness of the herbs make them the perfect complement to the dashi stock; you end up with very complex flavors and, yes . . . you can taste the forest.

If you want, you can still add sliced green onions, tofu, shredded greens, and all kind of goodies to make a wholesome, nutritious soup. You're also not stuck with making a dashi as a soup stock; you can experiment using a vegetable or chicken broth. It's your soup and you can do what you want!

SMOKED HAY (WILD OATS)
FERMENTATION

Come August and September, our local hills are turning golden brown under the relentless sun due to the sheer quantities of dried mustard and wild oats (*Avena fatua*). While during springtime you can create interesting ferments with fresh wild greens, I'd always found late summer to be a challenge. That is, until I remembered that in Belgium and France, we cook in hay. So why not try fermenting in it?

With that idea, I set out early one morning to avoid the scorching temperatures and foraged a bunch of dried wild oats in the local hills. I'm sure there are ways to do similar ferments by using different spice blends and using other "hays" than wild oats. In this recipe, I ended up smoking dry oat stems inside a jar using a blend of local mesquite, juniper, and fig wood. You can find a lot of small smokers online that you could use for this method. I use a Handi Smok, which is a bit on the expensive side (around $175), but it works very well.

Alternative ingredients for hay can surely be found in your area. If you know an organic farmer, you could use regular hay such as wheat, oats, barley, or even corn husks. For a wildcrafter, any harmless grass or herbaceous-type plants that have been dried are a possibility. Try to find something with good stems that are easy to remove when the fermentation is done, unless you want to do fancy experimentation.

Ingredients being fermented for a 1-quart jar (946 ml)

5 ounces (142 g) wild radish or
    daikon tender seedpods
3 small yellow beets, sliced
7 tiny pearl onions, used whole
4 garlic cloves, finely diced
¼ small red onion, diced
¾ ounce (18 g) dried oat stems

Spice mix

1 tablespoon (6 g) paprika
1 teaspoon (3 g) garlic powder
1 teaspoon (3 g) smoked chili powder/flakes
    of your choice
½ teaspoon (1.5 g) ginger powder
½ teaspoon (2 g) ground peppercorns
½ teaspoon (1.5 g) onion powder
1 teaspoon (4 g) brown sugar
1 teaspoon (5.5 g) salt

Brine

1 cup (236 ml) water
1 teaspoon (5.5 g) salt

1. In a bowl mix all your ingredients to be fermented with the spice mix. Prepare the brine and add ¼ cup (59 ml) to the bowl. Massage for a couple of minutes, then let the mix rest for 20 minutes so everything gets soft and juicy.
2. Meanwhile, using scissors, cut your "hay" to the right length and place it in a jar. Poke a hole in the lid with the scissors and enlarge it by twisting and pushing down until the hole is the right size for the smoker's tube to be inserted. (Don't hurt yourself!) Close the lid and smoke the hay a couple of times (or more). When you're done, screw a new lid back on and let everything rest for 10 minutes.
3. Remove the hay and line it up on the sides of a new quart jar. Place the mixed ingredients to ferment in the center. Add the remaining ¾ cup brine. The ingredients won't be under the brine, so the technique used (fermentation method 5, page 33) is to simply close the jar tightly and shake two or three times (or more) a day for a few seconds, then unscrew the jar a tiny bit so fermentation gases can escape. I usually close the lid tight, shake, and burp as necessary. The liquid will become acidic and will be distributed evenly. You can also place the jar upside down, with the lid tightly closed, from time to time.
4. Ferment for 7 to 10 days, and when the initial fermentation is complete (no more gases), place in the fridge. Enjoy whenever you want; the stuff will last for months.

My ferment ended up with some very nice smoky accents; I can taste grassy accents as well. But you'll have to try your own.

Infusing Wild and Local Flavors in Ferments

There are all kinds of interesting ways to add some zing to your wild ferments if you think creatively. Because of my upbringing in Europe and probably the influence of French cuisine, I used to think that we should place things strictly suited for eating in the food we prepare. But some ingredients, although inedible due to texture, can really influence the taste of a ferment.

Leaves, barks, branches, stems, and various types of woods have some fascinating potential for infusing local flavors. At home I have a collection of wood chips, pine needles, leaves, and around 20 aromatic stems that I use for brewing. I simply place them in the wort with the other components during the boiling process, then strain. Why not use them for lacto-fermentation?

You can use a similar technique and experiment a bit. Both fermentation processes, alcoholic and lacto-fermentation, are excellent at extracting the savory essence of "inedible" ingredients. Just make sure that what you use is not unhealthy or poisonous.

My first experiment was a smoked sauerkraut. As you know by now, I love smoky accents in my food, and I thought that a smoked sauerkraut would be awesome. Of course, I could have taken the easy route and purchased some liquid smoke at the store, but that would be cheating, wouldn't it? I had some mesquite wood chips that I foraged in Nevada, and I decided to experiment by placing roasted chips in my sauerkraut.

My method was super simple. I placed the mesquite chips on a metal tray covered with aluminum foil and roasted them in an oven set on broil for maybe 15 minutes. After I removed them, I finished them with a kitchen torch. The chips were cooled off and then deposited at the bottom of a 1-quart (946 ml) jar with a bunch of cabbage leaves on top.

I made a dandelion/sauerkraut ferment and placed the ingredients in the jar on top of the chips and cabbage leaves. The smoky flavors are transferred to the ferment through the brine; the trick is to close the lid tight from time to time and place the jar

Mesquite chips roasted in the oven.

upside down. The technique worked quite well, and my Smoked DandiKraut was a success.

Since then, I've created all kinds of unusual infused ferments with aromatic stems, branches, and berries. Some were delicious and some were "interesting," but I've learned a lot in the process. One of my favorites is my pin-yon pine branch sauerkraut. If you crack open a branch, an incredible aroma exudes from the wood and bark; it's an odd mix of pine, sweet perfume, and candylike qualities. There are some similarities to juniper berries, too. It's really a complex compound.

You don't need a lot; you just need to take one branch and split it in two (lengthwise), then place it into the ferment. It makes a simple sauerkraut taste like the local mountains! I make another similar ferment using our local juniper berries and a small cracked branch. Taste as the ferment ages and remove the branch (and berries) when you're happy with it.

Leaves are quite delightful, too! Of course, there are obvious choices like our local California bay leaves, but recently I infused a regular sauerkraut with a few mugwort leaves. I was pretty much sure it would not work, as the leaf's aromatics can be rather intense and there is a substantial amount of bitterness, but it ended up quite good and much mellower than I expected. You don't know until you try.

As a note, if you're using California bay leaves, make sure you dehydrate and age them for a couple of months at room temperature. Fresh, the flavor can be overwhelming and (from experience) can create stomach upset.

Dandelion sauerkraut fermented with smoked chips.

Sauerkraut fermented with juniper berries and pinyon pine branches.

Oak Trunk Fermentation

Speaking of wood and branches . . . Sometimes I have crazy ideas. Quite a few of my experiments fail, but then some others produce results way beyond my expectations. It makes all the failures worth it.

How far can you go into exploring wild flavors? The more I explore the possibilities, the more I realize they're probably infinite.

This all started because of a forest fire in December 2017. Pretty much my entire wildcrafting territory comprised ashes and fallen trees after that fire. I remember walking in what used to be my favorite forest; it was pretty much a desert. I sat down on a burned tree trunk and could not figure out what to do next. This was the place where I was teaching and giving my plant identification walks.

One thing I have learned in my life is to never give up. Everything can be a positive opportunity if you are creative enough. I try to use that philosophy in everything I do. Even when I think I'm getting older and my energy is not the same as it was in my twenties, I try to find advantages, and there are some: You can slow down a bit and take more time to appreciate and explore things, use your accumulated knowledge, and become wiser in your experiments. I appreciate life much more as I grow old.

In the case of my burned forest, I looked at ashes, burned trees, and broken branches and contemplated their potential. What can you do with ashes? I pondered the subject for a while and remembered that indigenous peoples cooked with some ashes as a source of calcium. In Europe and the Middle East, ashes are used to make lye water, which is part of the process of making soap. Chefs use some specific ashes for plating (making food pretty) and flavoring. In South America corn is cooked with hardwood ash to soften the food and make it more edible, while increasing the nutritional value (nixtamalization). I remembered that some French cheeses are covered with ashes to protect against mold, which inspired me to forage some oak ashes to use on my plant-based cheeses. If you take the time to contemplate, opportunities abound.

Next to me, one of my favorite oaks was down. It had lived a long life, probably over 100 years, and now its ashes would fertilize the ground for the next generation. Nothing is ever wasted in nature. At one end of the trunk, the fire had burned the inside, leaving the bark. The smoky smell was enticing. It looked like a giant barrel. With all the fermentation I do, it didn't take much imagination to contemplate the possibilities. I was deep into writing this book, so my first thought was, *What about making my own oak barrel and fermenting in it?*

I remember attending some survival classes long ago taught by my friend, the author and teacher Christopher Nyerges. That day we made some crude bowls by placing coals on top of a sliced piece of wood and scraping the inside to remove the burned parts and hollow it out. Surely that would work with a trunk!

That big oak trunk was much too large, but nearby, the firefighters had cut down some trees that were too damaged and hazardous (ready to fall). Pieces of all sizes were scattered on the forest floor. After a couple of minutes inspecting the place, I found the perfect piece, around 8 inches (20 cm) in diameter and 12 inches (30 cm) tall. I'm not sure if it was a piece of a big branch or the trunk of a smaller oak, but it was ideal, and I took it home.

At this point it was still just a concept and I had no idea if it would work. Oak wood is quite fascinating. There is a reason wine and Belgian sour beers are aged in oak barrels: Oak wood contains complex chemical compounds that contribute flavor notes. I think I remember reading about over 150 flavor compounds. Some oak wood will imbue hints of vanilla, wood, and tobacco as well as tannin, which helps with preserving the precious liquid but also provides character and structure. I think it is what gives a "noble" quality to some wines.

But not all oaks are equal. Usually only three oaks are used to make barrels: white oak in America (*Quercus alba*), along with sessile oak (*Q. petraea*) and pedunculate oak (*Q. robur*) in Europe. My problem was that I was dealing with coast live oak (*Q. agrifolia*), which is known to be loaded with tannin and thus quite bitter.

But I took a calculated chance. If you think about it, this oak would be a perfect representation of my local terroir, so I had to go with it. My reasoning was as follows: Fermentation was originally a cold-temperature preservation technique. Kimchi is a good example: The ingredients are gathered in fall and often fermented in a pot buried in the ground during the winter. Due to the higher temperatures where I live, I usually do an initial fermentation for a few days, then age the ferment in the fridge. It's true for sauerkraut and all the various ferments I make.

If I made a kimchi-like ferment (page 76) in the oak, I figured, with the seasonal temperature being in the mid-80s Fahrenheit (around 30°C), it should be ready for aging after 4 to 6 days of fermentation. It might be too brief for much bitterness to leach into the ferment and significantly affect the flavors. Thus, I decided to go ahead!

The method I used was quite archaic and simple. I purchased some mesquite charcoal briquettes at the store and placed a red-hot one in the middle of the top part of the trunk. I let it burn until it was reduced to ashes, then I scraped away the burned wood.

It's important to take your time with this. I made an average of three burns a day. Soon the indentation became large enough for two briquettes,

Start with one charcoal briquette and scrape.

Add more charcoal as the hole becomes bigger.

Scrape, burn, and scrape some more until you are satisfied with the size of your hole.

Check for water leaks.

Sand the inside, clean, and fill cracks with dough paste.

Fill leaks with pine resin glue on both sides.

Place the ferment in the barrel and mix the contents at least twice a day with clean hands.

Cover to protect from insects. Set a clean towel on top, too.

Taste your ferment and remove it when you're happy with the flavors. This one took me 4 days.

then three. I used a rounded gourd scraper to remove the burned wood, but I'm sure other wood scrapers would be appropriate. With careful scraping, you can determine the size of the hole you create. It's not a lot of work, but you need to supervise the burn, mostly as the hole becomes deeper. You don't want to light a fire inside the trunk and burn too much of the sides. I decided to leave the bark on the trunk for aesthetic reasons.

After 7 days I ended up with a hole that was 7 inches (17.5 cm) deep and would hold around 6 cups (1.4 L) of liquid. Enough to make ferments that can be transferred to a quart jar. I stopped there. Using sandpaper, I removed any burned wood inside. A couple of problems became obvious right away. I had quite a few cracks and some holes inside the wood made by some sort of beetle, which would create a leak later on. I did a test by filling the hole with water and found two obvious leaks.

I used two tricks to fill up the cracks and seals the leaks. In Belgium dough paste is sometimes used to fix leaky barrels; pine resin glue is perfect to fix leaks, too, and was even used in boatmaking. I applied one layer of sourdough paste (which contains lacto bacteria) inside the barrel and removed the excess with a clean sponge so only the cracks would be filled. I then made a pine resin glue by heating up some pinyon pine sap with sea-weed ashes (charcoal would work as well). The ratio was pretty much 2 parts sap to 1 part ashes. Ashes make the glue a bit more flexible, so it won't crack. I applied the pine glue to the obvious leaks both inside and out. I did one more test by filling the trunk with water—and the seal worked.

The next day I placed my kimchi-like concoction inside the barrel for fermentation. I set a wreath made of mugwort (an insect repellent) around the hole and a flat stone on top. As an added precaution against insects, I covered the top with a clean towel. This is pretty much open fermentation, so you need to work with it. Twice a day, with clean hands, I mixed the contents. The weather was hot, and 4 days was enough for the initial fermentation (by taste). The result was fantastic and the loss of liquid minimal. There was a hint of bitterness, but the oak flavor conveyed was perfect. The slight amount of tannin also kept the ferment crunchy. I did taste some smokiness, but as an accent. It was by far the best-tasting kimchi-like ferment I've done in 10 years, and nature can take the credit.

One problem I encountered, which is due to the open fermentation, was the appearance of kahm yeast when aging these ferments in jars after the initial tree trunk fermentation. Thus, when using this method, I eat my ferments young and don't age them much if at all. Wild kimchis are perfect for trunk fermentation. Before you use just *any* log to make a barrel, do some research on which types of wood are traditionally used, as I would imagine some can be somewhat toxic.

Fermenting in Leaves

I've always been fascinated by the possibility of making ferments and just using what nature can provide as containers—leaves, clay, bark, and so on. Most ferments are designed to be aged, but you can break that rule, too. When I used to teach survival skills many years ago, anything that could preserve the food, if only for a couple of days, was greatly appreciated. But these days I'm looking to go beyond mere survival; I'm more interested in flavors.

There are many examples of crude preservation techniques used throughout history with the intent of making food last a bit longer than usual. A good example is the humble hand pie. Meat and vegetables were placed in dough, then baked in the oven (or in ashes)—pasteurizing the contents, while the crust provided protection from possible bacterial contamination and oxygen. That simple process could make the food last a couple of days longer, which was very useful in the Middle Ages if you were traveling or working in the field.

We don't think about it much these days, but quite a few pastries originated as food preservation techniques, including some pies.

Lacto-fermentation is really an ideal method to keep food longer, even in the most primitive settings. If you forage ingredients such as roots, leaves, and even whole plants, add some salt, and create a crude container, you can protect the ferment from oxygen and outside elements, preserving that foodstuff for a while.

With the right spices, you can even turn it into gourmet food. Salt, along with many spices and herbs, inhibits specific bacterial or viral growth (*Clostridium*, *Escherichia*, *Listeria*, *Salmonella*, and so on), which is why you find a lot of spicy food in countries with a hot climate. Reading a scientific study* on the subject recently, I was amazed to find out that out of 30 spices used in a lab, 15 inhibited at least 75 percent of bacterial species. This included such spices as thyme, oregano, garlic, cumin, chilies, allspice, garlic, onion, bay, tarragon, cinnamon, and more.

But obviously lacto bacteria are not affected by them. A ferment like kimchi contains a considerable amount of garlic and chilies. It's really the beauty of fermentation, bacteria and flavors working together to ensure food safety.

In my opinion, kimchi-like concoctions are perfect for fermenting roots or plants in somewhat crude containers. The garlic and chili powder

---

* Paul W. Sherman and Jennifer Billing, "Darwinian Gastronomy: Why We Use Spices: Spices Taste Good Because They Are Good for Us," *BioScience* 49, no. 6 (June 1999): 453–63.

provide the initial protection, and the contents very quickly become acidic due to the fermentation process making the food safe to eat. That said, there's no need to be an extremist, and because of the primitive nature of the system, I still like to use a bit of Culture Starter to kick off the process.

Don't take risks with your health; always check the pH of your fermented food (page 36) before consumption, and if it is the first time you're trying a particular type of ferment, check the pH during the process as well so that you know your method is safe. As they say, better safe than sorry.

I usually eat kimchi-like ferments around day 4, and for this style of preparation, I'm looking for a pH of 4 or below.

WILD FOOD KIMCHI FERMENTED
IN MUSTARD LEAVES

You're not limited to mustard leaves for this kind of ferment; just make sure that the leaves you're using are not toxic in any way. While our locally invasive castor bean (*Ricinus communis*) leaves seem perfect for this type of project, for instance, it would be a bad idea to use them, as the plant is highly toxic.

Locally I have used curly dock, mallow, sycamore, and black mustard leaves, but you're not stuck with wild leaves—you could use kale or cabbage, for example.

Your leaves need to be soft and tender enough to be wrapped around the food, and you have the option of blanching or freezing them. My usual method is to clean the leaves, pat them dry, then freeze them for a couple of hours before use. While they're freezing, I make my wild food kimchi or similar ferment.

Ingredients for 5–6 large mustard leaves

6 ounces (170 g) cabbage, shredded
2 ounces (57 g) wild edibles, shredded
   (mustard leaves, chickweed, chervil)
3–4 garlic cloves, minced
1 mustard root, crushed (optional)
2–3 tablespoons (15–24.5 g) coarse chili
   powder (I used Korean chili powder)
2 tablespoons (10 ml) Culture Starter
1 teaspoon (5.5 g) salt

Equipment

5–6 large mustard leaves, for wrapping
1 straw (I used a wild oat stalk)
Yucca fibers, to tie the top around the straw
   (you can also use a regular string)

Procedure

1. With clean hands, massage and mix all of the ferment ingredients together in a bowl as you would for regular sauerkraut, then let it rest for 15 minutes (or more).

2. Remove the mustard leaves from the freezer and let them thaw thoroughly. Remove any excess stems.

3. Once they're thawed, carefully arrange the soft leaves inside a bowl. You want them layered. Then place your ferment inside. With love, wrap the leaves around your ferment, making sure there are no air pockets. Insert the straw through the top. The purpose of the straw is to let fermentation gases escape—and to be honest, it looks pretty, too! I'm not sure it's always necessary, but I don't want my "leaf bag" to rip open, either.

4. To make sure there is no opening where fruit flies and other critters can get in, use the yucca fibers to tie the leaves around the straw and also around the ferment, which is helpful to maintain a solid shape.

5. Cover the bowl with a couple of thawed leaves as an added protection. The straw is a perfect opening for insects to get in, so my solution is to use dehydrated mugwort leaf fluff to top the straw, but you could

use anything that works, including nontoxic moss, lichen, cattail fluff, or regular cotton. If you make this during the summer and you have numerous flies and such, placing the ferment in a closed container could be a good idea.

6. Ferment for 3 to 4 days. You can usually smell if the ferment is doing well, but this skill comes with experience. Open the contents and check the pH; it should be below 4. When I try new recipes using primitive systems like this, I make several ferments and check the pH daily by opening one to make sure it's working properly. Experimenting is awesome, but food safety is a must.

Clean, pat dry, then freeze the leaves you want to use as wrap for at least a couple of hours. Remove them from the freezer and let them thaw thoroughly.

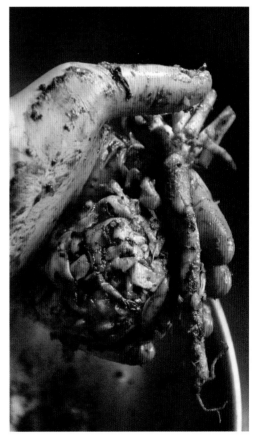

With clean hands, massage and mix everything together in a bowl as you would for regular sauerkraut, then let the contents rest for 15 minutes (or more).

Once they're thawed, carefully arrange the soft leaves inside a bowl (you want them layered). Place your ferment inside.

Gently wrap the leaves around your ferment, making sure there are no air pockets, and insert the straw through the top.

Place one or two large thawed leaves on top of the bowl as an added protection. Ferment for 3 to 4 days.

Open the ferment and check the pH. It should be around 4 or below.

Use of Tannic Leaves

Tannins are a class of naturally occurring astringent compounds found commonly in many species of plants, nuts, and fruits. They play a role in protecting the plants from predation and may help regulate plant growth. If you've ever bitten into a unripe grape or grape seeds, you instantly get a sour, dry feeling in your mouth—that's the typical reaction to tannin content.

Tannins are present in quite a few ingredients we commonly eat or drink. A good example is red wine. Some red wines will leave that dry feeling in your mouth or throat, but it's really part of their "character." A lot of foodstuffs we commonly consume contain tannins, too: coffee, tea, chocolate, many berries, apples, rhubarb, acorns, nuts, squash, legumes, and many others.

It seems like an odd concept, but traditionally tannic leaves have been used in fermentation to keep ingredients firm and crisp. Tannins have a role in protecting cells from damage: During the fermentation process they prevent cell walls from breaking easily, thus leaving the contents crunchier. And everybody likes a crunchy pickle . . . right?

Oak leaves, green banana peel, tea leaves, grape leaves, or horseradish leaves are usually used in fermented pickle recipes. Usually 3 or 4 grape or white oak leaves are used for a ½-gallon (1.9 L) jar.

So what does that have to do with wildcrafting?

Many of the plants, barks, and leaves you'll encounter during your foraging activities contain tannins, and you can use them in wild fermentation projects to keep ferments crunchy if that's a quality you're looking for. It works with cucumbers but will also work with many other ferments, including sauerkraut, roots, and fruits. Some leaves such as mugwort or bay have the additional benefit of adding flavors.

Which foraged ingredients can be used? I don't have a complete answer, but I know the list contains a lot more than what I've used so far. The problem (you might call it the exciting part) is that you'll need to experiment a bit if you decide to venture into the uses of foraged tannic additives for fermentation. For example, my local oak leaves are way more bitter than white oak leaves; if I use the traditional recipe, my resulting ferment will be quite crisp but not very enjoyable, if you know what I mean.

Doing some research in books and online, I've found people using wildcrafted sources of tannins for fermentation such as mesquite leaves (2 tablespoons / 10–12 g per quart or liter), olive leaves (1 tablespoon / 6 g per quart or liter), wild grape leaves, sour cherry leaves, and currant leaves.

For my part, I've used willow leaves (two to three per quart or liter), coast live oak leaves (one leaf per quart or liter), and roasted oak bark (page 172), which has the benefit of adding smoky flavors as well. I've also added

mugwort and California bay leaves to my ferments, but mostly for flavors.

What else could be used? I would need to research more but I'm interested in some of my local native currant leaves, which are very aromatic. Alder leaves are extremely tannic, so they could work. Crushed unripe currant berries, maybe? There's definitely lots of research and experimentation to do. Still, I wanted to bring the subject up in this book, even in an incomplete way, what with all the fermentation and culinary possibilities.

Note that some people are intolerant of tannins and can experience headaches/migraines or stomach issues. If you plan to serve your ferments, always check with each diner first. Willow leaves may also contain some salicin, the compound used in aspirin. Usually the bark is used in herbalism, but if you're allergic to salicin, it may not be a good idea to use willow.

Wild Seeds and Grains in Ferments

Making achar-type ferments with nutritious or aromatic seeds opened my eyes to new possibilities. Foraging seeds and grains isn't common among wildcrafters; these are a bit beyond the usual common wild edibles and require more advanced knowledge. (It's harder to identify a plant when it's going to seed, for instance.) My years of experience have taught me that we probably have over 200 edible wild seeds and grains locally, half of them being non-native such as fennel, mustard, cheatgrass (*Bromus tectorum*), and wild oats. It's a fascinating subject because in any culture seeds and grains to make

This daikon achar contains foraged mustard leaves, wild oats, and cheatgrass grains, roasted sesame seeds, and various other wildcrafted seeds (mustard, fennel, radish, and more).

Edible non-native or invasive grains and seeds.

gruels, porridges, or even fermented beverages like beers were a big deal, but nowadays foraging wild seeds and grains is a lost art. (Cheatgrass is on the chewy side, but at the same time is a good source of fiber. Some cheatgrass grains were found with other edible grains during archaeological research in the Alps region of France.)

There is often a misconception that seeds are labor-intensive, but in most cases it's really not. I could easily collect 6 cups of black mustard seeds in one morning, enough to make gourmet mustard for the year. From my wildcrafting perspective, I like to forage seeds with the intent of helping the environment. Some people complain about all the invasive grasses, but their culinary possibilities are begging to be explored. Frankly, I also consider not gathering wild seeds a form of food waste.

Crabgrass (*Digitaria* spp.) is a good example. It's one of those grasses that people spray with pesticides as a completely unwanted weed in a pristine lawn. Yet some people don't realize that they may be alive today because their ancestors used that plant. Crabgrass was actually an ancient crop in Europe and Asia, and is still a crop in Africa. Each year West African farmers devote approximately 750,000 acres (300,000 ha) to cultivating it, and the crop supplies food to three or four million people. And many others don't know foxtail is related to barley: Some varieties provide a large amount of seeds, which can be easily extracted.

Yesterday my neighbor was mowing and cutting weeds to preserve his beautiful lawn, but I noticed a bunch of unusual grass growing there. And what do you know! It's a native grass called smallflower melic (*Melica imperfecta*), which was also used as a staple in America. But people cut it like a weed because it doesn't fit the narrative of what the front of your house should look like. So fascinating!

Locally our hills are covered with wild oats, which are completely unused and considered invasive. Yes, it takes time to remove the grains from the husks, and each grain may need its own specific extraction method. It's not always about time, though; it's about a quality ingredient that, if used, can be part of the solution for our environmental issues, rather than the target of pesticides or a wasted resource. The grains can be harvested at their prime, dried, and used all year long.

Achar-type ferments are perfect for the addition of grains during the fermentation process and will add nutritional value as well. Grains and seeds are definitely not the main part of this ferment; they make up roughly 5 percent of the contents. Seeds can be added for flavors, too, such as fennel or black mustard seeds. Flavoring seeds are commonly used in ferments, such as caraway, coriander, fenugreek, and so on, but locally wildcrafted seeds and grains are another interesting way to explore a local terroir.

FERMENTED WILD GRAIN PORRIDGE

This is something I wanted to do for years: collect some wild edible grains and make a simple porridge the way people would have done in prehistoric times. Interestingly enough, this ferment was made with "weeds," the same ones now considered invasive and featured on commercials for herbicides; yet many of them are really ancestral food. It took me most of a day to collect and husk enough grains for this dish by hand, but I found the experience truly worthwhile. In this book I fermented the porridge as a good source of probiotics and added nutritional value, but it's not a must.

Ingredients for a ½-pint jar (236 ml)

Around ¼ ounce (6 g) foxtail grass grains (*Hordeum jubatum*)

1 teaspoon (3 g) crabgrass seeds

Around 3 ounces (85 g) wild oats grains

1 ounce (28 g) cheatgrass grains

¼ cup (59 ml) water

2 tablespoons (30 ml) Culture Starter

¼ teaspoon (1.5 g) salt

Procedure

1. Roughly grind the foxtail, crabgrass, and wild oats in a molcajete (stone grinder), adding a bit of cheatgrass.
2. Boil the remaining cheatgrass for 40 minutes.
3. Transfer the ground grains into your jar. Then added the cooked cheatgrass grains along with the water, culture starter, and salt.
4. Now simply stir the contents, close the jar, and let it ferment for 18 to 24 hours. Burp if necessary, but it's usually not an issue.

A Note on Grains

If you adventure in wildcrafting grains, make sure to do some research on proper storage, mold, and ergot. Ergot is a fungal infection of some grains. It can be toxic but is easily recognizable.

This ferment is quite sour, but in a good way. It's not overwhelming; it's as if someone added a dash of lemony vinegar to the mush, but with a trace of cheesy qualities as well. When serving, you can add a small amount of nutritional yeast (to taste) and miso to accentuate the cheese flavors. It's really a good base for creative tasty additions such as roasted sesame seeds, spices, herbs, or even soy sauce. It's so valuable that I serve a small amount on acorn crackers during some of my wild food tasting events.

Fermenting with Seawater

When I wrote about fermenting with seawater once on social media, it was probably one of my most controversial posts; I had no idea that so many people have a seawater phobia. Of course, because I live in Los Angeles people assumed that I had foraged the water there in the first place. (I hadn't.) But I received fascinating feedback full of opinions about pollution, toxic algae, high levels of radiation, and plastic particles. Add to that a few conspiracy theories and you get the picture. Having a backyard garden in a huge metropolis like New York, Los Angeles, Paris, or London and eating your homegrown vegetables is okay, but seawater is highly questionable and perhaps, in some cases, reprehensible.

I like common sense and doing the best you can with what you have—from an educated perspective. Yes, it's important to know the quality of the seawater you intend to collect for culinary uses, but you can't rely on rumors and speculations for that. Get facts! If you do your homework, you will find up-to-date online information on toxic algae blooms, radiation, and water quality based on actual water samplings. After a few weeks of research here and there, I finally found my perfect foraging location near the coast of Oregon, where the water samplings were awesome. Later on I found out that the area is also used for commercial seaweed harvesting.

Using seawater in culinary applications is hardly new. In fact, in some European countries such as Spain and Holland, you can purchase purified seawater at the supermarket. The water is used to cook potatoes, pasta, vegetables, shrimps, clams, crabs, and many other ingredients.

On average, seawater has a salinity of approximately 3.5 percent, which is perfect for fermenting pickles, but you can find wide variations due to the proximity of rivers, even underground ones. Based on taste, the seawater I collect in Northern California and Oregon is probably closer to 2.5 percent.

Pure seawater can work very well as a brine unless I'm fermenting pickling cucumbers, which are rather large. I use a brine between 2.5 and 3 percent for most vegetables—carrots, cauliflower, mixed vegetables, and so on. A brine of 2 percent is composed of around 1 teaspoon salt per cup of water (23 g per liter), and a 3 percent brine of around 1½ teaspoons salt per cup of water (29 g per liter).

PREPARING YOUR SEAWATER

The water you collect is very much alive with plankton, microbes, and—although unlikely at the location where I collect my seawater—the possibility of pathogenic viruses and bacteria. Very often you will also find sand and other organic particles. Thus, from a food safety perspective, you should filter and pasteurize it. There are all kinds of water filtration systems; some will even remove bacteria and viruses.

I'm mostly interested in removing sand, small rocks, and such, as the pasteurization process will take care of any bacteria or other microbes. A clean towel and colander will do the job.

Ingredients and equipment

1 large pot (more than 1 gallon)

1 gallon (3.78 L) seawater

Colander or something similar to strain/filter the water

1 clean towel

Container or jars for storing the water if you don't use it right away

Procedure

1. Once you've collected your seawater, don't let it sit around in the heat or at room temperature for too long. I once had seawater go rancid on me after I left it inside a bottle at room temperature for 4 to 5 days. I know it's weird, but maybe I was dealing with a lot of dead animalcules (microscopic animals or protozoa). It had a faint smell of rotten fish after a few days. Since then I either use the seawater within 24 hours or I freeze it.

2. Collect and filter your seawater. I use a clean towel placed in a colander positioned on top of a pot. I just want to remove sand, small rocks, tiny sharks, old Spanish gold coins, and any other unwanted particles. Pour the seawater inside the colander.

3. Remove the colander and towels then bring the filtered liquid to a boil for at least 12 to 15 minutes. You are basically pasteurizing it. Let it cool down and voilà! It's ready to be used as a brine in fermentation.

If you don't use the water right away, transfer it into bottles and refrigerate. I had no problem with 2-week-old bottles; once it's pasteurized, I think it would keep much longer. You can also freeze the water.

MAKING SALT FROM SEAWATER

Homemade salt is a very, very simple process—it's similar to preparing a seawater brine, with just a couple more steps. You end up with a very tasty and sharp salt that can be used like regular salt for cooking and/or fermentation.

Ingredients and equipment

1 large pot (more than 1 gallon)
1 gallon (3.78 L) seawater
Wooden spoon
Regular spoon or fork
Large plate to dehydrate the salt at the end
Colander or something similar to
    strain/filter the water
1 clean towel
Jar for storing the salt

Procedure

1. Collect and filter your seawater. I use a clean towel placed in a colander positioned on top of a pot. Pour the seawater inside the colander to remove any unwanted particles.

2. Remove the colander and bring the filtered seawater inside the pot to a boil. Don't cover the pot; the idea is to evaporate all the water. Continue boiling until you start seeing a white mush forming at the bottom. At this stage it's a good idea to turn down the heat to medium and let the liquid simmer. Continue until the mush has the consistency of wet sand. It's basically pure salt. A gallon of seawater may take 4 hours to get to this "mushy" stage.

3. Supervise the process closely when you're at the wet-sand stage. Reduce the heat to low. You may need to cover the pot with a mesh, because the concentrated salted mush can splash a bit. Use a wooden spoon to scrape the salt accumulating on the side of the pot and stir the contents a bit from time to time. It's possible to "burn" the contents at

the bottom of the pot, leaving you with a yellowish salt.

4. Your next step is to dehydrate the wet mush, so you end up with dry salt. You have several choices: solar dehydration, using your oven, or bringing in a dehydrator.

   Here in Los Angeles, my favorite method is solar dehydration. I transfer the mush to a flat surface (stone, tray, or plate) and place it in the sun. In summertime the whole process may take a couple of hours at the most.

   Or you can preheat the oven to around 180°F (82°C), remove the salt from the pot, and spread it flat on a large tray or plate. Place the tray in the oven and, every 15 minutes or so, stir the salt using a fork. It's very important to do this, or you will get a solid mass of salt (caking) instead of thin granules. Near the end of the process, you'll need to stir with your fork every 5 minutes until the salt is fully dried. If you use solar dehydration, you'll need to supervise and stir the salt, too.

5. Once the salt is dried, use a spoon or fork to crush any remaining solid bits. You should end up with a very fine salt, quite sharp. It will taste like the sea in a good way.

My experience is that 1 gallon of seawater should give you around ¾ cup—anywhere between 115 and 130 grams—of fluffy sea salt. This may be different for you given the salinity of your seawater. If you wildcrafted your seawater near a freshwater river, you'll end up with less salt.

Collect and filter your seawater using a strainer or colander and a clean towel.

Bring the filtered seawater to a boil, then simmer until most of the liquid is evaporated.

You'll need to supervise and stir the contents a bit when most of the water is evaporated. You end up with a sort of mush.

Place the salt mush on a dish and dehydrate in the oven or the sun. Stir the contents every 15 to 20 minutes so the salt doesn't cake into a solid mass.

Once the salt is dried, use a fork or spoon to crush the remaining solid bits.

Store in a sealed container.

SEAWATER FERMENTATION: CARROTS, WILD FENNEL, AND GINGER

Seawater has a salinity of around 3 to 3.5 percent, which corresponds to around 2 tablespoons of salt per quart of water or 33 grams of salt per liter. That's perfect for fermentation. Some people ferment carrots with a lower brine (2 percent), but 3.5 percent is perfect when you eat them, as I do, for a salty snack later on. You always have the option to add fresh water if you want to reduce the salinity.

Any fermented carrot recipe can be made with seawater, too; just substitute pure seawater for your brine. If you usually use a 2 percent brine, simply add some fresh water (around 30 percent).

Ingredients for a 1-pint jar (475 ml)

7 ounces (200 g) organic carrots, sliced (unpeeled, cleaned under cold water)

½ ounce (14 g) gingerroot, sliced

2 sprigs (7 g) wild fennel fronds (don't use the root with wild fennel)

Enough filtered, pasteurized seawater to cover the ingredients (the carrots are pretty tightly packed and will stay under the brine)

Procedure

1. Use fermentation method 2 (page 23). I simply close the jar and burp as necessary. If the carrots don't stay under the brine, just shake the jar a couple of times daily. It's that easy.
2. Ferment for a couple of weeks at room temperature, then place in the fridge.

Once they're fermented, you can eat the carrots as is, but for me a finished ferment is just a start. Taste and add spices if necessary. I like to marinate the carrots overnight in homemade wild beer vinegar sweetened with maple syrup (you can use seasoned rice vinegar, too) or a bit of lime juice, smoked chili flakes, and fresh wild chervil. But you get the idea: Be creative with your ferment.

Seawater Salt Fermentation: Cabbage and Seaweed

Fermenting in seawater is quite straightforward, but what about using your homemade salt in fermentations?

The salt you obtain from seawater is actually quite different from other salts in both texture and flavor. If you did a good job, you should have obtained a fine salt, but even if your salt is a bit rough, you still have the option of using a grinder. I kind of like to have a rough salt to start with; using my molcajete (Mexican stone grinder) gives me complete control of the texture I want. That's hard to do with an electric grinder. You don't want a salt that's powdered; a granular texture will help extract the moisture of the ingredients you ferment when you massage it into them.

If your sea salt becomes a bit humid over time, which can happen if you open the jar too often, you can dehydrate it in the oven before use.

The flavor of the salt is quite different from what you purchase at the store. It is very sharp and then goes away quickly. If I was to use a sea analogy, it's as if a big wave hits you and then recedes quickly.

This salt is also fantastic for other culinary uses. As I've mentioned, I think it tastes a bit like the sea in a good way, though that may be all in my head: The beauty of wildcrafting is that you can add beautiful memories to your ingredients. You can make any regular ferment with this sea salt; the only difference is that I use a bit more than usual, and that decision is purely based on taste. It seems a bit less "salty" and for 1 pound (453 g) of ingredients being fermented, I usually use around 0.45 ounce or 13 grams instead of the usual 0.38 ounce or 11 grams.

Your salt's origin makes absolutely no difference in technique. I once made a regular sauerkraut with my own sea salt, adding a bit of shredded seaweed to accentuate the sea flavors. For 1 pound (453 g), I used 1½ tablespoons of dried seaweed (3–4 g) and 2½ teaspoons (around 14 g) of my sea salt. I fermented as usual and, once the initial fermentation was complete, stored the sauerkraut in the fridge.

The only difference I've noticed is that ferments using homemade sea salt seem to start a bit faster than usual. I'm not sure why that is—maybe because the lacto bacteria like it so much.

CHAPTER 6

Foraged and Fermented Soups, Pastes, Spreads, and Sauces

There is a whole universe of delicious fermented possibilities with soups, sauces, spreads, and pastes. I love soups. When I was growing up in Belgium, our dinner often consisted of a soup freshly made from our garden vegetables, some bread, and fresh butter from the farm on the other side of the road.

I have only a few examples of fermented soups in this book, and these are really more concepts than recipes; you can research or buy books about raw soups and imagine the infinite number of creative concoctions you could ferment, with or without wild ingredients. I like to feature spring forest flavors, but you'll notice that I still use very common wild edibles found all over North America or Europe—chickweed, oxalis, wild fennel, et cetera. If you are an experienced forager, you can delve much deeper into local flavors by using more regional plants, mushrooms, and even odd savory ingredients such as roasted barks, roots, and so on.

Again, as with all ferments, think of fermented soups or soup stocks as a base to start with. You can add a lot of things before serving them. Try garnishes or fresh ingredients, vinegar, Worcestershire sauce, lemon juice, and many other yummy additives.

Most of my raw soups aren't fermented for very long. I like a happy compromise among freshness, flavors, and probiotics. Usually 2 to 4 days is enough. But you can experiment with aging them, too; it probably would work very well with some fermented soup stocks, which can be used as a savory additive to another existing basic soup stock. A good example in this book is adding a bit of fermented mustard root brine to a hot dashi soup.

Not everything in your soup stock has to be edible per se. For example, I use crushed roots and roasted oak bark as tasty additives. These are simply strained out when I create my final soup.

The fermentation process may change a food's color in some cases. Many of the photos on the following pages were taken when the ferment was very new. Over time the colors may become less vibrant, but the flavors will be accentuated, so it's a bit of a happy compromise.

While working on this book, I had a lot of fun researching and experimenting with sauces and pastes made with wildcrafted ingredients. I learned a lot, too. I fell in love with paste made from wild herbs and spices. It's quite wonderful to be able to experience spring flavors through the year, especially when Southern California turns into a desert later on. If you live in another state, fermentation will allow you to enjoy foods in the winter.

I've made fermented hot sauces for years; they are regular condiments in my classes and workshops, to the delight of my students. I absolutely adore very spicy food, so keep that in mind when you read the recipes. You can substitute milder chili powders or flakes if you want to tone down the amount used. Because a lot of Americans like the taste of vinegar-based hot sauces, I sometimes add vinegar when the fermentation process is done. It's your choice.

Have fun! Create!

FERMENTED WILDER GAZPACHO SOUP

This is a good example of rewilding a classic raw soup. This is a soup my mom would make during the summer with fresh ingredients from our garden. It's very refreshing and extremely tasty if you have high-quality ingredients. Tasteless tomatoes like the ones you buy at the supermarket don't do it justice. The specifics will vary based on the ingredients you have at hand. The base is mostly composed of tomatoes, garlic, and onion, to which you add minced or chopped vegetables and herbs. The contents are blended into a smooth or rough liquid and served with a bit of oil, vinegar, and salt.

Don't get hung up on the particulars of this recipe; keep the base of tomatoes, garlic, and onion, but from there you can definitely use your own local savory (wild) herbs.

Ingredients for a 1-quart jar (946 ml) (around 75 percent full)

½ cucumber (3 ounces / 85 g), peeled and chopped

½ red bell pepper, chopped

4 tomatoes, chopped (around 18 ounces / 510 g)

⅓ small red onion, chopped

¾ ounce (21 g) chickweed, chopped or minced

¾ ounce (21 g) miner's lettuce, chopped or minced

¾ ounce (21 g) wild chervil, chopped or minced

1 teaspoon (0.5 g) Herbes de Provence or Italian Herbs

¼ teaspoon (0.5 g) ground cumin

Salt

Procedure

The total weight was 1 pound 7 ounces (652 g). I used 1½ teaspoons (8 g) of salt. You could use 1 teaspoon (5.5 g) if you want the contents to be less salty. The jar will be around 75 percent full. You can add other spices such as pepper or chili flakes to taste. Process all the ingredients to the texture that you like in a blender and transfer to a clean quart jar.

Use fermentation method 3 (page 28). I like to shake the contents twice daily, close the lid, and burp as necessary. Taste as you go along. I prefer this ferment aged for just 3 to 4 days; if I don't use it right away, I'll place it in the fridge, but it's really best as a young ferment. You can add oil, vinegar, lemon juice, or more spices when serving.

FERMENTED FOREST RAW SOUP STOCK

This is a basic soup stock inspired by my local forest that can be used fresh but also aged quite a bit. I've refined the procedure I use over the last few months. The idea is to use this stock as a base for ingredients added later, a bit like the chicken or vegetable soup stock you can purchase at the store. Think of it as a concept and how you can build on it. You can even start with garden or store-bought ingredients like parsley, cilantro, and so on.

The forest stock is fermented for around 3 days and strained. Then you can add whatever you want: fresh greens, onions, tomatoes, avocado, nuts . . . or even more wild plants. Fresh lime juice, lemon juice, and vinegar are also options. Why not spices? Curry? Savory herbs? Chili powder?

The soup stock ends up a tad sour (in a good way) but loaded with fresh green and earthy flavors. Frankly, I've never been able to achieve this much deliciousness with just store-bought ingredients. It's an awesome source of probiotics, too. I used the same stock after aging it for 3 weeks; it was sourer but worked very nicely.

So yes . . . I love it! There are still some experimentations and tweaking that could be done. I plan to try different versions with what's available next spring. My goal is to make a fermented (wild) vegetable soup stock that can last and taste great for a whole year.

Don't like raw soup? Just cook the stock after fermentation.

Ingredients for a 1-quart jar (946 ml) (around 80 percent full)

4 ounces (113 g) celery, sliced

¾ ounce (21 g) chickweed and bur chervil, chopped

1 garlic clove, peeled

½ ounce (14 g) wild mustard leaves (Mediterranean mustard), chopped or sliced

½ ounce (14 g) juicy forest grass (young foxtail), cut in smaller segments

Tad of oxalis (lemony flavors)

2 cups (473 ml) water

Salt

2 ounces (57 g) mustard roots, crushed (contributes earthy flavors—optional)

Procedure

The total weight was 1½ pounds (680 g), including the water. I used 1 teaspoon (5.5 g) of salt.

1. Place everything but the mustard roots in a blender and make a pasty liquid out of it. Pour into a quart jar. If using, add the crushed roots to the jar as well. Place the top on. This time I used one of my favorite fermentation systems from Kraut Source; it's very effective and super pretty, but if you just use a regular jar, use fermentation method 3 (page 28), shake the contents a couple of times daily, and burp as necessary.

2. Ferment for 2 to 3 days (taste and stop when you like it) or experiment with aging your concoction. Add your fresh ingredients and voilà! Delicious raw probiotic soup. It's great for the environment, too— all the wild plants used are non-native and invasive.

HEARTY FERMENTED RAW WILD SOUP

Super delicious—sweet and sour, spicy, and lemony, with fantastic green flavors from the fresh ingredients added.

Ingredients for a 1-quart jar (946 ml) (around 70 percent full)

4 ounces (113 g) celery, sliced

1½ ounces (42 g) wildcrafted chickweed and bur chervil, chopped

1 garlic clove, peeled

2 cups (473 ml) water

Salt

Procedure

The total weight was 1½ pounds (680 g), including the water. I used 1 teaspoon (5.5 g) of salt.

1. Place everything in a blender and make a pasty liquid out of it. Transfer into a quart jar.
2. Use fermentation method 3 (page 28). I like to shake the contents twice daily, close the lid, and burp as necessary. Taste as you go along.
3. Ferment for 2 to 4 days (taste and stop when you like it) then place in the fridge. I don't age the ferment too much—I tend to use it within a week—but if you're into interesting sour flavors, by all means try aging it longer and see what happens.

The real fun is in creating the final soup. There is a bit of an art to it. If your fermented soup base is quite sour, you can add sweetness to balance it, such as maple syrup or honey. I added a dash of balsamic vinegar (to taste) to the fermented soup stock, then some chickpeas, organic red onion slices, freshly foraged chickweed and chervil, pinyon pine nuts, diced fermented oyster mushroom, and oxalis flower buds.

Salt and pepper to taste and add some smoked chili flakes if you like.

This is truly a delicious raw probiotics soup! Like a hybrid between a soup and a hearty salad.

FERMENTED RAW FOREST SOUP

This is a good example of how you can use the same (or very similar) basic stock and yet make a raw soup that ends up completely different. It's all based on your creativity and, of course, your taste buds.

As a wildcrafter, I find that my ingredients change all the time. The soups become a representation of the seasons. Springtime offers me a lot of fresh edible greens; I may add some wild berries during the summer, pickled or boiled seeds during fall, and mushrooms during winter.

But you can even go further than that and add some of your lacto-fermented ingredients in the mix. The soup pictured includes some fermented wild mushrooms; you could also add fermented stems, leaves, and so on. Maybe some root brine (page 127) could impart spicy flavors to the stock.

This soup stock is pretty much identical to the previous recipe with the addition of crushed mustard roots and bell pepper.

Ingredients for a 1-quart jar (946 ml) (around 70 percent full)

3 ounces (85 g) celery, sliced
1 ounce (28 g) green bell pepper, diced
1 ounce (28 g) wildcrafted chickweed and bur chervil
1 garlic clove, peeled
2 cups (473 ml) water
Salt
1 ounce (28 g) mustard roots, crushed (or you could add some fermented mustard brine from another ferment)

Procedure

The total weight was 1 pound 7 ounces (652 g), including the water. I used 1 teaspoon (5.5 g) of salt.

1. Place everything but the roots in a blender and make a pasty liquid out of it; pour into a jar. Add the crushed roots to the jar as well. Use fermentation method 3 (page 28). I like to shake the contents twice daily, close the lid, and burp as necessary. Taste as you go along.

2. Ferment for 3 to 4 days (taste and stop when you like it), then place in the fridge. I don't age the soup too much—I tend to use it within a week—but if you're into interesting sour flavors, by all means try aging it longer and see what happens. I added a bit of seasoned homemade elderberry wine vinegar before serving.

FERMENTED WILD OYSTER MUSHROOM RAW SOUP

Think of a fermented soup stock as a blank canvas open to creativity. You can add fresh ingredients, but you can also go with a more fermented flavor by aging it. Yes, it's on the sour side, but with the proper savory additions you can take it to the next level. Thinking simple is great, too. You don't always need to add tons of ingredients.

Ingredients for a 1-quart jar (946 ml) (around 70 percent full)

Soup stock, a variation of the Fermented Forest Raw Soup Stock

4 ounces (113 g) celery, sliced

¾ ounce (21 g) chickweed and bur chervil, chopped

1 garlic clove, peeled

½ ounce (14 g) mustard leaves (Mediterranean mustard), chopped or sliced

½ ounce (14 g) juicy forest grass (young foxtail), cut in smaller segments

Tad of oxalis (lemony flavor)

2 cups (473 ml) water

Salt

2 ounces (57 g) mustard roots, crushed (contributes earthy flavors—optional)

Procedure

The total weight was 1 pound 7 ounces (652 g), including the water. I used 1 teaspoon (5.5 g) of salt.

1. Place everything in a blender and make a pasty liquid out of it. Pour the contents into a quart jar.
2. Use fermentation method 3 (page 28). I like to shake the contents twice daily, close the lid, and burp as necessary. Taste as you go along.
3. Ferment for 4 days, then place the soup in the fridge for 6 days. It turns nicely sour, but not excessively.

Thai Soup Variation: Thai cuisine is very much about a good balance of four flavors: sweet, sour, spicy, and salt. Bitter can be part of it, too. To create a Thai version of this soup, I added a bit of sliced Thai chili peppers. (Just a bit—they're really hot!) The sour, sweet, and salty balance was achieved by adding lime juice along with some maple syrup and salt. The basic ratio is 2 parts sugar to 1 part salt. It's not complex; just check the flavors as you go along. Start with the lime juice, have a sip, then add your sugar and salt.

I garnished with some local bur chervil. If your diet is not plant-based, you can add fish sauce, too!

TURKEY TAIL MUSHROOM
FERMENTED SOUP STOCK

Turkey tail mushrooms are used in Chinese medicine for boosting the immune system. When I first experimented with using them in soup, I wasn't sure it would work, but I'm really happy about the final results. At first my soup was quite bitter, but it mellowed up quite nicely after 10 days of fermentation and I think it's quite tasty. If you live on the East Coast, chaga or reishi mushrooms might work, too.

Ingredients for a 1-quart jar (946 ml)
Around 2½ ounces (70 g) dried turkey tail mushrooms
½ gallon (1.9 L) water
3 garlic cloves, crushed
1½ teaspoons (7.5 ml) maple syrup or sugar
1 teaspoon (0.5 g) herb mix such as Herbes de
    Provence or Italian Herbs
2 teaspoons (11 g) salt, to make a 2 percent brine
3 tablespoons (45 ml) Culture Starter

Procedure
1. Place your turkey tail mushrooms and water in a pot, bring to a boil, then reduce the heat and cook at a low simmer for a couple of hours. My stove is eccentric and doesn't do low simmer well, so I add more water if necessary—you want to end up with enough liquid (around 2 cups / 473 ml) and mushrooms for a quart jar. Remove the pot from the heat, place it in cold water, and let the contents cool down to room temperature.
2. Transfer the contents to a quart jar, leaving around 1 inch (2.5 cm) headspace. Add the crushed garlic, maple syrup, herbs, salt, and culture starter. Shake the jar well and let it ferment for 10 days at room temperature. You could also add some other flavorings such as chili powder, bay leaves, or peppercorns—feel free to create.
3. Use fermentation method 2 (page 23). I close the jar and shake it a bit at least twice a day, burping as necessary. When you don't get any more fermentation gases (7 to 10 days), place the jar in the fridge, where it will keep for months. Strain the contents and use the liquid when you're ready.

I really like this soup stock; it's earthy with just the right amount of bitterness. Yes, it's quite salty, but think of it as a base from which you can create. You can add savory ingredients such as vinegar, lemon or lime juice, celery juice, and so on. I also love to add some of my Fermented Spicy Mustard Root brine. It's a great raw soup stock with cooked mushrooms, too.

Wildcrafted Dashi

Dashi is a basic soup stock made usually from fish and kelp, though there are many plant-based recipes as well. The broth is used in traditional soups (miso), sauces, and in Japanese cuisine.

Traditionally, dashi uses bonito flakes (bonito is a fish related to tuna). The fish is dried, fermented, and smoked for several weeks until it finally looks like a piece of dried wood. It is then thinly shaved and ready to use. Every Asian market sells it. The plant-based version uses mushrooms, often shiitake, as a source of umami (savor) instead of fish. Because of the large quantity of mushrooms I can find locally as a forager, I tend to go for the plant-based version.

Why do I like dashi and why is it part of this book?

Because it's an incredible savory broth that works well with the addition of fresh edible greens but also fermented ingredients or brines. To take it to the next level, you can add a bit of miso paste; the result, miso soup, is nearly addictive! If you're a lazy forager, you can simply go to an Asian market and buy some "instant" miso soup, but it's so much better if you do it yourself.

DASHI STOCK

This recipe is my version of dashi using local kelp and dried oyster mushrooms, which are plentiful during wintertime. Based on observation and for the best flavor, I dehydrate my oyster mushrooms in the oven at around 190°F (88°C). I tried dehydrating oyster mushrooms at a very low temperature, but they ended up pretty much tasteless; 190°F seems to be the sweet spot. Try to experiment with other tasty dried mushrooms such as morels or porcini. Once dried, I store them in a closed jar.

Feel free to use fermented wild greens in addition to or in place of kelp in this recipe (see Wild Gundruk on page 117). The flavor is not the same, but the method is very similar. The gundruk version is quite bitter, though—probably an acquired taste.

I've made dashi-type soup stock with mixed seaweed and it works well, too. If you live near the coast and the seawater is pure (not like Los Angeles), use edible seaweeds you can find locally. You can also purchase kelp (kombu) at your local Asian market.

Ingredients for 1 quart (946 ml)
4½ cups (1064 ml) cold water
1½ ounces (42 g) dried oyster or
    shiitake mushrooms
½ ounce (15 g) kelp, cut into 1- or 2-inch
    (2.5–5 cm) pieces

Procedure
Place 4 cups (946 ml) of the cold water and the dried oyster mushrooms in a pot. Leave them to soak for 2 to 4 hours. Meanwhile, soak the kelp pieces in a bowl with the remaining ½ cup (118 ml) cold water for around 20 minutes.

Cover the pot containing the mushrooms and bring to a boil, then simmer for around 15 minutes (30 minutes for shiitake mushrooms). When it's done, add the kelp and soaking water. Bring to a boil, then remove from the heat. After a couple of minutes, strain the soup and reserve the liquid. Transfer the stock to a jar and place in the refrigerator. Use within a week. You can also freeze it.

Miso Soup: Add 1½ to 2¼ teaspoons (8.5–13 g) of miso per cup (236 ml) of hot dashi broth before serving. You can use more if you prefer!

I dehydrate my wildcrafted oyster mushrooms at 190°F, then store them in a jar for later use.

To make plant-based dashi stock, first soak the mushrooms for 2 to 4 hours in a pot.

Meanwhile, soak the kelp pieces in ½ cup of cold water for around 20 minutes.

Cover the pot and bring the contents to a boil, then simmer for around 15 minutes (30 minutes for shiitake mushrooms). When it's done, add the kelp and water. Bring to a boil, then remove from the heat.

After a couple of minutes, strain the soup and reserve the liquid.

MISO AND FERMENTED MUSTARD ROOT SOUP

This is a wonderful comfort soup, and one of my favorite uses for the brine from Fermented Spicy Mustard Roots. You have a lot of freedom with this basic recipe. You can use more brine if you want, or a lesser amount. You can also increase the amount of miso if you like a very salty soup.

It's up to you how many wild greens you add to the soup, as well as how you garnish it (wildflowers are nice). I've made this soup with young mustard leaves, chickweed, miner's lettuce, bur chervil, lamb's-quarter, and many other wildcrafted ingredients.

Ingredients for 1 serving
1 cup (236 ml) Dashi Stock
½ tablespoon (8.5 g) miso (optional)
¼ cup (59 ml) Fermented Spicy Mustard
   Root brine
1 green onion, sliced
Small amount of fresh wild greens

Procedure
1. Bring the dashi stock to a boil and add the miso (if you're using it). Stir well to dilute the miso paste, remove the pan from the heat, and add the brine.
2. Place all your fresh ingredients in a soup bowl, then pour in the hot soup stock. Just before serving, garnish with a few edible wildflowers or a bit more of your wild greens, such as chickweed or wild chervil.

The miso is truly optional, by the way. You can make a similar soup by just adding the mustard root brine to the basic dashi stock.

FERMENTED MUSTARD LEAF SAUCE

This sauce uses wild Mediterranean mustard leaves and mallow. It's very similar to an Indian saag sauce, but the spinach is replaced by foraged herbs. The mustard leaves are a tad bitter; you can add a bit more maple syrup if you want.

It's a simple sauce that's good for the environment, too, since our local mustard is very invasive.

The photo shows the sauce served with foraged oyster mushrooms cooked in homemade mugwort beer, garlic, acorn miso, and a homemade herbs blend with French herbs and local sages. But you can just use your favorite sautéed mushroom recipe.

Ingredients for a 1-quart jar (946 ml)

10 ounces (283 g) wild greens (mustard leaves, mallow, and the like)

1–2 tablespoons (15–30 ml) olive oil

1 red onion, diced

2 bell peppers, diced (or you could use 2 tomatoes)

4–8 garlic cloves, minced, or 1–2 tablespoons (6–12 g) garlic powder

½ cup (118 ml) water

1 teaspoon (2 g) Curry Blend (double the amount if you like curry flavors)

1½ teaspoons (8 g) salt

Red pepper flakes to taste (optional)

½ cup (118 ml) coconut milk

¼ cup (59 ml) Culture Starter

2 teaspoons maple syrup

Procedure

1. Set a pot of water to boil. Place the wild greens in the boiling water for 3 to 5 minutes; remove and place in cold water. Take them out and squeeze the water out with your hand. Cut the greens into pieces.
2. Heat the olive oil in a pan and sauté the onion first (I like to brown them a bit), then add the bell peppers, garlic, and wild greens. Stir the ingredients, then pour in the water and add all the spices and salt. (You could also substitute ½ cup [118 ml] coconut milk for the water.) Cover and cook at medium heat for 10 to 15 minutes until the water is nearly evaporated. Add the coconut milk.
3. Transfer everything into a blender and make a smooth paste out of it. Remove from the blender, place in a bowl, and let it cool. To speed up the cooling process you can place the bowl in cold water. Once it's cooled, add the culture starter and maple syrup.
4. Place the sauce into a quart jar (should be quite full).
5. Use fermentation method 3 (page 28). I close the lid, shake or stir the contents in the jar a couple of times daily, and burp as necessary.

The sauce is usually fermented for 3 to 4 days just to give it a tad of sourness. It ends up nicely sour, with a good balance of bitter and sweet, spicy, and very good "green" flavors. I haven't experimented with aging it more than a few days.

FERMENTED WILD GREENS PESTO

Traditionally, a pesto is an Italian sauce made of crushed herbs (typically basil), pine nuts, garlic, and Parmesan or sheep's-milk cheese blended with olive oil. It's often served with pasta. Some versions include vinegar or lemon juice.

You can actually make pesto with all kinds of savory wild plants, so this basic recipe can be adapted for any of your local savory wild greens. I used local common weeds such as wild chervil, chickweed, and fennel, but if you live farther east, you could use garlic mustard, ramp leaves, and so on. And of course, you can mix in regular ingredients, such as basil and parsley.

Making pesto sauces is very common with foragers; it's a great way to enjoy the fresh flavors wild edibles can provide. But if you are interested in the probiotics or the usual tangy accents provided by fermentation, there are a lot of interesting experiments you can do. I had no luck with a stinging nettles pesto, but it's possible to add a small portion of nettles to your pesto, like 10 percent.

I use two steps to make the pesto. The first is fermentation.

Ingredients for a ½-pint jar (236 ml)

2½ cups (591 ml) minced savory wild greens, packed (I used minced chickweed, chervil, and a tad of fennel; my mix was probably 60 percent chervil)

2 ounces (57 g) pine nuts or walnuts

3–4 garlic cloves, peeled and minced

3 tablespoons (44 ml) Culture Starter

Procedure

1. You can use a blender to process the ingredients, but I prefer my Mexican molcajete (stone grinder). The texture is just too smooth with a Vitamix, and I have more control grinding by hand. When you're satisfied with the texture of the paste, transfer the pesto to your jar and pack the paste inside, leaving no air pockets if possible.
2. Use fermentation method 4 (page 32). Close the lid and stir the ferment a couple of times a day until the fermentation gases subside, usually in 7 to 10 days. You'll need to burp as necessary. When done, store the jar in the fridge. It's totally okay to eat it after 4 or 5 days if you want.

Once the pesto is fermented to your liking, feel free to add more flavorful ingredients before you serve it, but it's not a must. You could try:

- 4–6 tablespoons (12–18 g) nutritional yeast or Parmesan cheese
- ¼–½ cup (59–118 ml) olive oil
- Some chili flakes (why not?)

If your diet is plant-based, the nutritional yeast will give you the "cheesy" flavors associated with a traditional pesto, but again, it's not a must. Taste and decide for yourself. A bit of vinegar, or lemon or lime juice, can be welcome, too.

BRINE SAUCES

With a few flavorful additions—or even none at all—fermented brines can make delicious sauces. I use them all the time. For a simple salad dressing, I may add some apple cider vinegar to a kimchi-like brine, and I'm done. Even the brine of basic fermentation method 1 (page 16) can be used to make a very tasty dressing. Here are a couple of examples.

Spicy Mustard Root Brine Sauce

Ingredients for ¼ cup (59 ml)

3 tablespoons (44 ml) Spicy Mustard Root brine

1 tablespoon (15 ml) balsamic vinegar

½ teaspoon (1 g) Curry Blend or spice mix of your choice (completely optional if your brine was highly flavored in the first place)

Procedure

Mix all the sauce ingredients. Done! That was easy.

Sautéed Cauliflower Florets in Spicy Mustard Root Brine Sauce.

Sautéed Cauliflower Florets in Spicy Mustard Root Brine Sauce

When I give a wild food walk, I always serve all kinds of little snacks at the end. When I offered this humble dish, the participants could not get enough. Sometimes I must be reminded that the best things can be super simple.

It's a very easy dish, but you can't stop eating it. It would even work with raw florets if you're into raw food.

Pan-sear cauliflower florets in avocado oil for 6 to 8 minutes (you can use olive oil, too), stirring and churning the florets every couple of minutes until they're roasted on both sides. There is no need to add salt as the brine is already salty.

Gently pour the sauce into a soup plate or a bowl, then add the florets and serve.

Roasted Fermented Oyster Mushrooms, wild fennel, and radish flowers served with Sauerkraut Brine Wasabi Sauce.

Sauerkraut Brine Wasabi Sauce

Ingredients for ½ cup (118 ml)

2½ tablespoons (37 ml) avocado oil

2½ tablespoons (37 ml) sauerkraut brine

1 teaspoon (1.5 g) freshly grated gingerroot

½ tablespoon (3 g) wasabi
   (more if you like it spicy)

2 tablespoons (30 ml) lemon or lime juice

Procedure

Whisk everything together and transfer the sauce into a small dish or bowl. Add Roasted Fermented Oyster Mushrooms and a bit of minced fennel fronds for decoration and flavor. If you don't have fennel, dill would work quite well, too. I added a few wild radish flowers for aesthetics.

Pastes

Springtime offers an abundance of delicious and tender wild greens such as chickweed, miner's lettuce, wild chervil, tender young grass (foxtail), watercress, bitter cress, and countless others. Eating a freshly foraged salad is truly an epiphany of green flavors in your mouth: earthy, a punch of chlorophyll, grassy, the perfect balance of sweet and bitter. You cannot even approach those flavors with ingredients purchased at the store. And they can be preserved for use year-round in the form of pastes.

In North America and Europe, it's uncommon to use pastes or even find them in the supermarket. But elsewhere in the world, they're quite common—in Mexico, for example, you'll find a mind-boggling amount of mole. As you'll see in the following recipes, the concept is simple: Process tasty herbs in a blender, then add spices to create a highly savory paste. Fermenting it takes it to the next level and helps preserve it for months.

I used to make savory salted herb pastes and freeze them as soup stock, but fermentation became the key to unlocking a new layer of umami qualities. It's easy to experiment with edible plants that you can find locally; with very few exceptions, if they taste good in the first place, fermenting will work. With experience, you can invent some very complex blends that represent your wild terroir.

I use fermented pastes as a condiment or as a base for delicious soups. Adding a small amount on top of an egg toast is heavenly. You can make your paste very spicy if you add more chili powder. (From experience, I advise using stinging nettles sparingly and not as the main ingredient.) Note that you're not stuck with wild ingredients. You can make some very tasty pastes with herbs from your garden or purchased at the store—parsley, cilantro, arugula (bitter), basil, chives, and so on.

SPICY FOREST PASTE

I usually serve this paste on top of my acorn and wild seeds crackers, but it will work nicely on eggs, grilled steaks, and even fish. If your diet is plant-based, I would spread the paste on vegan pizza or simply use it as a savory side condiment.

Ingredients for a ½-pint jar (236 ml)

2 large jalapeño peppers, seeds removed, cut into large pieces

2½ cups (75 g) minced forest herbs (I use 60 percent chickweed, 20 percent chervil, 10 percent miner's lettuce, 10 percent others)

1 cup (30 g) lemon basil

1 cup (30 g) cilantro

7 garlic cloves, peeled

2 tablespoons (30 ml) Culture Starter

4½ tablespoons (27 g) paprika

2 tablespoons (15 g) Korean chili flakes

¾ teaspoon (2 g) ground coriander

1 teaspoon (2.5 g) chile morita or spicy chili flakes

¾ teaspoon (1 g) ground cumin

2 teaspoons (4 g) ginger powder
or 1 tablespoon (5 g) freshly grated gingerroot

1 teaspoon (3 g) garlic powder

½ teaspoon (1.5 g) ground black peppercorns

1 teaspoon (2 g) turmeric

Salt

Procedure

The total weight was around 8 ounces (227 g). I used 1 teaspoon (5.5 g) of salt.

Process the jalapeños, forst herbs, lemon basil, cilantro, garlic, and starter in a blender until you get a smooth paste. Place this in a bowl, and add the spices, stirring to combine. Mix the salt with the paste and transfer to a jar.

Use fermentation method 4 (page 32). Close the lid and stir the ferment a couple of times daily until the fermentation gases subside, usually 7 to 10 days. You'll need to burp as necessary. When done, store the jar in the fridge. I like to age this kind of ferment for at least a month before enjoying it.

FERMENTED FOREST FLOOR PASTE

Ingredients for a 1-pint jar (475 ml)

1 cup (30 g) minced chervil

½ cup (15 g) minced chickweed

¼ cup (8 g) minced nettle leaves

¼ cup (8 g) minced miner's lettuce

1¼ small red onions, minced

1 tablespoon (15 g) freshly grated gingerroot

3 garlic cloves, finely minced

1 green Thai chili, finely sliced
   (or fresh spicy green pepper)

1 teaspoon (2.5 g) chile morita
   (smoked dried jalapeño flakes) or
   regular spicy chili flakes

1½ teaspoons (9 g) salt
   (or more to taste)

Procedure

1. You can make the paste a bit rough by mincing the ingredients by hand, or you can make it very smooth using a blender such as a Vitamix. Personally, I like my paste to have some texture.

   If you don't use a blender, place all the ingredients in a bowl and, using clean fingers, mix/squeeze them together for a minute or so. It should end up quite juicy. Transfer into a pint jar.

2. Use fermentation method 4 (page 33). You'll need to stir the contents twice a day with a clean fork or spoon. There's no need for Culture Starter (page 44) with this recipe, but you can add a couple of tablespoons (30 ml) if you want; the contents will become acidic quite quickly, thus ensuring food safety. I close the lid, stir daily, and burp as necessary. If you experiment with different ingredients and the fermentation progress is not obvious—which can be an issue with pastes—checking the pH is wise. If it measures 4 or lower, it's acidic enough.

3. Ferment the paste at room temperature for 2 weeks, then transfer the jar to the fridge for aging. It will last a long time; I'm still enjoying a paste that I made 6 months ago, and I think the flavors are better after aging.

BASIC FERMENTED FOREST FLOOR SOUP STOCK

I like to use Fermented Forest Floor Paste as a condiment, but it really shines as a soup base. This dish will rival a good miso soup in its own unique way, and you can make it with local lacto bacteria instead of koji.

Ingredients for 1 serving

¾–1 tablespoon (12–15 g) Fermented Forest Floor Paste
1 tablespoon (15 ml) soy sauce (more if you like salty flavor)
1 teaspoon (3 g) garlic powder
1 cup (236 ml) water

Procedure

Place the paste, soy sauce, and garlic in a soup bowl, then bring the water to a boil and pour it into the bowl. Mix briefly with a spoon and let it rest for 3 to 4 minutes. I like to set a small plate on top of the bowl to keep it hot.

But don't stop there! Before you pour the hot water into the bowl, you can add all kinds of flavors or garnishes—wild or store-bought—such as mushrooms, seaweed, sliced green or red onions, tofu, and even more spices. The possibilities are really infinite. You can also opt to add fresh herbs just before serving.

CHICKWEED (OR CHERVIL) SPICY PASTE

This is a basic paste that should work with many of your local savory wild edibles such as chickweed, miner's lettuce, wild chervil, and so on. You could also use garden or store-bought ingredients such as parsley and cilantro. The only wild herb I would not use is stinging nettle. I haven't had success with that plant in large quantities; the smell and taste are quite rancid.

Ingredients for a ½-pint jar (236 ml) (90 percent full)

2 cups (60 g) chickweed or similar wild greens such as chervil, garlic mustard and the like

3 tablespoons (18 g) smoked paprika

1 teaspoon (2.5 g) chile morita or spicy chili flakes

4 garlic cloves, peeled

1 tablespoon (6 g) ginger powder *or* 3 tablespoons (15 g) freshly grated gingerroot

1 small red bell pepper (around 4 ounces or 113 g)

½ California or regular bay leaf (optional)

2 tablespoons (15 g) mild chili flakes (I use Korean chili flakes)

¼ cup (59 ml) Culture Starter

2 teaspoons (10 ml) maple syrup

Salt

Procedure

The total weight was around 8 ounces (226 g). I used 1¾ teaspoons (9 g) of salt. It's a salty sauce.

Place all the ingredients in a blender and make a rough paste. Transfer to a jar. Use fermentation method 4 (page 32). I close the lid and stir the contents twice a day with a clean fork or spoon, burping as necessary, although the fermentation gases should not be excessive.

I usually ferment the paste at room temperature for 10 days then transfer the jar to the fridge for aging. It will last a long time; I'm still enjoying the paste that I made 6 months ago, and I think the flavors are better after at least a month of fermentation.

CALITOPIAN PASTE

This fermented paste was inspired by a local Ethiopian restaurant. I go there around once a month, and I'm so in love with their spicy paste that I had to re-create it with my local wild plants. Smear this paste on a flatbread and add fresh or cooked ingredients on top—it's quite delicious!

Ingredients for a ½-pint jar (236 ml)

2 large jalapeño peppers, seeds removed, cut into large pieces

2½ cups (75 g) forest floor greens (I use 60 percent chickweed, 20 percent chervil, 10 percent miner's lettuce, and 10 percent others: oxalis, sow thistle, and the like)

1 cup (30 g) lemon basil

1 cup (30 g) cilantro

7 garlic cloves, peeled

2½ teaspoons (5 g) ginger powder

½ teaspoon (1 g) ground coriander

¼ teaspoon (0.5 g) ground nutmeg

½ California bay leaf or 1 regular bay leaf, ground

⅛ teaspoon (0.25 g) ground cloves

¼ teaspoon (0.5 g) ground cinnamon

⅛ teaspoon (0.25 g) ground allspice

½ teaspoon (1.5 g) ground black peppercorns

3½ tablespoons (26 g) paprika

2 teaspoons (5 g) Korean chili powder

2 teaspoons (6 g) chipotle powder or chile morita powder

Salt

1 tablespoon (15 ml) Culture Starter

Procedure

The total weight was around 8 ounces (227 g). I used 1 teaspoon (5.5 g) of salt.

Process the jalapeños, greens, lemon basil, cilantro, and garlic in a blender until you get a smooth paste. You should end up with a bit less than 1 cup of paste. Place this in a bowl, and add the spices and culture starter, stirring to combine. Mix the salt with the paste and transfer to a jar. Use fermentation method 4 (page 32). Close the lid and stir the ferment a couple of times daily until the fermentation gases subside, usually 7 to 10 days. You'll need to burp as necessary. When done, store the jar in the fridge. I like to age this kind of ferment for at least a month before enjoying it.

DANDHARISSA
(FERMENTED DANDELION HARISSA)

Harissa is a Maghrebi hot chili pepper paste. I think originally it's from Tunisia, but it's used widely in Morocco and Algeria as well. Growing up in Belgium, I had many Moroccan friends, and I fell in love with the sauce. Somehow the harissa sauces I've had in America are sweeter than the ones I remember in Europe, maybe because of the chili peppers used locally. Recently I found a bunch of dandelions and had my aha moment: Why not make a fermented harissa and add some dandelion greens for bitterness?

Ingredients for a 1-quart jar (946 ml) (a bit more than 80 percent full)

12 large dried red chilies (I used 8 dried ancho and 4 California chilies), pan-roasted
5 ounces (141 g) dandelion green tops, chopped
3 large bell peppers (2 of them roasted over a flame), chopped
12 garlic cloves, peeled
1 teaspoon (3 g) fennel seeds (use regular fennel seeds if you don't have wild fennel in your area)
1½ teaspoons (3 g) ginger powder
1 teaspoon (2 g) ground cumin
2 teaspoons (2.5 g) coriander seeds, ground
2 teaspoons (11g) sugar or honey
1½ teaspoons (1 g) dried mint
1½ tablespoons (22 ml) lemon juice
2 teaspoons (5 g) chili flakes
6 tablespoons (90 ml) Culture Starter
Salt

Procedure

The total weight was around 1 pound 10 ounces (737 g). I used 3½ teaspoons (20 g) of salt.

1. Process all the ingredients in a blender until you get a paste. The texture can be rough or smooth.
2. Use fermentation method 4 (page 32). I close the lid and, using a clean fork or spoon, stir the contents twice a day and burp as necessary, although the fermentation gases should not be excessive.
3. Ferment the paste at room temperature for 10 days, then transfer the jar to the fridge for aging. It will last a long time and is best when aged for at least a couple of months.

Fermented Wilder Hot Sauces

The hot sauces that you purchase at the store are vinegar-based and preserved using a method called water bath canning; bottles are usually used instead of jars. The principle is simple: By adding vinegar you make the sauce very acidic, which prevents harmful bacteria such as the ones that cause botulism to thrive in that low-oxygen environment and produce toxins. By placing the hot sauce bottles in boiling water for a specific amount of time, you also kill anything that's alive (pasteurization) and stabilize the flavors.

From a commercial perspective, it makes sense. If you buy a specific brand of hot sauce, you expect that sauce to taste the same year after year. Although rare, some commercial sauces such as Tabasco are fermented for 3 years (or more) in white oak barrels, after which vinegar is added. The sauce is then bottled and canned. Through the process of pasteurization, you make the sauce very safe to consume, but you also kill any beneficial probiotics. In the modern world of food preservation, it often seems that safe food is synonymous with dead food. The aisles of our local supermarket are lined with preserves in which everything has been boiled, salted, dehydrated, and chemically processed to death.

Fermenting your hot sauce offers a different perspective. Not only can the sauces rival similar products preserved with vinegar in terms of flavors, but they also keep alive the probiotics, which contribute to the diversity of your gut flora and your health in general. (Consuming dead food can't do this.)

The beauty of fermentation is also related to the evolution of flavors, especially when you're dealing with wild edibles. To a large degree, your fermented creations will mimic nature, evolving and maturing over time. This isn't limited to lacto-fermentation; a good wine or an authentic balsamic vinegar can become exceptional through the process of aging. Koji fermentation is another good example: Some soy sauces can be fermented for years before consumption, and their delicious complexity cannot be compared to what you normally find commercially.

Many of my wildcrafted fermented hot sauces benefit tremendously from aging. In some cases the young sauces are simply too hot to be edible, but with the passage of time the taste will mellow, and the flavors of the ingredients will blend beautifully. This is particularly true of savory but hot peppers such as habaneros.

The variety of fermented sauces you can create is mind-boggling and so are the savory wild ingredients you can use. They range from simple flavorful (wild) herbs and spices to unusual additions including roasted barks, dehydrated aromatic stems, toasted seeds, spicy or pungent roots, and wild fruits and berries.

I usually use a ratio of around 80 percent pepper mash and 20 percent wildcrafted additives. It's not a rule set in stone by any means, but things seem to work better that way for me. As always, feel free to experiment.

The recipes that follow are very basic, just enough to make you think about possibilities. It's up to you to research and create with your own terroir so you can make sauces that are a true representation of a place and time.

Can you add vinegar at the end? Sometimes I do. I have a whole collection of raw vinegars made with my wildcrafted wines, beers, and other boozy concoctions.

In the end, all you want is something that you love or that others will enjoy. Have fun!

WILDLY CRUEL HOT SAUCE

This is a super-simple hot sauce that I call Wildly Cruel because while you're going to love it, it will make you cry—and yet you can't stop loving it so you go back and taste it again. It's a vicious circle. The young ferment is almost too punishing to taste, but it will mellow over time. Wild food is used as a flavor accent; you don't need that much, but you can experiment, too. I've used lamb's-quarter, chickweed, chervil, dandelion, various mustards, and countless other wild edible greens, often a mix of them. Sometimes I even add a bit of roasted oak bark. I'm in love with habaneros; you can substitute other peppers, but the sauce just won't be as abusive.

Ingredients for a 1-quart jar (946 ml)

13 ounces (369 g) fresh habaneros

15 garlic cloves, peeled

2½ ounces (71 g) mixed wild edible greens

½ cup (118 ml) water

5 tablespoons (37.5 g) chili powder
(I use Korean chili powder)

2 tablespoons Culture Starter

Salt

Procedure

The total weight, including water, was around 1½ pounds (680 g). I used 5½ teaspoons (30 g) of salt, pretty much a 5 percent brine.

The wild edible greens you use will give you different savory accents. If you like a bit of bitterness in your hot sauce, you could use dandelion; for some earthy green notes, use chickweed.

Place all the ingredients in a blender and make a paste. Use fermentation method 4 (page 32). I close the lid and, twice daily, either shake the jar or unscrew the lid, stir the contents, and close the lid again. Burp as necessary. When the initial fermentation is complete, after around 10 days, I may stir or shake the contents once a week for another 2 weeks, then stop. I like to ferment this sauce at room temperature for at least 1 month, then place it in the fridge for further aging.

HABANERO AND SMOKED
JALAPEÑO "WILD" HOT SAUCE

This is a basic recipe that leaves *a lot* of room for experimentation. I started to make fermented hot sauces like this one in 2014 by mixing habaneros with wild greens, and over the years I've increased the number of habaneros quite substantially. The sauce is way too hot if you try to use it young; it needs to be aged for at least 1 month. My favorite one was aged for a month at room temperature, then 3 months in the fridge. The heat will mellow considerably over time, but this sauce is still challenging for those who have a shy palate. You're pretty much looking at a ratio of 75 to 80 percent habaneros and various chili powders to 20 percent wild edibles and 5 percent garlic.

The recipe changes based on the season, and thus the flavors will be a representation of a specific time and place. In springtime it's more fresh and green tasting. Summer is fruitier due to the possible addition of fruit juices and berries. Fall and winter have a bitter edge. But if you keep the ratio, I don't think you can go wrong. If the sauce is too hot for you, substitute milder peppers for some of the habaneros.

Ingredients for a 1-quart jar (946 ml) (a bit more than 70 percent full)

10 ounces (283 g) fresh habaneros

3 ounces (85 g) bell peppers

1 ounce (28 g) carrots

3 ounces (85 g) wild greens
(watercress, dandelion, mustard,
curly dock, and the like)

Salt

2 tablespoons (15 g) chile morita powder
(smoked jalapeño) or spicy chili flakes

3 tablespoons (23 g) mild Korean chili flakes
or (15 g) smoked paprika

¾ cup (177 ml) water or juice
(I use prickly pear juice)

10–25 garlic cloves, peeled
(I love garlic, so I use a lot)

Procedure

The total weight for the ingredients was around 1 pound 10 ounces (737 g). I used 1 tablespoon plus 2 teaspoons of salt (around 27 g). It's a lot of salt, but it works well with habaneros. You can try the recipe with a bit less salt if you want, say 1 tablespoon plus 1 teaspoon (around 22 g), adding more later on if necessary.

1. Roughly chop the habaneros, bell peppers, carrots, and wild edibles, place them in a bowl, and sprinkle with the salt. Next add the smoked chili morita and other chili powders you're using. Korean chili and smoked paprika are very mild but give a nice red color to the sauce. Massage everything for a couple of minutes (wearing gloves), then pour it into your blender. Add the water and garlic, then make a paste. (This can be smooth or chunky; I like it a bit chunky.)

2. Use fermentation method 3 (page 28). Transfer everything into a quart jar and screw the lid on, but not too tight. Two or three times daily, close the lid tight and shake the jar for a few seconds or stir the contents inside with a clean spoon (so you don't get mold on top). You can also keep the lid closed tight at all times and burp the jar as necessary. Because I like to work closely with my ferments, the latter is my favorite method. Still, shake (or stir) two or three times daily after burping.
3. Ferment the jar at room temperature. After a couple of weeks, you can close the lid tight and just shake/ stir it once a week or so. I don't think you'll need to burp it again, but monitor the pressure just in case. After a month, the contents inside will be very acidic, and I stop shaking or stirring it. Place the jar in the fridge for further aging.

If you like vinegar-based hot sauces, feel free to add vinegar after a couple of months (do it by taste) or when serving. Note that some people ferment whole peppers and other ingredients first, then blend everything together when the initial fermentation is complete. I prefer to blend the contents from the start, which gives me more control over texture and thickness.

Two gallons (7.5 L) of habanero and wild edible hot sauce after 3 months of fermentation.

ROOTS, BARK, AND STEMS
HOT SAUCE

This is a recipe you'll want to adapt to your local terroir; you may not have all the ingredients available to you (unless you live in Southern California). Think of it as a model. I picked up the oak bark from a large fallen branch. Inspect it to make sure there is no fungus or weird stuff on it; also, it shouldn't be too old. Once you get it home, clean it, then pasteurize it in the oven at 200°F (94°C) for 15 minutes. I break it in small pieces, around ½ by 1 inch (1.3 by 2.5 cm), and roast them with a kitchen torch, but you probably could use your stovetop, too.

Ingredients for a 1-quart jar (946 ml)

5 ounces (142 g) fresh habaneros

2 cups (473 ml) water

6 garlic cloves, peeled

½ California bay leaf (or 1 regular bay leaf)

1 tablespoon (7.5 g) spicy chili powder
   or flakes (I use chile morita)

2 tablespoons (15 g) Korean chili flakes
   or mild chili flakes

2 tablespoons (30 ml) Culture Starter

1 tablespoon (6 g) wild pequin chili peppers
   or spicy chili flakes

A bit more than 1 tablespoon (18 g) salt

4 ounces (113 g) wild mustard roots
   (I used Mediterranean mustard)

2 dehydrated mugwort stems
   (5 inches / 12.7 cm tall)

2 dehydrated California sagebrush stems
   (5 inches / 12.7 cm tall)

3 pieces of oak bark, roasted

Procedure

1. First clean the habaneros, remove the stems, and coarsely chop, then place them in your blender. Add the water, garlic, bay leaf, chili powder, chili flakes, culture starter, pequin peppers, and salt. Blend until you get the consistency you like. Cut and lightly crush the mustard roots using a stone (a stone grinder works well) or hammer. Transfer all those ingredients into a quart jar and finally add the aromatic stems and roasted bark pieces.

2. Use fermentation method 5 (page 33). I simply close the jar and shake the contents a couple of times daily, burping as necessary. When the initial fermentation is complete, after around 10 days, I may shake the contents once a week for another 2 weeks, then stop and place in the fridge to age.

WATERCRESS-JALAPEÑO
FERMENTED HOT SAUCE

I use wild watercress for this simple recipe, but you can substitute other wild or store-bought ingredients such as parsley, chervil, or chickweed. Though I haven't tried it, I think cilantro would also be terrific. Fermented watercress can be an acquired taste—maybe ferment a pint jar first and see if you like it.

Ingredients for a 1-quart jar (946 ml)

14 ounces (397 g) jalapeños, chopped
(you can leave the seeds if you want,
which will make the ferment spicier)
2 ounces (57 g) watercress, chopped
2 teaspoons (3.5 g) ginger powder
2 tablespoons (30 ml) Culture Starter
Salt
1 cup (236 ml) water
1 tablespoon (8 g) chopped red onion
25 garlic cloves, peeled

Seasoned Lime Juice

Add 1½ tablespoons (22 ml) of maple syrup and 1 teaspoon (5.5 g) of salt to ¼ cup (59 ml) of fresh lime juice. Stir well. Add Seasoned Lime Juice to hot sauce at a ratio of 2 parts hot sauce to 1 part lime juice.

Procedure

The total weight, including water, was around 1 pound 11 ounces (0.8 g). I used 1 tablespoon (17 g) of salt.

1. Place the jalapeños and watercress in a bowl, then add the ginger, culture starter, and salt. Massage everything for a couple of minutes (with gloves), then pour it into your food processor or blender. Add the water, onion, and garlic and make a paste. This can be smooth or chunky; I like it a bit chunky.

2. Transfer the contents to a quart jar and use fermentation method 3 (page 28). These days, I just close the lid tight, shake the contents a couple of times daily, and burp the jar as necessary. Because I like to work closely with my ferments, it's my favorite method. When the initial fermentation is complete, after around 10 days, I may stir or shake the contents once a week for another 2 weeks, then stop. I like to ferment this sauce at room temperature for at least 1 month, then place it in the fridge. The sauce once aged is quite sour. If it's too much for you, you can add some Seasoned Lime Juice before serving.

ROASTED OAK BARK HOT SAUCE

I like my sauce to have a bit of smoky flavor, which roasted oak bark imparts; oak can also provide a lot of complexity. It's an interesting way to explore true local flavors. I use bark from fallen coast live oak branches. Although the bark is quite bitter, it doesn't infuse too much bitterness into the ferment—more a hint. The smoky flavors will infuse well.

Ingredients for a 1-pint jar (475 ml)

6 ounces (170 g) fresh habaneros
9 garlic cloves, peeled
½ cup (118 ml) water
3 tablespoons (25 g) mild chili powder
    or flakes (I use Korean chili powder)
2 tablespoons (30 ml) Culture Starter
1 tablespoon (17 g) salt
4–5 pieces of roasted oak bark
    (see instructions on page 172),
      each around 1 inch (2.5 cm) square

Procedure

1. Place everything (except the oak bark) into a blender and make a paste. Transfer to a jar and add the oak chunks.
2. Use fermentation method 3 (page 28). I close the lid. Twice daily, I'll either shake the jar or unscrew the lid, stir the contents, and close the lid again. Burp as necessary.

This sauce is too hot to sample as a young ferment, but it will mellow over time, though it may still make you cry when you eat it. But those are tears of joy! I think . . . right?

CHAPTER 7

Wilder Cheeses

The year 2018 was an interesting one for me. For health reasons and on the advice of my doctor, I decided to embrace a mostly plant-based diet. Having a lot of knowledge about plants probably made the overnight transition quite easy. Instead of complaining, I took it as an opportunity to be more creative.

Interestingly, not eating meat wasn't an issue, but one of the foods I definitely craved was cheese. I grew up in Europe, where cheeses are a fundamental part of the cuisine and the variety that's available is absolutely mind-boggling. You truly can't compare artisanal cheeses to what you find in a regular American supermarket; the flavors and scents can range from subtle and grassy to extremely pungent. Some cheeses are even described as having barnyard qualities, and if you have ever visited a barn filled with animals, you get the idea. I was missing a huge range of flavors and savory qualities.

Fermented Plant-Based Cheeses

It didn't take me long to embark on a search for plant-based cheeses that would satisfy my craving. Within a couple of weeks, I tasted every single "vegan" cheese available at local stores, which ended up in a huge disappointment. None even came close to the flavors of a dairy-based cheese.

But in my determination and desperation, I decided to look for artisanal plant-based cheeses and see if I could find something better. After a quick search online, I found two local artisan cheese producers who offered tasting platters. I visited both on the same day. Most of the cheeses were made from common nut milks and pastes, such as cashew, almond, and macadamia. I'll be honest, they were enjoyable and much better than what I had purchased at local stores, but, in my opinion, still very far from dairy-based cheeses. The flavors were quite mild and the scent practically nonexistent. Not enough to satisfy my deep craving, but the tasting gave me some hope that making plant-based cheeses that could rival dairy versions might be possible.

My quest became an obsession! Thanks to the internet, I was able to do a lot of research online and found a few pioneers that were really pushing the envelope by fermenting vegan cheeses with the same bacteria and mold used for regular versions. It seemed that the secret was to use exactly the same techniques for regular and plant-based cheeses. Fermentation was the secret.

I probably spent a whole month making cheese daily. I made cashew Camembert, walnut blue cheese, and all sorts of fermented concoctions with special mold and bacteria purchased online. Guess what? It worked! My craving was finally satisfied.

Now, if you are a dairy-based-cheese lover, the idea of making plant-based cheeses can be provoking. In fact, when I post some of my cheeses on social media, I always have a couple of comments about the fact that those are not "real" cheeses. I think the controversy is a bit silly and unnecessary.

In fact, Merriam-Webster defines *cheese* as:

1. a: a food consisting of the coagulated, compressed, and usually ripened curd of milk separated from the whey
    b: an often cylindrical cake of this food
2: something resembling cheese in shape or consistency

Definition number 2 applies to fermented plant-based cheese just as it does to quince cheese, medlar cheese, or headcheese. Nondairy cheeses can be a welcome addition to the diets of people who are looking for alternatives. Frankly, I've stopped comparing them to dairy cheeses. They are beautiful and delicious in their own way.

FERMENTING WILD AND REGULAR PLANT-BASED CHEESES

The basic method I use to make my "wild" fermented cheeses is quite straightforward. First, I soak my ingredients (seeds and nuts) for at least 8 hours; then I use my blender (Vitamix) to make a thick paste. It's easier said than done; you need to add some liquid, or else the paste is so compact that your blender won't be able to do it or will overheat. It's a delicate balance to achieve. Too much liquid and you may have difficulties in making a hard cheese later on, but not enough and your blender can't do the job. The goal is to use just enough to make a thick, compact paste. Note that a regular blender usually isn't strong enough to turn seeds and nuts into a paste; we'll review possible economical options later.

To start up the fermentation, instead of adding regular water to the blender, I'll use the liquid of a Culture Starter (page 44). Most of the time I create a starter by making a quick sauerkraut a few days before, then add the juice while blending the paste in the Vitamix. This introduces the lacto bacteria that will initiate the fermentation process and intensify the flavor and tanginess of your cheese through aging.

Can you use the brine of an older sauerkraut? I'm not sure. I make a point of using the brine of a young ferment while it's very active, bubbling, and loaded with live bacteria. Once the fermentation slows down and stops producing gases, I stop using it.

To make the paste, you'll need to use the blender tamper and push the ingredients down from time to time. I use around 1½ cups or 12 ounces (340 g) of seeds/nuts (before soaking) when making a batch. If you use too much, your blender can't take it, and if you don't use enough, it won't work well in the blender. Again, you'll need to experiment and find the sweet spot with the blender you're using.

Start with the blender on low, add a bit of starter, and slowly increase the speed while actively pushing the ingredients down with the tamper. If the blades stop mixing the contents, add more sauerkraut brine. Usually, for 12 ounces (340 g) of nuts, I end up using ½ to ¾ cup (118–177 ml) of fermenting brine. Don't worry if you need more to do the job right, but try not to use too much, particularly if you want to make a hard cheese later on. For a fermented spread cheese, it's less of an issue. The goal is to blend at high speed for a minimum of 10 seconds until very smooth.

Next, using a spatula I remove the contents to a bowl and add some cheese flavoring such as nutritional yeast, miso, garlic powder, and so on. Taste the paste and add salt if necessary. (You want it to be salty.) From experience I've learned that the saltiness will go down a bit during fermentation.

To make a soft cheese, all you have to do is cover that bowl with a clean towel or plastic wrap and let it ferment at room temperature for 24 to 48 hours, then place it in the fridge.

If you want to make hard cheese, you'll need to remove as much moisture/liquid as possible. My way of doing this is to place the contents in a folded towel (two layers) and tie up the top. Regular cheesecloth doesn't work very well; you want the fibers and weaving to be tight enough that your paste won't go through. I use thin cotton towels that can be cleaned later on. My favorite brand is First Street White Flour Sack Towels, which can be purchased in the United States at stores such as Smart & Final. Flour sack towels can also be bought online.

I tried various ways to remove moisture and settled for the following: Place several layers of folded cotton or paper towels at the bottom of a bowl, then position your cheese on top. Add a few more layers above it, then position a stone or heavy object such as a plastic container with small stones in it. The weight will squeeze out any excess "juice," which will be soaked into the layers of cloth above and below your cheese. Feel free to research different techniques, but this one works extremely well. With experience, you'll even be able to judge the number of layers you need based on the liquidity of your original paste. So far I've never had an issue with too many layers.

You want to protect your cheese from flies. Trust me . . . I've made that mistake and it's not pretty. You can place the bowl inside a closed plastic or paper grocery bag or cover it with a large bowl upside down.

In the climate of Southern California, I let it ferment at room temperature for around 24 hours. In a colder climate 48 hours may be more appropriate. You can judge by smell. If it's fermenting well, a beautiful tangy, sour, and cheesy smell will emanate from the bowl.

When you're ready, remove the stone and cloth layers and open the towel wrapped around the paste. The inside should look like a solid cream cheese and separate from the towel easily.

Place the paste into a new bowl and taste. Does it need more salt? More flavorings? This is your opportunity to be creative. If you want to make a spicy cheese, you can add some chili

Soak your seeds or nuts overnight in a jar.

Once you remove them from the jar, clean your ingredients. These days I also use very hot water to kill any bacteria and clean one more time with cold water.

Transfer to your blender and add a bit of culture starter. Don't put in the whole amount yet—just enough to get started.

Using the tamper, slowly increase the blender speed while actively pushing the ingredients down. Add a little starter at a time. Take your time; go back and forth with speed. With experience, it will become second nature.

With a spatula, remove the paste from the blender to a bowl.

Add your flavoring agents—nutritional yeast, miso, garlic powder, aromatic herbs, and so on.

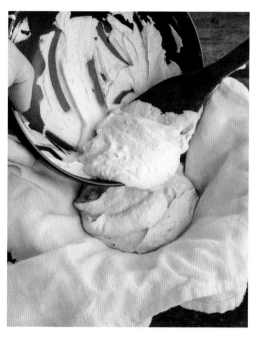

Mix all your spices and flavoring agents. Don't use any flours, such as acorn flour, at this stage; they may impede the extraction of moisture.

Fold a towel in two and place it in a bowl. Add the paste in the center.

Make a small bag containing your paste and close it with a string or rubber band.

Place several layers of folded cotton or paper towels at the bottom of a bowl, then position your cheese on top.

Add a few more layers above the cheese, then position a stone or heavy object such as a plastic container with small stones in it.

Ferment at room temperature for 24 to 48 hours. Don't forget to protect your cheese from flies during that period.

Place the paste in a new bowl and taste. Does it need more salt? More flavorings? This is your opportunity to be creative.

Put your cheese in the fridge or freezer to harden. Meanwhile, prepare a savory crust for it.

Remove the cheese from the fridge. Grab some of the paste and use your hand to form it into a ball around 2½ inches in diameter.

Place the ball on the plate with all the savory herbs/spices you're using for the crust. Roll the ball in the crust, then press it in gently.

You want the herbs or spices to cover the whole surface. Now, using the palm of your hand, press the cheese slowly into a wheel shape.

Place the shaped cheese into a dehydrator or in front of a fan for 12 to 24 hours; turn it over halfway through. Put it in the fridge to age.

flakes and smoked paprika. You can also add dried herbs for an herb cheese or Curry Blend to make an Indian cheese.

Once you've added your spices and stirred everything into the paste, place it back into the refrigerator or even freezer to harden a bit. It's important because the next step will be to shape it by hand. Five to 10 minutes in the freezer is usually enough, as you don't want to freeze it. Around 30 minutes in the refrigerator should be plenty.

Now remove the cheese from the fridge, grab some of the paste, and using your hands make a ball around 2½ inches (6.3 cm) in diameter. Place the ball on the plate with all the savory herbs/spices you're using for the crust. Clean and dry your hands quickly, then roll the ball back and forth on the plate. You want the herbs or spices to cover the whole surface. Then, using the palm of your hand, press the cheese slowly into a wheel shape.

By the way, you're not stuck with a wheel shape. You can make cylinders, cones . . . whatever shape you want. Have some fun.

Place the shaped cheese into a dehydrator or in front of a fan, but make sure it's protected from flies and other critters (see the photo of my setup on page 244). Ferment at room temperature for 12 to 24 hours. Turn the cheese halfway through the drying time. During the summer, when it's hot and dry, I may dehydrate my cheeses for less time—say, 10 to 12 hours. You just want a dry crust around your cheese. If it takes only 10 hours, that's fine.

Remove the cheese and place it in the fridge on a layer of paper toweling or, even better, a couple of layers of cheesemaking draining mats. I use embroidery plastic canvas, which is pretty much identical to cheese draining mats; I buy them in the craft section of my local dollar store. I place a few upside-down Mason jar screw bands on top of a paper towel, then a draining mat on top of the screw bands, and finally place the cheeses. That way, I get some airflow, which helps the dehydration process.

A modern refrigerator will continue the dehydration process and slow down the fermentation. You can age your cheese up to 10 days. I've noticed that after 12 days, the flavor will slowly dissipate, and you end up with a boring cheese. And nobody wants a boring cheese, right?

You can eat your cheese after 3 or 4 days; it should be hard enough at that point. My favorite aging time is around 6 days, as I think the flavor and texture are best then, but it's just an opinion.

During the whole process, cleanliness is very important. Use clean and fresh towels, no dirty hands, and wash any instruments you'll use—spatulas, spoons, blender, bowls, and so on. Hot water and soap are all you need. I've never had an issue with mold, but if it occurs, toss and restart from scratch. Don't take a risk with your health.

I know this is a lot of information, but once you get the hang of it, making plant-based cheeses is quite simple to do. I make all kinds of cheeses pretty much every week using this method; it's becomes second nature.

Creating Your Base

Plant-based cheeses start with a thick creamy base to ferment. In the beginning, you may want to use just one ingredient. As you gain experience, you can mix various nuts and seeds together to form your base—cashews, pine nuts, walnuts, and so on. I've experimented with all kinds of seeds and nuts, and these days I mostly use a base of cashew (around 70 percent); the rest is often foraged ingredients such as pinyon pine nuts, acorn flour, or walnuts.

Why cashew? I just like the texture; it's smooth and ferments very well. I've also fermented some interesting and delicious cheeses made entirely of freshly leached (hot method) acorns as well as walnuts and chestnuts. Almonds are my least favorite base due mostly to their texture. I haven't tried peanuts or pistachios myself, but I know people who have. By all means explore the possibilities with what you can find locally, wildcrafted or store-bought, and have some fun.

Here is a list, quite incomplete, of ingredients you could use to make your base:

> **Commercial nuts:** Cashews, almonds, macadamias, Brazil nuts, walnuts, pine nuts, peanuts, pistachios.
> **Wildcrafted nuts:** Acorns (leached or flour), walnuts, hazelnuts, pecans, pinyon and other pine nuts, chestnuts. If you're an experienced forager, you can probably find many other suitable ingredients in your local area.
> **Seeds:** Various seeds can be added to the base, including sesame, flax, pumpkin (shelled), and sunflower. I've made cheeses with mixed (wild) seeds such as nettles, lamb's-quarter, chia, plantain, and so on, but I usually add them after the fermentation process, when they can best contribute flavor, texture, and aesthetics (crust).
> **Grains:** I have not yet played with grains such as quinoa or oats in my cheeses. I think they could work in small quantities, mixed with your base or added later on for texture, but I'll leave it to you to experiment with them.

Creative Flavorings

Now that we've looked at the method and ingredients, let's talk a bit about flavorings. You can add spices, herbs, and other savory ingredients at specific stages of the cheesemaking process. I always recommend you taste as the process goes along.

When I was researching vegan cheese recipes, I found that most used store-bought probiotic capsules that contains live *Lactobacillus*. Usually the contents of a couple of capsules were added to the paste. I did some experimentation using capsules or liquid/brine from an active ferment, and the difference in flavor was quite noticeable. Lab-grown *Lactobacillus* (probably just a specific strain) could not compete with the variety of wild bacteria available from cabbage and other ferments, which add a "funkier" and sourer element to the taste.

But you can start your creative cheesemaking with the ferment you use as a starter. For example, if you want to make a spicy cheese, the juice of an active kimchi ferment is sure to add more flavorful complexities than store-bought capsules.

And I think it's exciting that you can start planning your savory plan of attack this early in the game. If you're an experimented fermenter, think of the possibilities! Use a fermenting hot sauce as a starter in the blender, for instance. Given the infinite number of flavorful hot sauces you can prepare, this should give you an idea how many hot cheeses you can make. And you can go even further and choose plants and herbs as a base, too. I once made a forest cheese by using as a starter the fermenting juice of wild edibles growing in my local forest—chickweed, miner's lettuce, grass, wild chervil, and more. It gave the cheese not only a beautiful "forest" color but also some grassy, savory notes. These can sometimes be found in dairy cheeses but are hard to reproduce in plant-based cheeses.

Introducing Cheese Flavorings

You want your cheese to have some of the flavors usually associated with dairy cheeses. The fermentation process will definitely help, but there are some specific ingredients that will impart savory "cheese" qualities. My four favorites are:

- Nutritional yeast.
- Miso.
- Garlic powder.
- Liquid smoke. I don't use this for every cheese, but it imparts a rich, smoky taste that's quite delicious.

Sometimes I sparingly add other ingredients such as:

- Kimchi or sauerkraut powder (dehydrated kimchi/sauerkraut ground into powder).
- Onion powder.
- Ginger powder.

Another good ingredient that can be found in Middle Eastern stores is dried lime powder. It's made from limes that have been boiled in salted water and then dehydrated in the sun. Quite sour but strong flavors. You can do some online research on "loomi" if you're interested to know more. I explain the process in my book *The Wildcrafting Brewer*. (Be aware that kimchi and lime powder will introduce a reddish hue to the paste.)

Some unfermented plant-based spread cheese recipes use lemon juice or even vinegar to impart a tart/sour note, but I strongly suggest that you add this *after* the fermentation process and just before serving. These ingredients alter the cheese's acidity and pH, which can impede a proper fermentation. I've had ferments that didn't do well, because the pH was too low to start with. They end up tasting more like vinegar-based pickled food than fermented food.

But I'll give you a little secret: Most of the time I only use garlic powder and nutritional yeast to make my plant-based cheeses, and it works very well. Those two ingredients are enough to give a good basic cheesy savor, and from there I can create with other flavorful spices and herbs.

As you'll see in the coming recipes, I'm not shy about the quantity of nutritional yeast and garlic powder I use. I like my cheese to have a good pungency. Try one of my recipes and see if you like it; if it's too strong for you, reduce the amount or flavoring.

Crusting Your Cheeses

Creating a crust is the final time you can add flavors to your cheese, but I think it's probably more important than the previous times because this is where your creativity can shine, in terms of not only savory possibilities but also aesthetics. I've always said that aesthetics are probably 20 percent of flavor: If something looks really pretty, people are already expecting it to taste good. And gosh, you can use savory crusts to make your cheeses look like a million dollars.

I like to create cheese crusts that are a representation of what the cheese is all about. If the cheese is spicy, I want the rind to have that red-hot color. A cheese containing wild aromatic herbs from the forest should look like the forest. I often go further and add leaves and small branches to make it look like the forest ground itself. While there may be some rules in terms of food flavors, I think there are no rules with aesthetics and how you present the food. Little sticks and leaves on cheeses are always very interesting to people and a great conversation starter. Just remove the sticks carefully when you slice the cheese. I often use beautiful willow leaves, which I

Miso, nutritional yeast, garlic powder, ginger powder, kimchi powder, onion powder, dried lime powder.

Various Cheese Crusts

Dried chickweed, wild chervil, nettles, willow leaves, mallow.

Curry and turmeric, nutritional yeast, salt.

Smoked paprika, Korean chili flakes, smoked jalapeño powder (chile morita).

Herb blend: thyme, California sagebrush, California bay leaves, white sage, black sage, peppercorns, rosemary, garlic powder, salt, oak ashes.

Oyster and reishi mushroom powder, dried oyster mushrooms, peppercorns, chili flakes, nutritional yeast.

Wakame seaweed, California kelp powder, peppercorns, smoked chili flakes.

collect in fall when they feature a striking red-orange color. The leaves' flavor is a tad bitter but works nicely as a pleasing balance to the other herbs.

You can use whatever you want to create your crusts as long as it is not poisonous or unhealthy. So far, I've used and mixed together the following ingredients:

- Spices (Curry Blend, chili peppers, black pepper, various spice blends).
- Herb blends such as Italian Herbs or Herbes de Provence, homemade or not.
- Seaweed.
- Dehydrated mushrooms.
- Dried autumn leaves.
- Ashes (oak or willow ashes collected after our local forest fires).
- Dehydrated wild herbs such as nettles, chickweed, mallow, and so on.

I haven't done it yet but next spring, I think I'll also wrap some of my cheeses with fresh leaves like wild grape, mallow, and sycamore.

Some ingredients used in crusts also help dehydrate the cheese and form a hard rind. This is especially true for dehydrated herbs, seaweed, and mushrooms. If I'm in a rush and need to make a somewhat hard cheese within 3 days, I'll go for an herb cheese. By mixing dry herbs in the cheese and on the crust, I can manage to make a cheese that holds its shape.

Dehydrating Your Cheese

Dehydrating helps your cheese hold its shape and creates a hard crust around it. There are no real rules as to how long you should dehydrate cheese. I've seen some people dehydrate for 2 or 3 days, but I don't go beyond 24 hours.

The dehydration is done at room temperature; you don't need a dehydrator unless your dehydrator allows you to use it with no heat involved.

It's very easy to make your own cheese dehydration system. My setup cost me around $20. I purchased a small fan, on sale for $14, at a local department store retailer (Target), then went to the local dollar store and purchased a plastic shoe box, two small rectangular storage containers, and a couple of 10-by-13-inch (25 by 32.5 cm) plastic canvas sheets (normally used for yarn stitching). Using a knife, I cut off both ends of the box to allow airflow.

Simply place the fan on a table and position your shoe box in front of it. To make sure it's at the right height, I put a small storage container below the shoe box; there's also a smaller one inside that places the cheeses right in the center in front of the fan. For airflow and ease of transportation to the refrigerator, I add a layer of plastic canvas sheets below the cheeses.

I switch the fan on high and let it run for 12 to 24 hours. Halfway through, I flip the cheeses so they can dehydrate well on both sides.

There is still one more issue we must deal with. I live just outside Los Angeles, close to many equestrian parks and horse boarding facilities. This means I have a decent number of flies in my area, and guess what? They're always interested in my cheeses. Because I'm not interested in making Casu Marzu—a traditional Sardinian sheep's-milk cheese that contains live insect maggots—I opt to protect the cheese.

Don't think flies can't be a problem for you. It takes just one fly and your cheese will start moving in a few days.

I tried all kinds of systems to address this and finally found the solution. I use French laundry pins (at strategic locations) to hold a cheese towel around my box; these pins have enough weight that the towel won't be blown away by the fan. The laundry pins, bought at the dollar store, are also perfect to hold the towel on top of the fan without interfering with the airflow.

Because you're dehydrating at room temperature, your cheeses will continue fermenting. You can experiment and see how various temperatures affect the process and flavors. A friend of mine ferments some of her cheeses at room temperature for 2 to 3 days, then places them in an oven set at 160°F (71°C) for a few hours; after that she puts them in the fridge to cool off just before serving. Her crusts are not as hard as I like mine to be, however.

The size of your cheeses is important. I've noticed that if my cheeses are too large, they have a tendency to crack, probably because fermentation is still quite active and gases can make their way through the crust. I try to keep the diameter of my cheeses to 2½ to 3 inches (6.5–7.5 cm) and the height around 1¼ inches (3–3.5 cm).

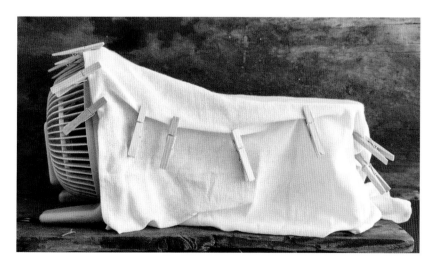

When I'm done using the fan to form the crusts, I put my cheeses in the refrigerator, where the dehydration continues. Modern refrigerators are very good at dehydrating. I have a small fridge dedicated to aging all my ferments, including those in jars. The top shelf is reserved for my plant-based cheeses. Near the temperature control knob, there is even a fan with cold dry air coming out from time to time. By placing the cheeses close to this fan, I can dehydrate them even faster if necessary.

Making a Basic Spread Cheese with Cashews

Before we make hard cheeses, let's start with some soft ones. Making fermented spread cheeses is a cinch. The cheeses can be used on toast or bread, but I also love to serve them on the side with my wild food salads.

A whole world of culinary creativity opens up when you add spices as flavorings. With a soft cheese you can include savory ingredients in the paste—chili flakes, curry, and various spice blends—but also fresh ingredients such as garlic and chives or even wild edibles like minced chervil, sweet white clover, and chickweed. Because it's a fermentation process, which can discolor fresh herbs and also alter the flavor profiles, I tend to add raw ingredients just before serving.

You can also add another layer of flavors and decoration by topping the cheese with herbs and spices.

The procedure is straightforward. First, I soak the cashews for at least 8 hours, then use my blender (Vitamix) to make a paste. You can alter the consistency by the amount of liquid you add when blending the ingredients.

To start up the fermentation, instead of just adding regular water in the blender to make the paste, I add the liquid of an active ferment. Most of the time I just use a Culture Starter, but you can probably use a ratio of 50 percent starter and 50 percent water. If I have some kimchi fermenting, I may add some of that juice as well.

Another option is to use water along with probiotics. For 2 cups (312 g) of raw cashews, you need the contents of 2 probiotic capsules. This introduces the lacto bacteria that will initiate the fermentation process and accentuate the "cheesy" flavor of the paste.

To make the paste, you'll need to use the blender tamper and push the ingredients down from time to time. I use around 2 cups or 11 ounces (312 g) of cashews (before soaking) when making a batch.

I start with the blender on low, add some Culture Starter, and slowly increase the speed while actively pushing the ingredients down with the tamper. If the blades stop mixing the contents, add a little more starter. For a soft cheese, I end up using around ¾ cup (177 ml) of starter, but you could use more if you want a lighter consistency. The goal is to blend at high speed for a minimum of 10 seconds until very smooth.

Next, use a spatula to remove the contents to a bowl and add some cheese flavorings. For around 2 cups (473 ml) of paste, I use the following:

4–5 tablespoons (16–20 g) nutritional yeast
1½ tablespoons (6 g) garlic powder
1 tablespoon (18 g) miso
½ teaspoon (2.5 ml) liquid smoke (optional)

Taste the paste and add salt if necessary; you want it to be salty. From experience, the saltiness will go down a bit during the fermentation. You can also add other spices and dry herbs at this stage such as chili flakes, curry powder, Italian Herbs or Herbes de Provence, and so on. Using the back of a spoon, spread the cheese evenly inside the bowl and clean the sides with a paper towel. Cover with a clean towel or plastic wrap and let the cheese ferment at room temperature for 24 to 48 hours, then store it in the fridge. For best flavors, eat the cheese within 8 days.

Taste when you're ready to use it and add more nutritional yeast, garlic powder, and spices if necessary. If you want to use fresh herbs (like chives and garlic), mix them in a few hours before serving. If you like, decorate the top with additional spices, herbs, or edible flowers.

Creative Spread Cheeses

There are no limits to the creative possibilities with spread cheeses. I usually make my final savory and fresh ingredient additions a few hours before serving, but if you use dried spices or herbs, you can also add them a couple of days prior to treating your guests. This would leave time for the dried herbs to infuse flavors.

A lot of fresh savory herbs from the store or garden will work well: parsley, cilantro, dill, chives, basil, thyme, marjoram, tarragon, oregano, and so on. A classic French mix would be fresh garlic and chives.

On the wilder side, I often use wild fennel, bur chervil, California sagebrush, chickweed, and different kinds of wild mint. On the East Coast you could use garlic mustard, wild garlic, ramps, and so on.

Various kinds of onions (red, sweet, yellow), shallots, and garlic cloves, minced or chopped, are good savory additions as well.

Fresh chili peppers are fantastic. I once made a "salsa" spread cheese by mixing standard and wild ingredients including minced jalapeños, red onion, wild chervil, cilantro, and a touch of garlic. The cheese top was

decorated with sliced tomatoes, cilantro, and some lime juice. Truly delicious.

If you're a skilled wildcrafter, you can dehydrate local aromatic herbs and make your own herb blend, but you can also purchase some interesting premade ones such as herbes de Provence, Italian herbs, and Cajun or Old Bay Seasoning mix.

You can find books and online information on creating spice and herb blends. I grew up with herbes de Provence so it's one of my favorite blends, but I often add local flavors with a bit of white sage, black sage, California sagebrush, and California bay.

Just mix the ingredients and taste as you go along. It's nearly impossible to go wrong if you have a delicious fermented cheese as your base.

Top: Fermented cashew and acorn flour spread cheese flavored with nutritional yeast, garlic powder, and miso. *Middle:* Fermented cashew, pine nut, and acorn flour spread cheese flavored with nutritional yeast, garlic powder, and miso. *Bottom:* Fermented cashew, pine nut, and acorn flour spread cheese flavored with nutritional yeast, garlic powder, and miso. I added my Curry Blend for flavoring. The pine nuts, around 15 percent of the mix, were soaked overnight with the cashew nuts.

MAKING SPICY HARD CHEESES

Let's make some spicy hard cheeses. This recipe is really the foundation for many others; using the same method you can substitute curry for the chili/ paprika powder; add a dried herb mix such as Herbes de Provence, Italian Herbs, or you own "wild" blend; and so on.

Here are the basic ingredients to start with. We'll add more spices and savory elements later during the process.

2 cups or 11 ounces (312 g) cashews (before soaking)
Around ½ cup (118 ml) Culture Starter; you may need a bit more (for my spicy cheese, I used some Fermented Wild Mustard Roots brine)
2 tablespoons (12 g) garlic powder
4–5 tablespoons (16–20 g) nutritional yeast
1 teaspoon (6 g) miso (optional)
1 teaspoon (4 g) spicy chili powder or flakes
2 tablespoons (13 g) smoked paprika
½ teaspoon (3 g) salt

Note that you have a lot of freedom with these ingredients. You can use less paprika or replace it with mild chili powder. If you want to make a curry cheese, replace the chili powder and paprika with around 2 teaspoons (4 g) of Curry Blend.

Soak your cashews overnight (at least 8 hours). Afterward, rinse the cashews with cold water once and then soak them in very hot water for a couple of minutes. The idea is to kill any unwanted bacteria. Rinse once more with cold water, then drain the cashews and transfer to a high-powered blender such as a Vitamix.

To make the paste, you'll need to use the blender tamper and push the ingredients down from time to time. I pour in ¼ cup (59 ml) of my starter (active sauerkraut brine or spicy brine) and start the blender on low, slowly increasing the speed while I actively push the ingredients down with the tamper. If the blades stop mixing the contents, add a bit more fermenting brine or starter. Your goal is to try to keep the starter to ½ cup (118 ml), but you may need more than that. If so, don't worry—but do try not to use too much. The goal is to blend at high speed for a minimum of 10 seconds until very smooth. If you prefer a cheese with some texture in it, however, you can stop blending whenever you like it.

Next, using a spatula I remove the contents to a bowl and add the remaining ingredients. Taste the paste and add more salt if necessary; you want it to be a tad too salty.

To make a hard cheese, you'll need to remove as much moisture/liquid as possible. Place the paste into a folded towel (two layers) and tie up the top. Regular cheesecloth doesn't work very well; you want the fibers and weaving to be tight enough that your paste won't go through. I use thin cotton towels that can be cleaned later on. My favorite brand is First Street White Flour Sack Towels, which can be purchased in the United States at stores such as Smart & Final. Flour sack towels can also be bought online.

Place a few layers of folded cotton or paper towels at the bottom of a bowl, then position the cheese on top. I use as many as eight layers. Add a few more layers on top, then position a stone or heavy object such as a plastic container with small stones in it. The weight will squeeze out any excess moisture, which will soak into

Transfer the spicy brine to a blender containing the cashews. To make the paste, you'll need to use the blender tamper to push the ingredients down from time to time (see the visual steps on page 241).

Next, use a spatula to move the contents into a bowl, add the remaining ingredients, stir, move the paste into a bag, and tie the bag closed with a string (see the visual steps on page 242).

Set the bag in a bowl between layers of folded cotton or paper towels, then add a weight on top. Place the bowl in a plastic or paper bag to protect your cheese from flies (see the visual steps on page 243).

Ferment for around 24 hours, taste, add more spices if necessary, then place in the fridge or freezer to harden (see the visual steps on page 244).

the layers of cloth/paper towels above and below your cheese. Feel free to research different techniques, but this one works extremely well. With experience, you'll even be able to judge how many layers you need based on the liquidity of your paste; so far I've never had an issue with too many layers. You can also check the paper towels and replace them with some new ones if they're soaked.

Place the bowl inside a closed plastic or paper grocery bag or cover it with a large bowl set upside down.

I ferment my cheese at room temperature for around 24 hours. In a colder climate, 48 hours may be more appropriate. You can judge by smell: If it's fermenting well, you'll smell a beautiful tangy, sour, and cheesy scent when you open the bag.

When you're ready, remove the stone and cloth layers and open the towel wrapped around the paste. The inside should look like a solid cream cheese and separate from the towel easily.

Place the paste into a new bowl and taste. Does it need more salt? More flavorings? This is your opportunity to be creative. If you want to make a spicy cheese, you can add some chili flakes and smoked paprika. You can also add dried herbs for an herb cheese or Curry Blend to make an Indian cheese.

For this spicy cheese, I added the following:

¼ teaspoon (1.5 ml) liquid smoke (optional)
1 tablespoon (6 g) garlic powder
2 tablespoons (8 g) nutritional yeast

Once you've added your ingredients/spices and stirred everything into the paste, place the bowl in the refrigerator or even the freezer to harden a bit. It's important because the next step will be to shape it by hand. Five to 10 minutes in the freezer is usually enough—you don't want to freeze it. Around 30 minutes in the refrigerator should be plenty.

Remove the paste from the fridge, grab some of it, and use your hands to make a ball from 2 to 2½ inches (5–6.3 cm) in diameter. Place the ball on the plate with all the savory herbs/spices you're using for the crust. Clean and dry your hands, then roll the cheese ball back and forth on the plate. You want the herbs or spices to cover the whole surface. Then, using the palm of your hand, press the cheese slowly into a wheel shape.

In this recipe, I made the crust with mild chili flakes (Korean chili flakes) and smoked paprika.

Place the shaped cheese into a dehydrator or in front of a fan, but make sure it's protected from flies and other critters (see the photo of my setup on page 253). Dehydrate at room temperature for 12 to 24 hours, turning the cheese halfway through. In summer, when it's hot and dry, I may dehydrate my cheeses for less time—say, 10 to 12 hours. You just want a dry crust around your cheese. If it takes only 10 hours, that's fine.

Remove the cheese and store it in the fridge. Modern refrigerators will continue the dehydration process and slow down the fermentation. You can age your cheese up to 10 days; it should be hard enough to eat after 3 or 4 days, though. My favorite aging time is around 6 days. I think the flavor and texture are at their best then, but that's just my opinion.

During the whole process, cleanliness is very important. Use clean and fresh towels, no dirty hands, and wash any instruments you'll use such as spatulas, spoons, blender, bowls, and so on. Hot water and soap are all you need.

I've never had an issue with mold but if it occurs, toss everything and start again from scratch. Don't take risks with your health.

MAKING A BASE CHEESE

Instead of making a specific cheese such as a spicy or curry version from the start, my current method is to begin by making a basic cheese and add my flavorings later on in the process. It's the same technique I used to make a spicy cheese on the preceding pages, but I add my spices when I'm about to shape the paste.

2 cups or 11 ounces (312 g) cashews
   (before soaking); you could also use walnuts,
   pine nuts, or mixed wild nuts
2 tablespoons (12 g) garlic powder
4–5 tablespoons (16–20 g) nutritional yeast
½ teaspoon (3 g) salt
Around ½ cup (118 ml) Culture Starter

Follow the same process used "Making Spicy Hard Cheeses" (starting on page 257): Soak the cashews, create the paste in the blender, add the flavorings, and transfer the paste into the folded towel. The cheese is then placed in a bowl with layers of paper towels on top and below, and a weight is added. Set an upside-down bowl on top (or put the setup inside a tied-up plastic bag) and ferment for 24 hours.

These days I use *a lot* of layers of paper towels and have discovered in the process that I don't think there is such a thing as too many layers. At some point the cheese itself will decide that it doesn't want to lose any more moisture.

Remove the cheese from the folded towel. I taste it at this point and evaluate what I should add, and this is where I decide what my cheese should be. Should I make a curry cheese? A spicy cheese? An herb cheese? Do I want to add some other wild ingredients inside such as acorn or burdock flour? More salt?

Recently I created six cheeses by dividing the amount of base cheese in three parts and three different bowls. Here are the exact amounts I used:

Curry Cheeses—Makes 2

1 tablespoon (4 g) nutritional yeast
1 teaspoon (2 g) garlic powder
1 teaspoon (2 g) Curry Blend
1 teaspoon (3 g) acorn flour

Spicy Cheeses—Makes 2

1 tablespoon (4 g) nutritional yeast
1 teaspoon (2 g) garlic powder
1 teaspoon (2 g) smoked paprika
½ teaspoon (1.5 g) chili powder

Herb Cheeses—Makes 2

1 tablespoon (4 g) nutritional yeast
1 teaspoon (2 g) garlic powder
1 teaspoon (1 g) Herbes de Provence
1 teaspoon (3 g) acorn flour

I mixed all my ingredients into each bowl, then placed the bowls in the freezer for 5 to 10 minutes. Meanwhile I prepared three different crusts, each representing what the cheese was about. As an example, for the curry cheese I used a crust made of ground coriander, nutritional yeast, turmeric, and curry powder.

I removed the various savory pastes from the freezer one at a time, and for each one I made a couple of balls with my hands, each the size of an egg, and rolled the cheese balls back and forth onto the plate with the crust ingredients. I then shaped the cheeses and placed them in front of the fan for 12 hours, flipping them once halfway through. Then I put the cheeses in the fridge to

continue the dehydration process. I think creating a base cheese to start with can allow you more creative options later. I usually eat the cheeses after 4 or 5 days and up to 10 days.

Seaweed, Spicy, Curry, Wild Sages.

Place fresh acorns on a towel so they don't roll, cut them in two with a knife, and remove the insides. You'll need around 2 cups. Soak for 2 to 3 days in cold water. I change the water at least once daily. I like to keep the jar in the fridge.

PURE ACORN CHEESE

In most of my wild fermented cheeses, I use acorn flour, but in a recent year we had so many acorns that I was able to explore the possibility of making a cheese from freshly leached acorns. It was something I'd wanted to do for a long time.

You can use this method to experiment with making cheeses from wild nuts such as chestnuts, walnuts, hazelnuts, and so on. Each ingredient may require a different approach to start, but the basic method of making the cheese should be quite similar. For example, instead of leaching (as I did with my acorns), chestnuts need to be cooked or boiled first. Hazelnuts were so tough that I had to blend them 50–50 with cashews; in retrospect, I think I would have had more success by using a flat stone grinder (*metate*) instead of my Vitamix.

This cheese was made with 100 percent coast live oak acorns.

First, place the acorns on a towel, so they don't slide, then carefully cut them in two and remove the insides. This method works well with coast live oak acorns because they are long. You may need to crack yours open.

Then put the cut acorns in a jar with water for 3 days, changing the water every 12 hours. This doesn't leach them, but it removes the (very) bitter skin around the acorns. The skins will detach and float. You can get rid of 90 percent of the skins that way; the rest will detach during the leaching process.

I use the hot leaching process explained in my book *The New Wildcrafted Cuisine*. Basically, place the acorns in cold water, bring it to a boil for 20 to 30 minutes, change the water with *very* hot or boiling water, and continuing redoing this process until the acorns are no longer bitter. If you change the water with cold water, you will bind the tannin to the acorns' starch; it's pretty much impossible to make them edible after that. During the process, I also stir the contents from time to time and remove any floating skins. It's okay to stir vigorously; this helps in removing the bitter skins.

For this cheese, my acorns required five changes of water. You probably will need less time, as the acorns I used are quite bitter to start with. When you're done, strain the boiled acorns and remove any leftover skins by rubbing them with your (clean) fingers. Let the acorns cool to room temperature.

Transfer the acorns to your blender or metate (flat stone grinder) with the addition of Culture Starter (page 44). You'll need around ½ cup (118 ml) of starter and possibly a bit more.

The base recipe is:

2 cups or 11 ounces (312 g) leached acorns
2 tablespoons (12 g) garlic powder
4–5 tablespoons (16–20 g) nutritional yeast
½ teaspoon (3 g) salt
1 teaspoon maple syrup
   (source of food for lacto bacteria)
Around ½ cup (118 ml) Culture Starter

Once you've made your paste, add the flavorings and transfer the paste into a folded towel. Place your acorn cheese into a bowl with layers of paper towels on top and below, then add a weight on top. Cover with an upside-down

On days 2 and 3, pour the acorns into a bowl, remove the floating skins, and put them back in the jar. Gently rubbing the acorns between your hands will help greatly with skin removal.

Place the acorns in cold water and bring to a boil, then simmer for 20 minutes. Change with very hot water and repeat until the acorns are no longer bitter. Depending on the acorns, it may take three to five cycles, or more.

When you're done, strain the boiled acorns. Let them cool to room temperature like the other cheeses. Blend them with your Culture Starter to make a paste, then add seasoning.

Put the seasoned paste in a two-layer folded flour sack towel. The idea is to extract the excess moisture so you can shape the cheese later. Twist or tie the top of the towel.

Add layers of paper towels on the bottom and top of the wrapped paste, then place a weight on top to help extract excess moisture. Protect from flies by setting the bowl into a closed plastic bag, or cover it with an upside-down large bowl.

Let the paste ferment for around 24 hours, then remove it from the bowl and open the wrapping. Transfer the paste to a new bowl.

Meanwhile, prepare savory ingredients for the crust on a dish. Remove the paste from the refrigerator and, using your hands, form a ball, roll it into the herbs/spices of your choice, then shape it.

Using a fan, dehydrate the cheese for around 12 hours, then place it in the fridge to continue the dehydration process. My favorite aging time is around 6 days.

bowl as a protection from flies; you can also place the contents into a tied-up plastic bag.

You can use *a lot* of layers of paper towels; there are rarely too many. At some point the cheese itself will decide that it doesn't want to lose any more moisture.

Ferment for 24 hours, then remove the paste from the folded towel, place the contents into a bowl, and taste.

For my acorn cheese, I didn't want to use too many fancy spices; I was more interested in the nutty flavors of the leached acorns. I wanted maybe a bit of spiciness, no more. But you could divide your cheese and experiment with various spices if you wanted to. I used the following flavorings after tasting:

2 tablespoons (8 g) nutritional yeast
1 tablespoon (15 ml) maple syrup
  (the paste was a tad bitter)
1 teaspoon (2 g) garlic powder
½ teaspoon (1.5 g) chili flakes
½ teaspoon (2.5 ml) liquid smoke

Once you've stirred everything into the paste, place the bowl in the refrigerator or even freezer to harden a bit. It's important because the next step will be to shape your cheeses by hand. Five to 10 minutes in the freezer is usually enough, as you don't want the paste to freeze. Around 30 minutes in the refrigerator should be plenty.

Remove the paste from the fridge, grab some of it, and use your hands to form a ball from 2 to 2½ inches (5–6.5 cm) in diameter. Place the ball on the plate with all the savory herbs/spices you're using for the crust. Clean and dry your hands, then roll the cheese ball back and forth

on the plate. You want the herbs or spices to cover the whole surface. Then, using the palm of your hand, press the cheese slowly into a wheel shape.

You should be able to make around six cheeses with the ingredient quantities given here. For my acorn cheeses, I used a special blend of local aromatic wild herbs such as black sage, white sage, and California bay. I also mixed in some thyme, rosemary, ground peppercorns, oak ash, willow leaves, and even small sticks. The sticks are ornamental; I remove them before slicing the cheeses. I just thought that they should look like the forest they came from.

Place the shaped cheeses into a dehydrator or in front of a fan, but make sure they're protected from flies and other critters (see the photo of my setup on page 253). Dehydrate at room temperature for 12 to 24 hours, turning the cheeses over halfway through. During the summer, when it's hot and dry, I may dehydrate my cheeses for less time—say, 10 to 12 hours. You just want a dry crust around your cheese. If it takes only 10 hours, that's fine.

Remove the cheeses and put them in the fridge. Modern refrigerators will continue the dehydration process and slow down the fermentation. You can age cheese up to 10 days; you can eat it after 3 or 4 days, though, when it should be hard enough. My favorite aging time is around 6 days. I think the flavor and texture are at their best then, but that's just my opinion.

The flavors of this cheese are quite awesome, nutty with still tiny hints of bitterness—a unique product! Adding liquid smoke worked well, too. I served this at one of my wildcrafting classes, and the students could not get enough.

Stone Cheeses

I teach all my workshops outdoors if possible. When you deal with wild ingredients, being in the middle of nature truly gives a context to your activities. You feel as one with the world around you; you don't have the sense of disconnection that living in the city can create. People who understand the richness and value of the environment will want to nurture and protect it, not trash it with beer cans or plastic bags.

This year I decided to hold a wild cheese workshop at my usual teaching location, a beautiful private property in the Angeles National Forest. The only problem was the lack of electricity. It was impossible to use a blender and make a paste of the seeds and nuts.

But a challenge can easily become a creative opportunity. When faced with a challenge, I often ask myself: How can I use this for my advantage? How can I be creative with it? For example, as I grow older I don't have the same energy I used to have as a young man. Thus I've learned to relax more and use my time for creative research, writing books, and spending more time playing with ingredients at home instead of hiking for hours in the wilderness. I think aging has made me more creative.

In fact, we don't need electricity and aren't stuck with having to use powerful blenders to make cheese. Even if you're on a budget, there is no need to spend hundreds of dollars. The key is to think simple. Locally I can buy a molcajete stone grinder for $20 and a metate for $80. Both will last for my lifetime and can be handed down to the next generation. You can even make your own metate by finding appropriate stones.

Since the dawn of humanity, people have made all kinds of flours and pastes using traditional wood or stone mortars. In Mexico metates are still used to grind corn and make tortillas.

There is a physical quality to foods prepared in a stone grinder that cannot be achieved with an electric blender. We are much more in control over the texture of our cheese. I think we also form a deep connection to our own past, nature, and spirit through using stones. My favorite cheeses are made that way.

When I make a cheese paste using a metate, I just add some Culture Starter while I grind the nuts and create the paste. It takes a bit of practice and it's a bit messy in the beginning, but once you get the hang of it, it's truly a pleasurable endeavor. It takes me 20 to 30 minutes to make enough paste for two or three cheeses. When I'm happy with the texture, I place the paste into my folded towel and continue with the usual method.

CHAPTER 8

Creative Dishes and Plating

Ferments are usually thought of as condiments and served as small side dishes or savory additions to the main course. That's completely fine, but I think we're limiting ourselves by doing so. You can absolutely create a cuisine based around fermentation as the main ingredient. Ferments are also an awesome way to create tasting menus or appetizers. Here in Los Angeles, we had a very successful restaurant (Baroo) whose cuisine incorporated a lot of koji and lacto-fermentation. It ended up being nominated for a James Beard award and was voted one of the top five restaurant in America by *Bon Appétit* magazine, to name a few of its recognitions. If you are into plant-based cuisine, fermentation is an awesome addition to your creative toolbox.

There is also a bit of a misconception in the fermentation world that ferments must be "raw"; that it's all about probiotics and gut health. But what about flavors? Why can't you ferment for flavors first? When I post about a cooked ferment on social media, I often get the comment, "But you're killing all the good bacteria!"—as if I were doing something terribly wrong!

Yes, you can ferment for health reasons, but you're limiting your culinary horizons if you just want raw ferments and reject other options. Cooking ferments is not new ground, by the way: Quite a few traditional ferments are cooked, such as kimchi or miso soup. In Belgium my mom used to ferment our French fries to give them a nice tangy touch before frying them. In many cuisines fermentation is the key to creating that fifth basic taste, umami.

I view a lot of the ferments in this book as a creative springboard and outlet. Lacto-ferments can be transformed into sauces, drinks, soups (cooked or raw), dehydrated to create spices, and much more.

For example, when I was working with Chef Ludo Lefebvre (Trois Mec restaurant), I used to make a lot of preserves and drinks using wild food. At one point I started to introduce some ferments, but the sour and tangy flavors were not readily accepted by the American public. Which makes sense: A lot of Americans grew up on sweet vinegar-based condiments such

as sweet dill pickles and relishes. After a little bit of thinking, I decided to experiment and replace the brine of some ferments with sugary vinegar. They became much more popular. If you want to do a quick experiment yourself, simply marinate some kimchi overnight in a bit of seasoned rice vinegar. You end up with a different flavor profile.

There is also nothing wrong with freezing or even canning your ferment. Recently I blended and fermented some raspberries into a thick sauce, and I loved the flavors after a couple of weeks. Rather than let it ferment and become sour over time, I simply froze it so I could use it in desserts later on.

Working with your ferments is also important. I like to taste them during their fermentation process and don't hesitate to add spices, sugar, or salt if necessary. I do the same before serving them.

As a good exercise, try to stop thinking of fermented food as a condiment. Make it the main dish.

The photos in this chapter depict some of the dishes I've made with ferments. If you're interested to see more, follow me on social media such as Instagram (Pascal Baudar). I often share recipes there, too.

Flavorful Additives for Wild Ferments

It's important to taste your ferments. You can add more salt, peppers, or chili or curry powders if you want, or even fresh herbs. Because I make my own vinegars, I love to use them in ferments as well. Seasoned vinegars, due to their sweetness, add a nice balance to a ferment sourness. You can purchase commercial seasoned rice vinegar, but it's much better to make your own from natural ingredients.

If I use vinegar, I usually marinate the ferment in it overnight or for around 8 hours before serving. I don't use a lot; for a ½-pint (236 ml) jar of ferments, I may add a couple of tablespoons of vinegar. Each ferment is unique, however, so taste and adjust as you go along. The vinegar flavor will mellow overnight.

I also like to mix various ferments together from time to time. For example, the Black Mustard Leaves Fermented in Their Own

Seasoned Rice Vinegar

To make seasoned rice vinegar, combine ¼ cup (59 ml) of the vinegar with 4 teaspoons sugar and ½ teaspoon salt. You can also use more natural ingredients—for example, I make seasoned elderberry wine vinegar with maple syrup or honey as well as homemade sea salt. I've also made a seasoned prickly pear vinegar that used prickly pear molasses as the sugar source. Feel free to experiment with the sweetness level.

Sautéed plant-based scallops (fermented king oyster stems), olive oil, garlic, parsley, and lemon juice. Salt and pepper to taste.

Soft acorn cheeses wrapped in mallow leaves.

Fermented king oyster mushroom stems roasted with garlic and herbs.

Fermented blueberry galette in an acorn-and-wheat crust.

1. Roasted and Fermented Oyster Mushrooms. 2. Fermented Mustard Stems. 3. Mixed Wild Greens and Daikon Achar. 4. Korean radishes in Forest Floor Brine Ferment. 5. Spicy MustaKraut. 6. Fermented mustard greens, Korean radish, and wild turnip roots. 7. Black Mustard Leaves Fermented in Their Own Seeds. 8. Mallow Stem Relish.

Seeds would have made a nice mix with the Spicy MustaKraut. Your finished ferments are just the beginning of the creative process. It's possible to turn a "meh" ferment into something sublime.

Invasivore Fermentation

For the last couple of years, I've been looking at ways to use wildcrafting to address environmental issues. Here in Los Angeles, unwanted plants have taken over the environment: wild radishes, more than 10 different types of mustards, non-native grasses, and so on. As I mentioned earlier in this book, a lot of those plants are also considered edible crops in other countries, but here they are called "weeds."

The two options usually used to control these plants are to spray pesticides or to uproot them and throw them away. I like to look toward food solutions instead. Presently, their extermination represents a huge waste of potential food resources. I know full well that I'm not making a dent in their populations, but I like to make people think. Those plants that are called "evil" or "nasty" can be turned into gourmet food.

Locally, the city is using various agencies to deal with the problem. Their role is mostly destruction, removing those pesky plants through whatever means are available. Maybe one day someone will have the bright idea to create a subsidized agency focused on removing all those edible plants, using them to feed those who cannot afford healthy organic food. Creation instead of destruction. A win-win for the environment and for social issues.

Perhaps I'm a completely unrealistic dreamer. But as a wildcrafter I also see my role as planting seeds in people's heads about "preposterous" ways to help the environment via the delicious bounty that surrounds us.

Top shelf (left to right): Wild mustard leaf and field mustard root achar with cheatgrass and foxtail barley grains. King oyster mushrooms fermented with garlic and black mustard seeds. Rehydrated shiitake mushrooms fermented in soy sauce as brine. Crushed Mediterranean mustard roots for soup stock fermented with ginger, garlic, and chili flakes. Shiitake mushrooms fermented with cheatgrass grains, a pinch of spicy chili flakes, crushed garlic, and soy sauce. *Middle shelf (left to right):* Cubed field mustard root achar with wild grains and lamb's-quarter leaves. Whole shiitake mushroom achar. Burdock roots fermented with soy sauce as the brine, garlic, wild oats, and cheatgrass grains. Fermented sliced wild fennel stems (extremely aromatic!). Cooked lamb's-quarter fermented with soy sauce, garlic, and thyme. *Bottom shelf (left to right):* Oyster mushroom stems fermented in brine with Korean chili flakes and garlic. Sunchokes fermented in seawater, Herbes de Provence, and garlic. Wild fennel sauerkraut. Sliced wildcrafted oyster mushrooms in seawater with Italian Herbs and garlic. Sliced wildcrafted oyster mushrooms fermented with Curry Blend, ginger, and a small amount of garlic. Sliced wildcrafted oyster mushrooms fermented in seawater with garlic, Korean chili flakes, and smoked jalapeño flakes (chile morita).

Working on this book about lacto-fermentation of wild edibles has been an eye-opening experience. Through the process of fermentation, I used the parts of plants that some people consider inedible. For example, I can turn our most "invasive" Mediterranean mustard into fermented delicacies from roots to leaves, stems, flowers, and seeds—small dishes that have a lot of meaning and context. I'm currently working on a tasting menu of around eight courses that will explore the culinary possibilities of invasive plants. For each dish I can provide a creative and meaningful narrative. Even the plating (the aesthetic of a dish) can be part of the story. For instance, people are quite fascinated when they find out that the seeds from some of our most invasive grasses such as cheatgrass and crabgrass have been found in prehistoric sites. Within such a narrative, ferments become the main course and not just a condiment.

In fact, let's create a whole gourmet invasivore cuisine to find creative ways to heal the planet. It couldn't be more timely, given the obvious effects of climate change that we are already witnessing.

I don't think of this book as a recipe book. It's really about ideas and concepts that can be applied to all kinds of wild or standard ingredients. It's about experimenting, creating with ferments, and researching flavors.

I'd like to end this book with a look at some of the ferments I currently have in progress. I probably have 30 jars of such concoctions in all. Some will be so unusual, they're destined to be main dishes. Others may be paired with insects or fish. I may add vinegars, lemon or lime juice, brine sauces, seasoned wild beer or wine vinegars, and fresh greens. I may use some of the brines as tasty soups. I'll taste each one, then work with it—and play with it!—to create a tasty dish.

A truly invasivore ferment: diced field mustard roots, black mustard seeds, Mediterranean mustard leaves, and seeds from various grasses that have taken over our local environment, such as wild oats, crabgrass, cheatgrass, plantain, and more. Fermented with Curry Blend and toasted sesame oil. In the background are dried wild fennel fronds—that plant is a real problem locally. The sticks were cut from mule fat (*Baccharis salicifolia*) branches, and the dish is oak bark found on the ground after a local forest fire.

RESOURCES

———

Books About Fermentation I Recommend

Wild Fermentation by Sandor Katz
The Art of Fermentation by Sandor Katz
Fiery Ferments: 70 Stimulating Recipes for Hot Sauces, Spicy Chutneys,
 Kimchis with Kick, and Other Blazing Fermented Condiments by
 Kirsten K. Shockey and Christopher Shockey
Fermented Vegetables: Creative Recipes for Fermenting 64 Vegetables &
 Herbs in Krauts, Kimchis, Brined Pickles, Chutneys, Relishes & Pastes by
 Kirsten K. Shockey and Christopher Shockey
DIY Fermentation: Over 100 Step-by-Step Home Fermentation Recipes by
 Rockridge Press
The Noma Guide to Fermentation by René Redzepi and David Zilber

Books About Plant Identification in the United States

This list includes a few books I'm familiar with, but it is very incomplete. A
simple search online or on Amazon.com should point you toward plant
identification books you can use to learn about your local wild edibles.

SOUTHWEST

Foraging California: Finding, Identifying, and Preparing Edible Wild
 Foods in California by Christopher Nyerges
The Forager's Harvest: A Guide to Identifying, Harvesting, and Preparing
 Wild Edible Plants by Samuel Thayer
California Foraging: 120 Wild and Flavorful Edibles from Evergreen Huck-
 leberries to Wild Ginger by Judith Lowry
Nuts and Berries of California: Tips and Recipes for Gatherers (Nuts and
 Berries Series) by Christopher Nyerges

NORTHEAST

Northeast Foraging: 120 Wild and Flavorful Edibles from Beach Plums to
 Wineberries by Leda Meredith
Edible Wild Plants: A North American Field Guide to Over 200 Natural
 Foods by Thomas Elias and Peter Dykeman

SOUTHEAST

*Southeast Foraging: 120 Wild and Flavorful Edibles from Angelica to Wild
Plums* by Chris Bennett

NORTHWEST

*Pacific Northwest Foraging: 120 Wild and Flavorful Edibles from Alaska
Blueberries to Wild Hazelnuts* by Douglas Deur
*Foraging the Mountain West: Gourmet Edible Plants, Mushrooms, and
Meat* by Thomas J. Elpel and Kris Reed

CENTRAL

A Field Guide to Edible Wild Plants: Eastern and Central North America
(Peterson Field Guides) by Lee Allen Peterson and Roger Tory Peterson

RECIPE INDEX

INDEX

Note: Page numbers followed by "f" refer to figures.

bell peppers
  in brine, 14, 23, 24
  in salsa, 29, 70
berries, 143–51
  blanching of, 143, 145
  blueberries. *See* blueberries
  in brews and drinks, 152, 153, 155, 158
  cranberries, 144, 146, 150–51
  dehydrated, 148
  with local aromatics, 145
  yeast in, 145, 153
beverages. *See* drinks
Billing, Jennifer, 182n
bittercress, hairy, 127
black mustard, as invasive, 48, 50, 51
black mustard leaves, 50
  in achars, 94
  cutting of, 39
  fermented in own seeds, 112, 271, 274
  in gundruk, 114, 115
  kimchi fermented in, 184
  in sauerkrauts, 53, 56, 57, 58, 82
black mustard roots, 125
black mustard seeds, 24, 48, 276f
  in achars, 92, 99
  black mustard leaves fermented in, 112, 271, 274
  in curry blend, 79
  foraging of, 190
  in MustaKraut, 58
black mustard stems, 40, 139
black sage, 50, 145, 149, 158, 160
blueberries, 150
  dehydrated, 148
  flavor of, 144
  with local aromatics, 145
  salt for, 143
  in soda, 153
  yeast in, 143, 145
bok choy, 76, 106–7, 108
bonito, in dashi, 168, 210
bottles for fermented drinks, 155, 157f
botulism, 37, 114–15, 227
Brassica nigra, 24. *See also* black mustard

Brassica rapa, 40. *See also* turnips, wild
brine, 14, 23–27, 140–42
  in cheese, 130, 257, 258f
  in forest floor ferment, 142
  in liquid ferments, 28
  loose ingredients in, 15, 33
  for pickles, 25–26
  potatoes in, 129, 130–31
  recipe for, 22
  roots in. *See* root brine
  salt percentage in, 23t, 24, 25, 192, 197
  in sauces, 218–19
  sauerkraut. *See* sauerkraut brine
  seawater as, 192, 197
  in soups, 206, 208, 213
  in starter culture, 44–45
  yellow beets in, 141
brine, keeping ingredients under, 16–17, 20, 39
  with commercial kits, 21, 55
  with pasteurized stone, 16, 19f, 25, 55, 58, 82
  with tannic leaves, 23
broccoli, 24
Bromus tectorum, 188. *See also* cheatgrass
bur chervil, 24
  in forest floor ferments, 164
  in sauerkrauts, 53
  in soups, 202, 205, 206, 207, 213
burdock root, 14, 125, 132
  cutting of, 40, 132
  in Forest Medley, 106–7
Bureau of Land Management, 50
burping jars, 20, 22, 34–35
  airlock alternative to, 22
  in brine-based ferments, 25
  in liquid ferments, 14, 31
  in loose ingredient ferments, 33
  in sauerkrauts, 17, 55, 58
  in starter culture, 44
button mushrooms, 95, 97, 100, 101

C
cabbage
  in basic sauerkraut, 13–14, 16–22, 39

in black mustard sauerkraut, 57
in CattailKraut, 61
in DandiKraut, 53–55, 172–73
in fennel sauerkraut, 57
in Forest Medley, 106–7
in gundruk, 117
in kimchi, 76, 184
in Mediterranean mustard sauerkraut, 56
in MustaKraut, 58, 86
in seawater salt fermentation, 198
with spice blends, 72
in spicy gingery greens, 67, 68
in starter culture, 43–45
in WaterKraut, 56
in WildKraut, 82
wild turnip roots with, 133
in yucca ferment, 63
Cajun spice blend, 84
California bay leaves, 23, 24, 173
  in curry blend, 79
  dehydration of, 24, 173
  in hot sauce, 233
  in pickle brine, 25
  tannins in, 187, 188
California juniper, 24
California sagebrush, 24
  in berry and fruit ferments, 146, 149
  in brews and drinks, 154f, 158, 159, 160
  in hot sauce, 233
Calitopian Paste, 225
Callirhoe involucrata, 125
Campanula rapunculoides, 125
caraway seeds, 190
Cardamine hirsuta, 127
cardamom, 79, 83, 91
carrots
  in achar, 92
  in pickle brine, 13, 14, 23, 24, 25–26, 27f
  salt content of brine for, 23t, 192, 197
  in seawater fermentation, 197
  in spicy sauce, 81
  wild (*Daucus carota*), 125
carrot tops, 70, 82, 164

cashews in cheese, 246, 254, 256f, 257, 258f, 260
castor bean, 184
cattail, 60–61
    cutting of, 40, 137
    foraging of, 60, 80
    in Forest Medley, 106–7
    in sauerkraut, 60–61
    in spicy sauce, 80–81
CattailKraut, 61
cauliflower, 14, 23, 24
    in mustard root brine sauce, 218
    salt in brine for, 192
    in spicy sauce, 81
celery, 10, 24, 140
chaga mushrooms
    in medicinal brew, 161
    in soup stock, 208
chard, in WildKraut, 82
cheatgrass, 190
    in achars, 189f, 274
    as non-native, 188, 276
    in porridge, 191
cheeses, 6, 11, 52, 237–68
    acorn, 263–66
    aging of, 245, 259, 265f, 266
    basic recipe, 260–61
    blending of, 239, 241f, 254, 257, 258f, 260
    brines in, 130, 257, 258f
    cleanliness for, 245, 259
    crust of, 243f–44f, 245, 248, 250f, 251, 259, 260, 265f, 266
    curry, 260
    dehydration of, 244f, 245, 251–54, 259, 260–61, 265f, 266
    flavorings for, 240, 241f–42f, 245, 246–48, 254, 255–56, 259, 263, 266
    hand shaping of, 244f, 245, 259, 260, 266
    hard, 240–45, 257–59, 260
    herb, 260
    probiotics added to, 247
    protection from flies, 240, 243f, 245, 252, 253f, 259, 265f, 266

removing moisture from, 240, 242f–43f, 245, 257, 258f, 260, 264f–65f
    size of, 252
    soft, 239, 254–56
    spicy, 260
    spread, 255–56
    starter culture for, 43, 239, 247, 254–55, 257, 260, 263, 264f
    with stone ground ingredients, 263, 267–68
Chenopodium album, 3. *See also* lamb's-quarter
Chenopodium californicum, 64–65
cherry leaves, 187
chervil
    as brine flavoring, 140, 142
    bur chervil. *See* bur chervil
    in cheese, 247
    cutting of, 40, 42f, 53
    in forest floor ferments, 142, 166
    in Forest Medley, 106
    in hot sauces, 229, 234
    in kimchi, 184
    in pastes, 220, 221, 222, 224, 225
    in pesto, 216
    in salsa, 70
    in sauerkrauts, 53, 61
    in soups, 201
chestnuts, 246, 263
chickweed, 3, 50
    in achars, 92, 99
    as brine flavoring, 140, 142
    in cheese, 247
    in cooked greens, 88, 89
    cutting of, 40, 42f
    in forest floor ferments, 142, 164, 166, 167
    in Forest Medley, 106
    in hot sauces, 229, 234
    in kimchi, 184
    in pastes, 220, 221, 222, 224, 225
    in pesto, 216
    in salsa, 70
    in sauerkrauts, 53, 61
    in soups, 201, 202, 205, 206, 207, 213

chiffonade technique, 39–40, 41f
    for kimchi, 76
    for pepperweed, 40, 53.67
    for sauerkraut, 53, 56, 58
chile morita, in spice blends, 73, 84, 99
chili powder
    in achars, 91
    in spice blends, 83, 84
Chinese cabbage, 76, 106–7, 108
chipotle powder, in spice blends, 73, 84
chives, 164
chlorine in water, 25, 127, 153, 158
chopping technique, 40, 42f, 53
Christmas Cranberries, 151
chutney, 91
cilantro
    as brine flavoring, 140
    in forest floor ferments, 164
    in herb blends, 85
    in pastes, 221, 225
    in salsa, 29, 70
    in sauerkrauts, 53, 56
cinnamon, 83
Claytonia spp., 70. *See also* miner's lettuce
cleavers, 142, 164, 166
Clostridium botulinum, botulism from, 37, 114–15, 227
cloves, 23, 25
    in achars, 91
    in spice blends, 83
coffee grinder, 72, 79, 83, 87
commercial fermentation supplies, 6, 7, 20–21, 25, 55, 202
containers for fermentation, 10, 155, 157f
    crocks, 10, 13, 38–39
    jars. *See* jars
    leaves, 182–86
    oak trunk, 175–81
coriander, 190
    in achars, 91, 92, 94, 97, 99
    in spice blends, 79, 83, 84
crabgrass, 190, 276
    seeds in porridge, 191
cranberries, 144, 146, 150–51
creeping bellflower, 125

ground ivy, 152
gundruk, 114–19, 211

H

habanero peppers, 80, 102, 129
habanero peppers, in hot sauces, 4, 14, 227, 229, 233
    roasted oak bark, 235
    with smoked jalapeño, 230–31
hairy bittercress, 127
HandiSmok, 170
hard cheese, 240–45, 257–59, 260
harissa, 32
    dandelion, 15, 34–35, 72, 226
hay, smoked, 170–71
hazelnuts, 263
herb blends, 85, 167
    in brews and drinks, 152
    in cheese, 255, 260
    mushrooms with, 100, 109
    potatoes with, 111
Herbes de Provence, 85
    in cheese, 255, 260
    in gazpacho, 201
    greens with, 89
    in mallow stem relish, 136
    mushrooms with, 100
Hesperoyucca whipplei (yucca), 6, 50, 52, 62–63
Hirschfeldia incana, 48. *See also* Mediterranean mustard
honey, 144, 153
hops, 152, 159
Hordeum spp., 48. *See also* foxtail grass
horehound, 152, 154f, 158, 159, 161
horseradish leaves, 23, 187
horseradish roots, 167
hot sauces, 14, 28–31, 200, 227–35
    aging of, 4, 227, 229, 230
    frequent shaking of, 28, 39
    habanero and smoked jalapeño, 230–31
    pH of, 36
    roasted oak bark, 235
    roots, bark, and stems in, 233
    salt in, 28

    vinegar in, 28, 200, 227, 228, 231
    watercress and jalapeño, 234
    Wildly Cruel, 229
huckleberries, 143, 150
Hydrion pH test strips, 36

I

identification of plants, 51–52, 164
Incredible Wild Edibles (Thayer), 125
invasive plants, 5, 48–51, 163, 274–76
    castor bean as, 184
    definition of, 48
    grasses as, 48, 190, 191, 276
    in kimchi, 76
    mustards as, 5, 48, 49f, 50, 51, 214, 274, 276
    in soups, 202
iodine in salt, 12
Italian herbs, 85, 89, 136

J

jalapeño peppers
    in hot sauces, 230–31, 234
    in pastes, 221, 225
    in salsa, 29, 70
    in spice blend, 73
jar lids, 34–36
jar openers, 35
jars, fermentation in, 6, 7, 10, 13, 20, 38
    airlocks for, 20, 22, 36
    brine-based, 25–26, 27f
    burping of. *See* burping jars
    of drinks, 155
    explosion of, 34
    lids of, 34–36
    of liquid ferments, 14, 28, 29–31
    of loose ingredients, 33
    monitoring pressure in, 14, 22, 34–35
    of pastes, 32
    of salsa, 29–31
    of sauerkrauts, 14, 16–21
julienne cutting, 40, 42f
juniper, 24, 173
    smoking with, 170

K

kahm yeast, 181
kale
    in gundruk, 114, 119
    spicy gingery, 66
    in WildKraut, 82
kelp, in dashi, 168, 210, 211, 212f
kimchi, 2, 3, 4, 10, 269
    aging of, 22
    brine for, 23t
    commercial kits for, 20
    dehydrated, 86, 247, 248
    Lactobacillus in, 43, 182
    leaves as containers for, 182–85, 185f–86f
    mushroom, 101
    oak trunk fermentation of, 176, 181
    pH of, 36, 37
    spice blends in, 72
    Wild Food, 76, 86, 184–85
    yucca in, 63
Kimshroom, 101
king oyster mushrooms, 97, 105
knife cutting techniques, 39–40, 41f–42f
    for roots, 40, 132
    for sauerkrauts, 39, 53, 56, 58
    for stems, 40, 137
koji fermentation, 227, 269
kombu (kelp), in dashi, 168, 210, 211, 212f
Korean radish, 92, 94, 97, 273f
Kraut Source Fermentation Kit, 21, 202

L

lactic acid, 23
    iodine affecting, 12
    sugar converted to, 9, 10, 38, 153
Lactobacillus bacteria, 9
    in achars, 91
    in berry and fruit ferments, 143, 145, 148
    in brews and drinks, 152, 153
    on carrots, 25
    on dock leaves, 123
    heat affecting, 135
    in kimchi, 43, 182

carrots, fennel, and ginger in, 197
culinary uses of, 192
fermentation with, 4, 192–93, 197–98
filtration and pasteurization of, 193, 197
safety of, 4, 192, 193
salt content of, 192, 197
salt made from. *See* sea salt
seaweed
    with cabbage in sea salt, 198
    in dashi, 168, 210, 211, 212f
    flavor of, 198
    salt in, 10
seeds, 188–91
    in achars, 99
    in cheese, 239, 246
    in mushrooms with bok choy, 108
    mustard. *See* mustard seeds
sessile oak, 176
shellfish, 130
Sherman, Paul W., 182n
shiitake mushrooms, 95, 100, 168
    in dashi, 168, 210, 211, 212f
shimeji mushrooms, 95, 97, 100, 101, 103
    spicy garlicky, 102
Shockey, Christopher, 91
Shockey, Kirsten K., 91
Shroomchi, 101
slicing techniques, 40, 42f, 132
smallflower melic, 190
smoke, liquid, 172
    in barbecue spice blend, 73
    in cheese, 247, 255, 259, 266
smoking, 172–73
    of oak stems, 170–71
    of sauerkraut, 172–73
sodas, 152, 153, 154, 160
soft cheese, 239, 254–56
Sonchus spp., 53. *See also* sow thistle
sorrel, 123
    in forest floor ferment, 167
    wood sorrel. *See* oxalis
soups, 14, 28–31, 199
    dashi, 128, 168–69, 210–11, 212f

forest floor ferments in, 163, 168–69, 202, 207, 223
gazpacho, 201
miso, 210, 211, 213, 269
mushrooms in, 168, 206, 207, 208, 210, 211, 212f
mustard leaves in, 202, 207, 213, 214
mustard roots in, 202, 206, 207, 213
raw, 10–11, 199, 201–7
shaking or stirring of, 28, 39, 202
sourdough paste, sealing oak trunk with, 179f, 181
sow thistle
    in cooked greens, 88, 89
    in forest floor ferment, 164, 166
    in paste, 225
    in sauerkraut, 53
spices, 71–89
    in achars, 90, 91, 99
    and bacteria, 91, 182
    barbecue blend, 72, 73, 75
    in brine-based ferments, 14, 23, 24, 25
    Cajun blend, 84
    curry blend, 79–82
    from dehydrated ferments, 86–87, 163
    in forest floor ferment, 167
    Garam Masala, 83
    in loose ingredient ferments, 15, 33
    Mexican-style, 83
    in pickle brine, 25
    for potatoes, 111
    in sauerkrauts, 14
    stone-ground, 72, 79, 83
    Thai blend, 84
spinach, 89, 122
splitgill mushrooms
    in Forest Medley, 106–7
    in medicinal brew, 161
    with oyster mushrooms and bok choy, 108
spoilage, 7, 13
    acidity reducing, 9–10, 23, 33, 153, 155
    closed containers reducing, 10

of liquid ferments, 28
salt reducing, 9, 24
spread cheese, 255–56
starter culture, 43–45. *See also* culture starter
Stellaria media, 3. *See also* chickweed
stems, 134–39
    cutting of, 40, 137
    dandelion, 134, 137
    in hot sauce, 233
    mallow, 136, 137, 273f
    mustard. *See* mustard stems
    watercress, 134, 135
stinging nettle, 4
    as brine flavoring, 140
    in forest floor ferment, 167
    odor of, 53
    in pesto, 216
    in sauerkrauts, 53
stone grinding
    of berries, 151
    of dehydrated ferments, 87
    of grains, 191
    of mustard, 58, 112, 141
    of nuts, 263, 267–68
    of pesto, 216
    of roots, 15, 33, 126, 127, 129
    of salt, 198
    of spices, 72, 79, 83
stone used as weight, pasteurization of, 16, 19f, 25, 55, 58, 82
sugar, 9, 10, 38
    for bacteria, 9, 10, 38, 64
    in berry and fruit ferments, 143, 144
    in brews and drinks, 153, 154
sunchokes, 111
sustainable harvest, 7–8, 50–51, 163
sycamore bark, 154f, 158
sycamore leaves, 184

T

Tabasco, 28, 227
table salt, 12
tannins, 23, 166, 187–88
    in oak leaves, 23, 187
    in oak trunk fermentation, 176, 181

tarragon, 85
tea leaves, tannins in, 23, 187
terroir, local
    definition of, 47–48
    drinks representing, 152–61
    exploration of, 5–6, 47–70
    oak in, 176
Thai cuisine
    mushrooms in, 103
    soup in, 207
    spices in, 84
Thayer, Samuel, 125
thistle
    dehydrated, 86
    in forest floor ferment, 166
    sow. See sow thistle
thyme, 85
tomatoes, 143
    in gazpacho, 201
    in salsa, 29, 70
Tropaeolum spp. (nasturtium),
    50, 53
turkey tail mushrooms
    in forest brew, 154f, 158
    in medicinal brew, 161
    in soup, 208
turmeric
    in achars, 91, 97, 99
    in curry blend, 79
turnips, prairie, 125
turnips, wild, 133
    in achars, 92
    cutting of, 40
    in kimchi, 76
Typha spp., 40. *See also* cattail

U

Umbellularia californica, 24. *See
    also* California bay leaves
Urtica dioica, 4. *See also*
    stinging nettle

V

vinegar, 2, 269–70, 271
    in achars, 90, 91

acidity of, 9–10, 36, 227
apple cider, 26, 218
balsamic, 205, 218, 227
beer, 58, 112, 197
in brine sauces, 218
in cheese, 248
elderberry wine, 133, 206, 271
in food preservation, 9–10,
    91, 227
homemade, 133, 197, 206,
    228, 271
in hot sauces, 28, 200, 227,
    228, 231
in mushroom ferments, 95, 98,
    100, 102, 103
in pesto, 216
rice, 95, 271
in root ferments, 132, 133
in salad dressings, 126, 128,
    130, 218
seasoned, 26, 95, 271
in soups, 199, 201, 202, 205,
    208
in stem relish, 136
Vitamix
    seeds and nuts ground with,
        239, 254, 257
    spices ground with, 72, 79, 83

W

walnuts, 52
    in cheese, 246, 260, 263
    cultivation of, 50, 51f
wasabi and sauerkraut brine
    sauce, 219
water
    bacteria in, 60, 193
    chlorine in, 25, 127, 153, 158
    seawater, 4, 192–98
watercress
    in achars, 92, 93f, 94, 97
    as brine flavoring, 140
    in cooked greens, 88, 89
    cutting of, 53
    in forest floor ferments, 167

in Forest Medley, 106–7
    in hot sauces, 230, 234
    in pastes, 220
    in sauerkrauts, 53, 56, 61,
        82, 134
    stems of, 134, 135
WaterKraut, 56, 134
water mint, 50
Weil, Andrew, 95
white fir *(Abies concolor),* 144,
    151, 160
white oak, 176, 187
white sage, 50, 79
The Wildcrafting Brewer (Baudar),
    152, 248
Wild Fermentation (Katz), 9
WildKraut, 82
willow bark and leaves, 23
    aspirin-like compound in,
        161, 188
    in forest brew, 154f, 158
    in mushroom brew, 161
wood sorrel. *See* oxalis
wormwood, 152, 159

Y

yarrow, 24, 50
    in brews and drinks, 152, 153,
        159, 160
yeast, 5, 152
    in alcoholic fermentation, 143,
        145, 153
    in berries, 143
    in honey, 144, 153
    in oak trunk fermentation, 181
yeast, nutritional, in cheese, 239,
    247, 248, 255, 257, 259
    in acorn cheese, 263, 266
    in basic recipe, 260
yellow beets
    in mustard brine, 141
    in smoked hay fermentation,
        171
yerba santa, 149, 158, 160
yucca, 6, 50, 52, 62–63

ABOUT THE AUTHOR

Photo courtesy of Mia Wasilevich.

Pascal Baudar is the author of *The Wildcrafting Brewer* and *The New Wildcrafted Cuisine*. He works as a wild food researcher, wild brewer, and instructor in traditional food preservation techniques. Over the years, through his weekly classes and seminars, he has introduced thousands of home cooks, local chefs, and foodies to the flavors offered by their wild landscapes. In 2014 Baudar was named one of the 25 most influential local tastemakers by *Los Angeles Magazine*, and in 2017 his instructional programs, taught through Urban Outdoor Skills, were named one of the seven most creative cooking classes in the LA region.